European Commission

General Report
on the Activities of
the European Union

2006

Brussels • Luxembourg, 2007

The *General Report on the Activities of the European Union — 2006* was adopted by the European Commission on 26 January 2007 under reference number SEC(2006) 1000 final.

**Europe Direct is a service to help you find answers
to your questions about the European Union**

Freephone number (*):
00 800 6 7 8 9 10 11

(*) Certain mobile telephone operators do not allow access to 00 800 numbers or these calls may be billed.

A great deal of additional information on the European Union is available on the Internet. It can be accessed through the Europa server (http://europa.eu).

Cataloguing data can be found at the end of this publication.

Luxembourg: Office for Official Publications of the European Communities, 2007

ISBN 92-79-02100-1

Printed in Belgium

PRINTED ON WHITE CHLORINE-FREE PAPER

The President of the European Commission to the President of the European Parliament

Sir,

I have the honour to present the *General Report on the Activities of the European Union for 2006*, which the Commission is required to publish by Article 212 of the EC Treaty and Article 125 of the EAEC Treaty ([1]).

Yours faithfully,

Brussels, 13 February 2007

José Manuel Barroso
President

([1]) In accordance with the procedure described in the declaration on the system for fixing Community farm prices contained in the accession documents of 22 January 1972, the Commission will shortly be sending Parliament the *Report on the Agricultural Situation in the European Union*. And, in accordance with an undertaking given to Parliament on 7 June 1971, the Commission is preparing its *Annual Report on Competition Policy*.

Contents

Note to readers

*The General Report and its role as a source of information
on the activities of the European Union*

Regular readers of the General Report will have noticed a major change in presentation starting with the 2005 edition, published in February 2006. Following the adoption of a transitional solution for the 2004 edition the Report now has a new format and is more compact in size and more concise in content.

This simplification was triggered by a desire for rationalisation, which in turn was largely dictated by the continuing increase in the number of Community languages following successive waves of enlargement, culminating in the defining moment reached in 2004. Ensuring fair treatment for all these languages in a report which is required by the Community Treaties and records the activities of all the Union institutions over the course of a whole year reflects a genuine commitment to transparency vis-à-vis members of the public who wish to keep in touch with the life of the European Union.

At the same time, the concern to make the General Report more readable has meant changing its focus to concentrate on the highlights of the past year, both general trends and key policy activities, including legislative measures. From a methodological point of view, this quest for readability goes hand-in-hand with the need to take account of the wider system of information on Union activities available to the public from numerous co-existing sources, including:

- the wealth of information now available online on **Europa**, the 'Gateway to the European Union' (http://europa.eu/index_en.htm), which can be consulted using various search criteria — activities by subject, institutions, documents or services (statistics, library, contacts, etc.);

- the frequently updated **databases** on the servers of the various Community institutions (e.g. Commission DG websites) or sources outside the institutions; links to these databases and references to Europa are included among the 'General references and other useful links' at the end of each section of the General Report;

- the real-time record of events contained in the *Bulletin of the European Union*; produced by the Commission in three languages (English, French and German) and — since the beginning of 2006 — available **only in electronic form** (http://europa.eu/bulletin/en/welcome.htm), the Bulletin provides a detailed summary of all Community activities, direct references to official texts, and hyperlinks to the relevant information and databases; the Bulletin is designed as a monthly review but information is posted online at more frequent intervals, so that readers can learn about all the activities in a given month as and when these updates appear; the Bulletin is therefore an **essential companion to the General Report**, for which it is also one of the key sources of information; together they form the lynchpin of an information service for readers who want both a general overview of the European Union's activities and a tool for conducting more detailed research.

With this system of comprehensive coverage, there is no longer any need for detailed information to be systematically reproduced in the General Report, which is now more concise in form and content in line with its dual role of providing a panoramic view of current events and highlighting key trends Union-wide.

Introduction

European Union activity in 2006 was in many respects shaped by the major initiative of the previous spring, namely the review and revision of the Lisbon agenda, which was to provide the basis for a genuine partnership for growth and employment.

Although doubts had surfaced in 2005 following the 'no' votes in the referendums in France and the Netherlands on ratification of the Treaty establishing a Constitution for Europe, the momentum generated by the relaunched Lisbon strategy was a powerful push factor for progress in several key areas and for ambitious new projects in others. The last-minute consensus at the December 2005 European Council on the new financial perspective for 2007–13 was another clear pointer in the same direction.

So the ground was prepared for numerous initiatives to bear fruit in 2006 and, in particular, for a number of important legislative proposals to reach the statute book. But there was another dynamic which provided inspiration for what was to be achieved in 2006 — the re-opening of the debate on Europe's role and added value in the 21st century. This was the context in which the Commission produced its blueprint for a genuine 'citizens' agenda' and formulated the practical proposals to back it up.

This introduction will highlight both the political climate which provided the backdrop for Union action in 2006 and the broad trends in work done to realise the strategic objectives set by the Commission when it took office, which are extensively shared by all the Union institutions.

*   *   *

The fresh air breathed into the better regulation initiative in 2005 was one of the main influences on Community activities throughout the year. In November the Commission undertook a strategic review of the better regulation programme. Its analysis showed that much remained to be done if the expectations of citizens and businesses were to be met and improved regulation was to make a positive difference to their daily lives. But tangible results were there to be seen in such key areas as further simplifying existing legislation and improving the assessment of new legislative proposals. And initiatives were taken to attain and reinforce the better regulation objectives, with the Commission continuing to give priority to ensuring that its proposals are of the highest quality, pressing on with the simplification process and lightening the administrative burden borne by business. The strategic analysis was accompanied by two Commission working papers: one, on measuring administrative costs and reducing administrative burdens, sets out a variety of options and ideas to prepare the ground for the action plan that the Commission will be presenting in 2007; and the other reports and updates the 2005 rolling simplification programme.

Better regulation is a joint responsibility involving not just the Commission but also the other institutions and the Member States, and efforts were made there too. Following an agreement between the institutions on a common approach, the European Parliament and the Council have begun conducting their own impact assessments, and have also supported the simplification process. And a number of Member States have initiated exemplary action to cut administrative costs.

All these efforts also bore the imprint of another initiative reflecting the growing concern to improve the information flow to Member States' national parliaments on the elaboration of Community policies. At the same time the Commission pressed on with the European transparency initiative launched the previous year, and an extensive public consultation exercise was conducted on the basis of a Green Paper put out in May. The June European Council outlined a comprehensive policy on transparency in Council proceedings. More generally, the Commission drew on a White Paper on a European communication policy, published in February, to push on with action begun in 2005 and to issue a mobilisation call to all key players in the European Union.

The process surrounding the Treaty establishing a Constitution for Europe continued to make slow progress with further ratifications by some Member States, but another development emerged from the reflection on Plan D for Democracy, Dialogue and Debate on the future of Europe, launched by the Commission in 2005. In May the Commission proceeded from an initial summing-up of the reflection process to present 'a citizens' agenda'. This calls for a two-track approach. First, results have to be delivered for Europe by means of a programme of practical measures matching the needs of Europe's citizens and gaining their support for the European cause: to this end the Commission is proposing a detailed review of the single market to identify what still needs to be done, and an in-depth stocktaking of the realities of European society with a view to deepening the Community's social dimension. And second, the implementation of Union policies must be accompanied by a gradual approach to solve the current institutional difficulties. This two-track approach recommended by the Commission was endorsed by the June European Council.

Meanwhile, a major obstacle to progress was lifted in May with the interinstitutional agreement between the European Parliament, the Council and the Commission on the new financial framework for Union activity for the period 2007–13. This consensus unblocked a series of correlated initiatives for implementing mechanisms (Community funds and programmes) in a wide range of fields.

As for the actual structure of the Union, final preparations were made for Bulgaria and Romania to become members on 1 January 2007, raising the total number of Member States to 27. In parallel with this ongoing process the Commission, acting at the request of the European Council, launched reflections on the Union's integration capacity, faced as it is with further applications for membership, and together with the Member States reminded Turkey of the need to fulfil certain commitments if negotiations are to continue. The general enlargement strategy was on the European Council agenda in December. But preparations for another type of enlargement were being made in the field of economic and monetary union, to result, also on 1 January 2007, in Slovenia becoming the 13th member of the euro area, making it the first of the 10 new Member States from the 2004 enlargement to adopt the single currency. Also worth noting is that a new component was added to Europe's identity in April when the new top-level Internet domain '.eu' came into operation with great success.

* * *

The strategic objective of prosperity in the European Union remained at the root of measures implementing the partnership for growth and employment as the spearhead of the Lisbon strategy relaunched in 2005. New priorities were set by the spring European Council, including investing more in knowledge and innovation, unlocking business potential (particularly that of smaller firms), responding to globalisation and ageing of the population, and moving towards an effective European energy policy.

In this context, work continued on existing projects and new initiatives were launched in numerous areas, including: the modernisation of universities, the future establishment of a European Technology Institute, and a new generation of research programmes; reform of the cohesion policy clearly focused on the Lisbon strategy; adoption of the services directive and measures for the further liberalisation of postal services; rules on chemical products (REACH) and the establishment of a European Chemicals Agency; reform of State aid in the context of modernising competition policy; a new generation of customs and tax programmes; and possible prospects for revision of the regulatory framework for electronic communications.

The objective of prosperity, like the objective of solidarity, in particular with future generations, is closely bound up with the concept of all aspects of sustainable development — economic, social and environmental. Based on the platform for action presented by the Commission in December 2005, a new strategy was adopted by the June European Council in synergy with the revised Lisbon strategy.

In the context of the solidarity objective, other initiatives were launched, also relating to the concept of sustainable development.

At the beginning of the year the Commission published a Green Paper on a European energy strategy defining the basis for a policy geared to three major objectives: sustainable development, competitiveness, and security of supplies. The last of these topics was discussed in detail with the Russian President at the informal European Council in Lahti in October. The Commission also proposed a Union strategy for biofuels. And the European Parliament and the Council adopted a directive on energy efficiency.

The Commission launched an extensive consultation process in June with a Green Paper on maritime policy in the European Union. In seeking the advice of public opinion on how the seas and oceans should be managed, it aims to lay the basis for a new vision of an integrated maritime policy. The Commission also adopted a communication outlining a policy strategy to halt the loss of biodiversity by 2010.

On the social front, 2006 was European Year for Workers' Mobility, and a wide range of awareness measures were organised. Several Member States relaxed or abolished restrictions on the free movement of workers from the countries that acceded in May 2004. The Commission also proposed establishing a European Globalisation Adjustment Fund to assist the vocational reintegration of workers made redundant because of major structural changes in world trade patterns. And new strategic guidelines were proposed for economic and social cohesion.

In agriculture, the Council approved a far-reaching reform of the common organisation of the sugar market. The Commission began work on far-reaching changes to the banana market and on exploring avenues for reforming the wine market.

With regard to the security objective, further progress was made on implementing the Hague programme to consolidate the area of freedom, security and justice. Special attention was paid to external border management and immigration, and the Commission adopted a communication on future priorities in the fight against illegal immigration from third countries. It also proposed the setting-up of rapid border intervention teams so that Member States facing exceptional difficulties in controlling their external borders could temporarily draw on other Member States' skills and human resources, particularly at maritime borders. More generally, the Commission continued its reflections on security reform as an integral part of the Union's external assistance to various regions in the world.

On 8 June, in support of the objective of strengthening the Union's role as a global player, the Commission adopted a major communication presenting a series of practical proposals to bring greater coherence, effectiveness and visibility to Europe in the world, and calling inter alia for better strategic planning with the Council.

By the same token the Union, as the largest aid donor in the world, sought ways and means of making its development aid operations more efficient. In March the Commission adopted a package of communications to this end. At the end of

August, by way of follow-up to the 2005 European development policy consensus between the European Parliament, the Council and the Commission, the Commission presented a communication calling for a harmonised approach in the European Union to governance in the developing countries.

New strategic approaches were devised in relations with the various regions of the world. In the case of the African, Caribbean and Pacific (ACP) countries, while Africa remains the priority concern, in particular the countries in crisis, enhanced partnership strategies were also worked out for the Caribbean and Pacific countries. Following the review of the Cotonou Partnership Agreement in 2005, decisions were taken jointly with the ACP countries regarding implementation of the 10th European Development Fund, with resources of nearly EUR 22 billion for 2008–13.

A new strategic approach was also proposed for relations with China.

Finally, the Union continued to devote special attention to reconstruction in Iraq and to the Middle East peace process, heavily compromised by the summer hostilities between Israel and Lebanon, and to relations with Iran and North Korea with regard to their nuclear programmes.

Chapter I

General policy framework

Governance and better regulation

Background

In order to achieve the objectives laid down by the Treaties, European legislation has created conditions favourable to economic growth, environmental protection and higher social standards, in particular by establishing the single market. At a time when the world is changing so rapidly it is impossible to consider this body of legislation — built up over a period of nearly 50 years — without addressing the issue of the effectiveness of European law and how it can be modernised and simplified. The political objective of improving the quality of European legislation and a desire for better regulation are thus prime concerns of the European Union today.

A new impetus was given to better regulation in 2005, when it was placed at the heart of the Lisbon strategy for growth and employment. The Commission reviewed the action plan for improving the regulatory environment, which it had launched in 2002, and agreed on a series of new approaches aimed at making progress more tangible. If the venture is to succeed, however, all the European Union institutions involved in the legislative process and the Member States must genuinely make the objective their own. Better regulation is, in this sense, a joint responsibility.

Better regulation

On 14 November the Commission presented the results of a strategic review of the progress achieved and the challenges that still have to be overcome if the process of improving regulation has to be taken forward more vigorously ([1]). The aim is to ensure that the regulatory environment for Europe's businesses and citizens delivers on European objectives such as the creation of a fair and competitive marketplace, the

---

([1]) COM(2006) 689.

welfare of its citizens and the effective protection of public health and the environment, while at the same time cutting the administrative costs which hamper productivity and job creation. The strategic review was accompanied by two Commission working papers: a first progress report on the strategy for the simplification of the regulatory environment (¹) and a paper on measuring administrative costs and reducing administrative burdens in the European Union (²).

Policymaking

The main tool for producing better legislation is the impact assessment — a systematic and integrated approach to identifying and anticipating the potential economic, social and environmental implications of new proposals. Since 2003 more than 160 impact assessments have been carried out, enabling the Commission to base its policy and legislative initiatives on sound assessments of the consequences of its action. A common methodology for measuring the administrative costs associated with new initiatives has been developed and was incorporated into the Commission's guidelines on impact assessments in March.

Quality impact assessment is crucial to achieving the objectives of better legislation. In November the Commission accordingly took steps to upgrade its monitoring system by setting up an Impact Assessments Committee composed of senior officials working independently of the competent policy departments and answerable to the President of the Commission. The committee will carry out an independent study of the quality of all impact assessments before the final stage of formulation and, if necessary, provide methodological support for the departments responsible. An external evaluation of the Commission's impact assessment system is also under way.

Following the agreement between the institutions on a common approach to impact assessment, which came into force in July, the European Parliament and the Council have undertaken to produce their own impact assessments of substantial amendments to Commission proposals. Since September summaries of the Commission's impact assessment reports have been translated into all official languages.

So far, 68 proposals pending before the Council and the European Parliament have been withdrawn following screening to determine their compatibility with the principles of better regulation and with the growth and employment priorities set by the Barroso Commission. In a resolution adopted on 16 May the European Parliament expressed its overall support for this screening process and welcomed the fact that the Commission had re-examined these proposals in the light of the objections it had formulated. To complete the process, the Commission announced in its work programme for 2007 the withdrawal of 10 further proposals, most of them dating from 2004. It will continue its regular examination of the legislative proposals still pending

---

(¹) COM(2006) 690.
(²) COM(2006) 691.

before the legislature to assess their general relevance and their compatibility with the principles of better regulation.

In addition to making greater use of wide-ranging public debates, such as those prompted by Green Papers, the Commission has, since 2005 in particular, made every effort to promote an extensive system of public consultations. A number of high-level groups have been set up to enable the parties concerned to discuss issues involving key sectors of the economy or horizontal matters. The constructive dialogue with the Member States continued in 2006 with the new high-level group of national experts on regulation. The aim is to help disseminate best practice and to strengthen cooperation with a view to improving regulation at Community and national levels.

Modernisation of existing legislation

The body of current legislation is an essential point of reference for the public and for businesses. Recognising this, the Commission launched a major simplification programme in October 2005 for a period of three years (2005–08) ([1]). Some 50 simplification proposals were presented under this programme in 2006 relating to areas ranging from the Community customs code to the framework directive on waste, the common organisation of the markets in the agricultural sector, payment services and structural statistics on businesses. Given that over 20 proposals are still before the European Parliament or the Council, procedures for accelerating their adoption might be considered.

The Commission updated its simplification programme in November, adding a further 43 new proposals with a view to increasing its impact and producing tangible economic benefits, particularly by cutting the administrative costs arising from legislation. The Commission has included the simplification programme in its annual work programme, thereby signalling that priority will now be given to simplifying existing legislation. The Commission's priorities for simplification correspond closely to the views expressed by the Parliament's committees on the multiannual simplification programme. Forty-seven initiatives are planned for 2007.

The Commission has proposed launching an ambitious strategy to cut administrative costs and has suggested that the spring 2007 European Council set a joint target with the Member States with a view to achieving a 25 % reduction by 2012.

On 14 November the Commission also adopted a communication on reduction of the response burden and simplification and priority-setting in the field of Community statistics ([2]). This sets out a strategy for continuing the efforts to reduce the burden on businesses resulting from the collection of statistics.

([1]) COM(2005) 535.
([2]) COM(2006) 693.

Work has started again on the process of repealing instruments that are no longer part of the active *acquis* and codifying Community acts to reduce their volume. After a slower start than initially intended, largely because of the need for translations into a growing number of official languages, the codification programme has been reviewed and extra resources have been allocated. It covers approximately 500 legislative acts in all fields. The Commission has so far finalised 85: 52 of these have been adopted and published in the *Official Journal of the European Union* and 33 are awaiting adoption by the European Parliament and the Council. These 85 acts replace 300 existing pieces of legislation. The 500 acts covered by the programme will replace approximately 2 000 instruments in all. The Commission plans to complete the programme in 2008 ([1]).

In a resolution adopted on 16 May the European Parliament expressed its firm support for the process of simplifying the Union's regulatory environment to ensure that it is appropriate, simple and effective. It feels that priority should be given to simplifying regulations rather than directives and to repealing outdated and obsolete acts, and considers codification and recasting to be important instruments for simplifying the Community *acquis*.

The June European Council welcomed the simplification programme and urged all its configurations to give priority to simplification proposals.

Application of Community law

As guardian of the Treaties, the Commission has made monitoring the application of Community law one of its strategic objectives. The coexistence of 25, 27 on 1 January 2007, legal systems within the European Union and the volume of the Community *acquis* — nearly 3 000 directives — represent new challenges. Compliance with the provisions of Community law in all Member States is essential to ensure that citizens and businesses benefit promptly and fully from the advantages of Community law.

The Commission continued to examine this policy during 2006 as part of the follow-up to its 2002 communication on better monitoring of the application of Community law ([2]). In doing so it took account of Parliament's recent resolution of 16 May on the application of Community law. As part of its ongoing work, the Commission continued to examine the various monitoring methods available, in order to increase their effectiveness and improve the provision of information on monitoring activities. Its analysis focused on:

- making greater allowance for possible difficulties with transposal when preparing each new directive;

([1]) Consolidated versions of 1 800 of the 2 000 acts in force which have been amended are available on the EUR-Lex website (http://eur-lex.europa.eu/en/index.htm). Two thirds of these are available in 19 languages.

([2]) See COM(2002) 725, 11 December 2002, at: http://ec.europa.eu/governance/docs/comm_infraction_en.pdf.

- planning monitoring that is proportionate to the nature of each directive during the transposal period; and

- the value of Member States providing tables correlating national provisions with the provisions of the directives.

The Commission continued to analyse ways of reducing the number of cases of non-compliance with Community law and the time they take to process, bearing in mind the existing or potential mechanisms for providing an immediate solution to problems affecting individuals arising from the incorrect application of Community law. In its response to Parliament's resolutions on the better regulation initiative the Commission has undertaken to find answers to these problems. Another issue under discussion has been the need to provide systematic information in response to the interest generated by questions associated with Commission action in the field of monitoring the application of Community law.

Subsidiarity and proportionality

At its meeting in June, the European Council recalled that the confidence of citizens in the European project can benefit from European legislation reflecting more strongly the added value of Union action rather than action at the different national levels. It therefore called on the European Parliament, the Council and the Commission to consistently check the correct application of the principles and guidelines laid down in the 'Protocol on subsidiarity and proportionality'. The European Council also welcomed the initiative taken by the Austrian Presidency to hold a conference on subsidiarity in St Pölten, in April, as a follow-up to the conference in The Hague in 2005 under the Dutch Presidency.

On 13 June the Commission presented its 13th report on better regulation relating to the application of the principles of subsidiarity and proportionality in 2005 ([1]).

Transparency

In connection with the launch of a European transparency initiative in November 2005, the Commission adopted a Green Paper on 3 May marking the start of a public consultation procedure which lasted until 31 August ([2]). The consultation was on transparency in relations between European Union institutions and lobbyists, ways of providing better information to the general public on the recipients of European Union funding, and perceptions of the Commission's consultation practices.

In October, in an effort to ensure greater transparency in budgetary matters, the Commission decided to give the public access to two Internet sites on Europa

---

[1] COM(2006) 289.
[2] COM(2006) 194.

containing information about Community grants and public contracts ([1]). By showing the way as regards the Community funds that are administered centrally, the Commission is trying to encourage the Member States to adopt the same approach for the Community funds which they administer jointly (for example in the areas of cohesion, agriculture and fisheries), which represent three quarters of all Community financing.

In a resolution adopted on 4 April the European Parliament asked the Commission to present a proposal for legislation on the public right of access to Parliament, Council and Commission documents.

In another resolution adopted the same day the European Parliament endorsed the European Ombudsman's recommendation to the Council that it reconsider its refusal to hold its meetings in public when it is acting as legislator. At its June meeting the European Council, convinced of the need to make the Council's work more transparent, adopted an overall policy on transparency based on the following measures: opening to the public all Council deliberations on legislative acts adopted under the co-decision procedure and the first deliberations on other legislative acts which, given their importance, are presented orally by the Commission in Council sessions; organising regular public debates on important issues affecting the interests of the Union and its citizens; opening to the public the deliberations of the General Affairs and External Relations Council on its 18-month programme, as well as the debates of other Council configurations on their priorities; and public presentation of the Commission's five-year programme, its annual work programme and its annual policy strategy, with the ensuing debates also held in public.

Interinstitutional cooperation ([2])

On 17 May, following a compromise between the three institutions on the 2007–13 financial perspective, the European Parliament, the Council and the Commission signed an interinstitutional agreement on budgetary discipline and sound financial management ([3]). This agreement, which comes into force on 1 January 2007, contains a new chapter on financial management and a number of institutional commitments to more effective budget implementation.

It also contains a clause on reviewing the financial framework, to be implemented as of 2008–09, and gives Parliament a major role in this overall review exercise covering all aspects of European Union funding and expenditure.

([1]) http://ec.europa.eu/grants/beneficiaries_en.htm   and   http://ec.europa.eu/public_contracts/beneficiaries_en.htm.
([2]) Relations with national parliaments are dealt with under 'Commission' in Chapter VI of this Report.
([3]) OJ C 139, 14.6.2006. See also Section 3 of this chapter.

Economic governance

On 20 December the European Parliament and the Council established a revised statistical classification of economic activities in the European Community (NACE Rev. 2) ([1]). The revision is fundamental to the Commission's current efforts to reform Community statistics. By ensuring more comparable and reliable data the new classification can help improve economic governance at both Community and national levels.

General references and other useful links

- Better regulation:
  http://ec.europa.eu/governance/better_regulation/index_en.htm

- Impact assessment:
  http://ec.europa.eu/governance/impact/index_en.htm

- Civil society:
  http://ec.europa.eu/civil_society/index_en.htm

- EUR-Lex:
  http://eur-lex.europa.eu/

Section 2

Communication strategy

Background

Aware of the widening gap between a large sector of public opinion and the European project, which was highlighted in certain Member States by the debate surrounding the Treaty establishing a Constitution for Europe, the Union institutions worked throughout 2005 on developing a new approach to communication policy and measures, with greater emphasis on connecting with and listening to citizens.

Having consequently made communication one of the strategic objectives for its term of office, the Commission itself took two key initiatives in 2005. The first of these was to adopt an internal action plan aimed at its own staff to ensure more effective communication, and the second the preparation of a White Paper setting out its policy vision and the initiatives to be undertaken in the medium and long term.

([1]) Regulation (EC) No 1893/2006 (OJ L 393, 30.12.2006).

White Paper on a European communication policy

The Commission published its White Paper ([1]), which it began drafting in 2005, on 1 February. The principal aim is to get all the key players actively involved: European Union institutions and bodies, Member States, regional and local authorities, political parties and civil society. It identifies five areas for joint action.

- To ensure that all citizens of the Union have the right to information and freedom of expression, the White Paper proposes drawing up a European charter or code of conduct on communication which the national and European Union institutions will be able to subscribe to on a voluntary basis.

- The White Paper speaks of 'empowering citizens', by providing the tools and instruments to: improve civic education (e.g. teachers' network, digitally connected European libraries); connect people with each other (e.g. physical and virtual meeting places); and strengthen relations between citizens and institutions (e.g. minimum standards for consultation).

- The White Paper aims to involve the media more effectively in communicating about Europe, placing the accent on exploiting the information potential of new technologies such as the Internet. It also envisages upgrading 'Europe by satellite' to provide the media with more and better material and introducing European training programmes in public communication for officials of national and European Union institutions.

- To better anticipate and understand trends in public opinion by pooling resources and exchanging best practice, the White Paper puts forward two options: setting up a network of national experts in public opinion research and establishing an independent observatory for European public opinion.

- Lastly, the White Paper again underlines the need to 'do the job together' by means of a partnership involving all the key actors: European Union institutions, Member States, regional and local authorities, political parties and civil society organisations.

The European Economic and Social Committee issued an opinion on the Commission White Paper on 6 July ([2]). Expressing reservations about a code of conduct setting out general principles, the Committee called on the Commission to reflect further on how genuine synergies and interinstitutional cooperation can be facilitated at a decentralised level.

([1]) COM(2006) 35.
([2]) OJ C 309, 16.12.2006.

New homepage for the Commission

As part of the continued drive for better — and consequently more successful — communication with European citizens, the Commission's new homepage has been designed specifically with them in mind ([1]).

The page now contains topical news items about the Union which are written daily and translated into all the official languages of the Union as quickly as possible. This represents real progress as, until now, the European Commission has not been able to present daily news in all the official languages. Mindful of the new emphasis on 'going local', the new-look homepage also introduces a section 'Around Europe — News from Member States', which publishes local news items in cooperation with the Commission representations in the Member States. Other content includes a section covering the activities of Commissioners, an 'On the agenda' section with interesting events and, last but not least, an invitation to take part in the 'Debate Europe' discussion forum.

The main navigation features of the homepage have been revamped to accommodate more effectively the needs and interests of the public. It still covers all Commission activities, but priority is given to the topics visitors are looking for.

Translation of Internet sites

In view of the increasing use of the Internet as a means of communication, the Commission's Directorate-General for Translation has allocated resources specifically to website translation.

General references and other useful links

- Directorate-General for Communication:
  http://ec.europa.eu/dgs/communication/index_en.htm
- Information sources and contact points for the European Union:
  http://europa.eu/geninfo/info/index_en.htm

([1]) http://ec.europa.eu/index_en.htm.

Section 3

The future of Europe

Constitution (¹)

> **Background**
>
> *The Treaty establishing a Constitution for Europe was signed in Rome on 29 October 2004 by the Heads of State or Government of the European Union and submitted for ratification in accordance with the respective constitutional procedures of all the Member States. This process began in 2004 and by the end of 2005 it had been completed by 13 of the 25 Member States. However, the 'no' votes in referendums organised in France and the Netherlands mean that it has not as yet been possible to ratify the Treaty in either country.*

The ratification process continued in 2006. The text was approved by Belgium by the parliamentary method on 8 February, by Estonia on 9 May and by Finland on 5 December. As at end 2006 seven Member States had still not taken a final decision.

Plan D

> **Background**
>
> *At the European Council meeting in June 2005, the Heads of State or Government of the European Union agreed to launch a 'period of reflection' to encourage a broad debate on the future of the Union following the 'no' votes on the Treaty establishing a Constitution for Europe in France and the Netherlands. In October 2005 the Commission presented its own Plan D for Democracy, Dialogue and Debate on the future of Europe, proposing new ways of involving citizens and helping them take ownership of Community policies, policies which in the process would become easier for them to understand.*

On 27 March, as part of Plan D, the Commission set up a discussion forum (²), now accessible in the 22 official languages of the Union, with a view to facilitating in-depth discussion and debate with European citizens on topics such as economic and social development, their perception of the Union and its tasks, and Europe's borders and its role in the world.

On 10 May, with an eye to the June European Council, the Commission adopted two communications as part of the ongoing debate. The first, 'The period of reflection and

---

(¹) http://europa.eu/constitution/index_en.htm.
(²) http://europa.eu/debateeurope/index_en.htm.

Plan D' ([1]), summarises the discussions and focuses on the lessons already learned from Plan D. These conclusions tie in with a second communication, 'A citizens' agenda — Delivering results for Europe' ([2]), which sets out some 12 practical proposals, including reviewing the single market, particularly from the point of view of solidarity and citizens' rights, improving the decision-making process, taking forward the debate on the value added of enlargement and the absorption capacity of the Union, continuing measures under the better regulation initiative, and accelerating work on public access to documents. As to method, the Commission is proposing a two-track approach — making the most of the possibilities offered by the existing Treaties in order to achieve concrete results while at the same time finding a way to continue the reform process.

This contribution was welcomed with interest by the European Council of 15 and 16 June, which endorsed the recommended two-track approach. It also welcomed the various initiatives taken by the Member States in the framework of national debates, like the conference organised in Salzburg in January by the Austrian Presidency, and expressed its gratitude to the European Parliament for having organised together with the Austrian Parliament the parliamentary meeting in May on the future of Europe. Essentially, the European Council felt that after a year of useful reflection it was now vital to focus on delivery of results and implementation of projects.

A first consultation of citizens was held in Brussels on 8 and 9 October. This event, co-financed by the Commission, brought together some 200 people, who identified three areas for future discussion at national level: energy and the environment, social welfare and the family, and the role of Europe in international affairs.

On 29 November the Commission adopted an information note from Vice-President Wallström to the Commission entitled 'Plan D — Wider and deeper debate on Europe', which takes stock of the implementation of Plan D one year after its adoption and sets out a roadmap to further widen and deepen the debate following the extension of the reflection period ([3]).

([1]) COM(2006) 212.
([2]) COM(2006) 211.
([3]) SEC(2006) 1553.

Financial perspective for 2007–13 (¹)

Background

The December 2005 the European Council reached political agreement on the main aspects of the financial framework for 2007–13. Following a period of intensive negotiations between the European Parliament, the Council and the Commission, the 'Interinstitutional agreement on budgetary discipline and sound financial management'(²) was signed by the three institutions on 17 May. The agreement sets expenditure ceilings for each heading (categories of expenditure) over the seven-year period and sets out the rules for cooperation between the institutions on budgetary issues.

The total appropriations provided for in the 2007–13 financial framework amount to EUR 864 316 million in commitments (1.048 % of Union gross national income (GNI)) and EUR 820 780 million in payments (1.00 % of GNI). The breakdown by heading is as follows.

- 1. Sustainable growth: EUR 382 139 million, of which:
    - – 1a. Competitiveness for growth and employment: EUR 74 098 million
    - – 1b. Cohesion for growth and employment: EUR 308 041 million

- 2. Preservation and management of natural resources: EUR 371 344 million, of which:
    - – Market-related expenditure and direct payments: EUR 293 105 million

- 3. Citizenship, freedom, security and justice:
    - – 3a. Freedom, security and justice: EUR 6 630 million
    - – 3b. Citizenship: EUR 4 140 million

- 4. European Union as a global player: EUR 49 463 million

- 5. Administration: EUR 49 800 million

- 6. Compensation to new Member States (Bulgaria and Romania): EUR 800 million

Greater flexibility in the use of European Union funds has been achieved through additional tools outside the financial framework, namely the Emergency Aid Reserve, the European Union Solidarity Fund, the Flexibility Instrument and the European Globalisation Adjustment Fund. The rules for managing these instruments and the procedure for mobilising them are set out in the interinstitutional agreement.

The agreement also includes a number of commitments from the institutions on the sound financial management of European Union funds, relating in particular to the

---

(¹) http://ec.europa.eu/financial_perspective/index_en.htm.
(²) OJ C 139, 14.6.2006. See also 'Interinstitutional cooperation' in Section 1 of this chapter.

internal control of Community funds, the future renewal of the financial regulation, and annual financial programming.

In a declaration annexed to the agreement, in accordance with the conclusions of the European Council the Commission is requested to undertake a wide-ranging review covering all aspects of European Union spending, including the common agricultural policy, and of resources, including the United Kingdom rebate, and to report in 2008/09.

Chapter II

Prosperity

Section 1

Economic and social environment

The Lisbon strategy: partnership for growth and employment

Background

In March 2005, drawing on lessons learnt from five years of implementation, the European Council decided on a fundamental relaunch of the Lisbon strategy. It agreed to refocus priorities on jobs and growth, by mobilising to a greater extent all national and Community resources in the three dimensions of the strategy (economic, social and environmental) with a view to tapping more effectively into their synergies in the general context of sustainable development. At their informal meeting at Hampton Court in October 2005, the Heads of State or Government gave further political impetus to the revised strategy by emphasising in particular the way in which European values can underpin modernisation in our economies and societies in a globalised world.

In July 2005, with a view to implementing the strategy, the Commission presented a Community programme covering all Community actions for growth and employment. At the end of the year, the Member States sent their national reform programmes to the Commission, which began examining them for the spring 2006 European Council.

On 25 January 2006 the Commission presented to the European Council its 2006 annual report on the revised Lisbon strategy, in the form of a communication 'Time to move up a gear — The new partnership for growth and jobs' ([1]). In it the Commission gives its analysis of the 25 national reform programmes presented by the Member States, pointing out their strengths, so as to promote a fruitful exchange of ideas, while proposing concrete actions to remedy a number of shortcomings highlighted in the report.

([1]) COM(2006) 30.

The Commission sets out four areas for priority action and presents specific proposals, later approved by the European Council at its meeting of 23 and 24 March, including:

- investing more in knowledge and innovation: in particular, specific objectives are laid down for each Member State as regards the proportion of national wealth to be devoted to research and development between now and 2010 and for improving innovation policies; in addition, the removal of constraints on universities and researchers is strongly recommended, as are a number of initiatives put forward by the Commission, such as setting up a European Institute for Technology and encouraging the development of venture capital funds;

- unlocking business potential, particularly that of SMEs: the European Council committed itself to improving the conditions for setting up businesses;

- responding to globalisation and ageing of the population: prioritising the effort to create jobs on certain categories, with 'flexicurity' seen as the type of integrated approach that the Lisbon strategy aims to encourage; and

- moving towards an efficient European Union energy policy: the Green Paper ([1]) presented by the Commission just before the European Council was welcomed as a solid basis for discussion and future decisions in this area with a view to achieving sustainability, competitiveness and security; the European Council tasked the Commission with developing this policy and drawing up an action plan to be presented for its approval at its spring 2007 session.

The March European Council also stressed the vital need to develop specific measures to create a real sense of ownership of the partnership for growth and jobs among citizens themselves. The European Council also adopted the Commission proposal for organising exchanges of good policy ideas and practices ('sharing success'). With that in mind, the Commission organised, jointly with Portugal, an initial high-level seminar on excellence and 'knowledge partnerships' between universities, research centres and businesses.

At their informal meeting in Lahti (Finland) on 20 October and on the basis of a Commission communication ([2]), the Heads of State or Government developed a strategic approach to innovation against the background of the consensus forged during the discussion of the renewed Lisbon strategy. They identified key areas in which Community action is required to create more favourable conditions for innovation in Europe ([3]).

In a resolution adopted on 15 March the European Parliament expressed satisfaction with the presentation of national plans by the Member States and called for them to be implemented rapidly and efficiently.

([1]) See 'Energy' in Section 2 of this chapter.
([2]) COM(2006) 589.
([3]) See also 'Innovation and competitiveness' in Section 2 of this chapter.

In addition to its general approach outlined above, the Commission issued communications on more specific aspects related to the implementation of the Lisbon strategy. These aspects (entrepreneurship, business transfers, corporate social responsibility, etc.) are dealt with under the relevant subject headings of this Report.

On 12 December the Commission presented its report for the spring 2007 European Council, based on the progress reports submitted by the Member States ([1]). The report sums up the progress achieved in implementing the strategy at both Community and Member State levels, reaffirms and develops the areas for priority action and puts forward specific suggestions for taking the strategy forward. It also gives detailed assessments of the progress made by each Member State in implementing its national reform programme.

The sustainable development strategy

Revision of the sustainable development strategy

Background

Sustainable development can be defined as a better quality of life for all, today and for future generations. It is a vision of progress which embraces economic development, environmental protection and social justice.

In June 2001 the Gothenburg European Council approved a strategy for sustainable development proposed by the Commission. This strategy, which complements the more general economic strategy adopted a year earlier in Lisbon, proposes measures aimed at the welfare of European citizens facing such challenges as climate change, poverty and health risks.

At the same time as the Lisbon strategy was relaunched in 2005 in the form of the partnership for growth and employment, the idea of revising the sustainable development strategy began to gain ground. A solid basis was laid in December 2005 with the presentation by the Commission of a communication aiming to refine the strategy adopted in 2001 and develop the existing framework ([2]).

In June 2006, based on the platform for action presented by the Commission the previous December and on contributions from, in particular the European Parliament, the Council and the European Economic and Social Committee, the European Council adopted a new sustainable development strategy for an enlarged European Union in the context of the necessary world solidarity. The new strategy also reflects the guiding principles for sustainable development approved by the European Council in June 2005.

([1]) COM(2006) 816.
([2]) COM(2005) 658.

One of the main strengths of the new sustainable development strategy is synergy with the Lisbon strategy, in that both aim to support the necessary structural changes to enable the Member States' economies to flourish, whilst ensuring social equity and a healthy environment. In addition, the sustainable development strategy sets out an approach to better policymaking based on better regulation and on the principle that sustainable development is to be integrated into policymaking at all levels.

The new sustainable development strategy pinpoints seven key challenges, with general objectives, operational objectives and relevant measures:

- to limit climate change and promote clean energy;

- to ensure that our transport systems meet society's economic, social and environmental needs;

- to promote sustainable consumption and production patterns;

- to improve management and avoid overexploitation of natural resources;

- to promote good public health on equal conditions and improve protection against health threats;

- to create an inclusive society by taking into account solidarity between and within generations and to secure and increase the quality of life of citizens as a precondition for lasting individual well-being; and

- actively to promote sustainable development worldwide and ensure that the European Union's internal and external policies are consistent with such development and its international commitments.

In order to ensure that European Union funding is used and channelled in an optimum way to promote sustainable development, Member States and the Commission are asked to adopt a coordinated approach in enhancing complementarities and synergies between various strands of Community and other part-financing mechanisms such as cohesion policy, rural development, LIFE+, research and technological development, the competitiveness and innovation programme and the European Fisheries Fund.

The Commission is also asked to mainstream sustainable development in its information, awareness-raising and communication activities and to mobilise stakeholders by organising events and meetings on the various strands of the SDS.

As regards follow-up, the Commission will in September 2007 and every two years thereafter submit a progress report covering both the implementation of the SDS in the European Union and the Member States, and future priorities, orientations and actions. For its part the Council will, at regular intervals, examine progress with regard to sustainable development indicators. On the basis of the Commission progress report and the Council's contributions, the European Council will review progress and priorities every two years. It will also provide general orientations on measures, strategies and instruments for sustainable development, taking account of priorities under the Lisbon strategy for growth and jobs. This approach will allow coherent treatment of cross-cutting issues such as climate change, energy efficiency, ageing of the population and social cohesion.

The macroeconomic framework

General approach

In its communication of 12 July entitled 'Joint harmonised EU programme of business and consumer surveys' ([1]) the Commission stresses that data from such surveys have become an indispensable tool for economic surveillance in the European Union and for monitoring the economic prospects for economic and monetary union as well as the development of the candidate countries' economies. The Commission therefore wishes to strengthen the role of the programme in the future, in particular by presenting every three years, starting in 2008, a report on implementation over the previous period.

Stability and Growth Pact

Background

The Stability and Growth Pact, based on a political agreement reached at the Amsterdam European Council in June 1997, is intended to ensure sound management of public finances in the Union in order to prevent a lax budgetary policy in one Member State from penalising the other Member States via interest rates and undermining confidence in economic stability. It also seeks to encourage sustained and durable convergence of the economies of the Member States belonging to the euro area.

In view of the difficulties and inadequacies identified in recent years in implementing the pact, the basic provisions were updated in 2005 to enable it to be applied fairly and consistently in all countries and to be understood by the general public. The reform allows more account to be taken of economic trends, though the two lynchpins of the pact — the 3 % reference figure for the deficit-to-GNP ratio and the 60 % reference figure for the debt-to-GNP ratio — have been maintained. The reform reinforces the commitment to a sustainable minimum structural adjustment. Changes were made to the pact's preventive arm, introducing the possibility of differentiating the medium-term budgetary objectives according to the level of debt and the potential for growth and even, in certain circumstances, of temporarily deviating from these budgetary objectives in the case of major structural reforms. Amendments were also made to the corrective arm of the pact in order to reflect more accurately the realities of an enlarged European Union of 25 Member States.

([1]) COM(2006) 379.

In a communication of 13 June (¹) the Commission gave a positive assessment of the first year of application of the revised Stability and Growth Pact. The revision allowed Member States in a situation of excessive deficit to move back below or close to the 3 % threshold by means, in particular, of more pragmatic deadlines and structural measures. In the view of the Commission, the new pact has thus regained credibility, although its preventive arm calls for additional efforts from the Member States, which are asked to consolidate their public finances. On 11 July the Council also gave a positive assessment of the first year and wanted to take the opportunity afforded by the favourable economic situation to pursue and accelerate budgetary consolidation efforts. However, at its February session (²) the European Economic and Social Committee had taken the view that, since reform of the pact was still not complete, guidelines were needed on strengthening European economic governance. Similarly, in a resolution adopted on 17 May, the European Parliament expressed concern at the difficulties in implementing the pact.

Alongside this assessment of the reform of the pact itself, the Community institutions conducted their annual review of the situation in each Member State.

On the basis of Commission recommendations, the Council successively adopted its opinions on the updated stability and convergence programmes of the EU-25: on a case-by-case basis, it found that they complied fully, broadly or partially with the requirements of the revised Stability and Growth Pact.

At its spring session the European Council noted that 12 Member States were in excessive deficit (the Council had judged the United Kingdom's deficit to be excessive in January) and that the debt levels were above 60 % of GDP in several Member States. It called upon Member States to use the opportunity of the evolving economic recovery to pursue fiscal consolidation in line with the Stability and Growth Pact. On 11 July (³), in the light of the recovery of the situation in Cyprus, the Council repealed a previous decision on the existence of an excessive deficit in that country. Similarly, on 29 November the Commission recommended that the Council close the excessive deficit procedure opened in respect of France in view of the improvement of its public deficit (⁴). On the other hand, on 14 March the Council adopted a decision giving Germany official notice to bring its public deficit as quickly as possible — in 2007 at the latest (⁵) — below the threshold of 3 % of gross domestic product laid down in the Treaty. On 10 October the Council issued for the third year running a recommendation to Hungary concerning the worsening of its budgetary deficit and the general deterioration of its public finances. On 28 November the Council noted the failure of Poland to take effective measures to reduce its deficit (⁶). In view of its

---

(¹) COM(2006) 304.
(²) OJ C 88, 11.4.2006.
(³) Decision 2006/627/EC (OJ L 256, 20.9.2006).
(⁴) SEC(2006) 1529.
(⁵) Decision 2006/344/EC (OJ L 126, 13.5.2006).
(⁶) Decision 2006/1014/EC (OJ L 414, 30.12.2006).

inability to comply with the Council's previous recommendations — it had been given until the end of 2007 to introduce corrections — Poland will be set a new deadline.

Quality and sustainability of public finances

At its spring session the European Council stressed the need for a number of Member States to undertake ambitious new reforms to improve the sustainability of their social security systems and to obviate the economic and budgetary consequences of the ageing of the population. Invited by the European Council to undertake a comprehensive assessment of the sustainability of public finances in the Member States, the Commission presented a communication on this on 12 October ([1]): it points out that such an assessment must be based on long-term age-related government expenditure projections and on budgetary strategies presented in the stability and convergence programmes, and confirms that the three-pronged strategy decided by the Stockholm European Council in 2001 (reducing debt at a fast pace, raising employment rates and productivity, and reforming pension, healthcare and long-term care systems) is appropriate and needs to be pursued.

For its part, the Council commented on several occasions in the course of the year on the quality of public finances. In its conclusions of 10 October, in stressing that budgetary rules vary considerably as between Member States, it highlighted a series of common characteristics that add to the effectiveness of national rules against a background of healthy public finances and compliance with the stability pact.

Economic and monetary union (EMU)

On a general level, the Commission on 12 July adopted its annual statement on the euro area ([2]), along with the annual report on the euro area. These annual reports highlight the common political challenges facing euro area members as a result of their growing economic interdependence as a result of EMU. As regards the Member States outside the euro area, on 5 December the Commission presented a convergence report ([3]) to help some of those Member States with their efforts to meet the requirements for adopting the euro.

In a communication of 14 July the Commission presented various components of, and supporting activities for, an actions programme for the promotion of research and analysis of issues related to the European economic and monetary union ([4]).

With a view to the celebration of the 50th anniversary of the Treaties of Rome on 25 March 2007, the Council called for the issue of a two-euro commemorative coin bearing a common design on the national side.

([1]) COM(2006) 574.
([2]) COM(2006) 392.
([3]) COM(2006) 762.
([4]) COM(2006) 389.

On the basis of a report from the European Central Bank and its own 2006 convergence report on Slovenia ([1]), the Commission proposed a decision on Slovenia's adoption of the euro. The proposal was received positively by the June European Council and, following a favourable opinion from the European Parliament, was adopted by the Council on 11 July. It will take effect on 1 January 2007 ([2]). Slovenia will thus be the first of the 10 Member States that joined the European Union in 2004 to adopt the euro. In addition, the Commission adopted its third report (22 June) ([3]) and fourth report (10 November) ([4]) on the practical preparations for the future enlargement of the euro area. These reports deal essentially with Slovenia, as detailed above, and Cyprus and Malta, both of which have designated 1 January 2008 as the target date for the adoption of the single currency.

The activities of the European Central Bank (ECB) are discussed in Chapter VI of this Report.

On 22 November the Commission adopted a communication in which it reviews the European Union economy in 2006 ([5]), and defines inter alia the key policy priorities for strengthening the euro area.

Taxation

General approach

As pointed out in a major Commission communication in October 2005 ([6]), taxation, like the customs union, is an important factor in helping the European Union achieve the Lisbon objectives.

This link with the revised Lisbon strategy was highlighted in 2006 by the proposal drawn up by the Commission for a decision of the European Parliament and of the Council establishing the Fiscalis 2013 programme ([7]). The programme aims to improve the operation of taxation systems in the Member States by continuing to develop cooperation between tax administrations in areas such as the common application of Community tax legislation and the smooth functioning of the internal market through the combating of tax avoidance and evasion.

---

[1] COM(2006) 224.
[2] Decision 2006/495/EC (OJ L 195, 15.7.2006).
[3] COM(2006) 322.
[4] COM(2006) 671.
[5] COM(2006) 714.
[6] COM(2005) 532.
[7] COM(2006) 202.

Combating tax evasion or fiscal fraud was the subject of a Commission communication of 31 May (¹). The communication launches a debate on a coordinated strategy on this issue. The Council welcomed the initiative in its conclusions of 7 June.

Direct taxation

Strong emphasis was placed on the link between direct taxation and implementation of the Lisbon strategy in a Commission communication of 5 April, which reports on progress to date on a common consolidated corporate tax base (next steps towards a CCCTB) (²). It also draws attention to those areas where further political support and direction is desirable, without seeking commitments from Member States to the legislative proposal. The European Economic and Social Committee had, at its February session, delivered an explanatory opinion on the creation of such a common tax base (³), followed, at its May session, by an opinion on tackling the corporation tax obstacles of small and medium-sized enterprises in the internal market (⁴).

On 22 November the Commission adopted a communication concerning a more effective use of tax incentives in favour of research and development (⁵), examining the legal constraints on measures of this type and presenting general principles to guide Member States in drawing up and implementing them.

On 4 December the Commission proposed a recast of Directive 69/335/EEC concerning taxes on the raising of capital (⁶). The purpose of the proposal is to simplify a very complicated piece of Community legislation, phase out capital duty, which is recognised as a significant obstacle to the development of European Union companies, and reinforce the prohibition on creating or levying of other similar taxes.

On 19 December the Commission adopted a communication announcing a series of initiatives intended to improve the coordination of Member States' direct tax systems (⁷). The aim is to ensure that national direct tax systems are compatible with Community rules and that they operate coherently among themselves. These initiatives are intended to eliminate the discrimination and double taxation suffered by taxpayers, whether individuals or businesses, while avoiding tax evasion and the erosion of the tax base. On the same day the Commission adopted two communications concerning two areas in which a coordinated approach would be possible: exit taxation (⁸) and the tax treatment of losses in cross-border situations (⁹).

(¹) COM(2006) 254.
(²) COM(2006) 157.
(³) OJ C 88, 11.4.2006.
(⁴) OJ C 195, 18.8.2006.
(⁵) COM(2006) 728.
(⁶) COM(2006) 760.
(⁷) COM(2006) 823
(⁸) COM(2006) 825.
(⁹) COM(2006) 824.

As regards transfer pricing, in November the joint transfer pricing forum adopted a report on procedures to resolve disputes in this area. On the basis of that report, the Commission is drafting a communication setting out guidelines for advanced pricing agreements in Europe. It was also decided that the forum would be reappointed for another term.

Indirect taxation

In 2006 the Council adopted a number of legislative proposals concerning indirect taxation, including:

- on 14 February, a directive extending until 31 December 2010 the experiment consisting in applying reduced rates of valued added tax (VAT) to labour-intensive services [1]; on 7 November, for the implementation of the new directive, the Council authorised 17 Member States to begin applying or to continue to apply, as the case may be, these reduced rates from 1 January 2006 to 31 December 2010 [2]; in addition, the Commission proposed similar provisions to authorise Romania to apply the reduced rates from 1 January 2007 [3];

- on 27 June, a directive extending until 31 December 2006 the period of application of the value added tax arrangements applicable to radio and television broadcasting services and certain electronically supplied financial services [4];

- on 24 July, a directive amending the sixth VAT directive, to give Member States the possibility of rapidly adopting measures to counter tax evasion or avoidance in certain specific and identified sectors [5]; the directive also lays down measures to simplify application of the tax in certain cases where the taxable persons concerned are facing financial difficulties;

- on 5 October, a directive codifying the system of exemption from taxes of imports of small consignments of goods of a non-commercial character from third countries [6]; and

- on 28 November, a directive on the common system of value added tax [7], which recasts the sixth VAT directive, thus considerably improving the readability of the existing legislation.

For its part, the Commission proposed:

- on 22 February, to modernise the rules on the exemption from valued added tax and excise duty of goods imported by persons travelling from third countries [8], in

---

[1] Directive 2006/18/EC (OJ L 51, 22.2.2006).
[2] Decision 2006/774/EC (OJ L 314, 15.11.2006).
[3] COM(2006) 739.
[4] Directive 2006/58/EC (OJ L 174, 28.6.2006).
[5] Directive 2006/69/EC (OJ L 221, 12.8.2006).
[6] Directive 2006/79/EC (OJ L 286, 17.10.2006).
[7] Directive 2006/112/EC (OJ L 347, 11.12.2006).
[8] COM(2006) 76.

order to adapt the system of tax reductions in the light of the enlargement of the European Union and the fact that the Community's external borders now extend as far as Russia, Ukraine and Belarus in particular;

- on 8 September, to increase the minimum rates of excise duty by amending Directive 92/84/EEC on the approximation of the rates of excise duty on alcohol and alcoholic beverages ([1]);

- on 19 October, to codify the arrangements for mutual assistance for the recovery of claims relating to certain levies, duties, taxes and other measures ([2]); this initiative is a follow-up in particular to the Commission report of 8 February ([3]) on the matter; and

- on 24 November, to extend until 31 December 2008 the period of application of the value added tax arrangements applicable to radio and television broadcasting services and certain electronically supplied services ([4]); this directive was adopted by the Council on 19 December ([5]).

Moreover, in a communication adopted on 30 June ([6]), the Commission presented the results of a review of the derogations that expire at the end of 2006 and concern the application of the 2003 directive restructuring the Community framework for taxation of energy products and electricity ([7]).

Competition

Background

Modernisation of European Union competition law

Between 2000 and 2005 the principal building blocks for a modernisation of European Union competition law were progressively put in place.

The accession of 10 new Member States on 1 May 2004 coincided with the entry into force of two pillars of this reform concerning competition and businesses:

- *a set of rules ([8]) implementing the EC Treaty provisions on restrictive agreements (Article 81) and abuses of dominant positions (Article 82); and*

- *a new regulation on mergers ([9]).*

([1]) COM(2006) 486.
([2]) COM(2006) 605.
([3]) COM(2006) 43.
([4]) COM(2006) 739.
([5]) Directive 2006/138/EC (OJ L 384, 29.12.2006).
([6]) COM(2006) 342.
([7]) Directive 2003/96/EC (OJ L 283, 31.10.2003).
([8]) Regulations (EC) No 1/2003 (OJ L 1, 4.1.2003) and (EC) No 773/2004 (OJ L 123, 27.4.2004).
([9]) Regulation (EC) No 139/2004 (OJ L 24, 29.1.2004).

> *In 2005 the reform was taken forward by the Commission with the presentation of an action plan (¹) designed to lead, over a five-year period, to a comprehensive reform of State aid policy. This process took concrete form at the end of 2005 with the adoption of new guidelines on national regional aid. In December 2005 the Commission also adopted a Green Paper on damages actions for breach of the EC antitrust rules.*

In 2006 the Commission continued to concentrate its competition activities on sectors of major importance for the economy of the European Union and for its citizens, consistent with the implementation of the Lisbon strategy. Competition policy saw considerable new developments, of which State aid reform was a major component.

Competition and State aid

With the publication at the beginning of the year of the results of the public consultation on its action plan launched in June 2005, the Commission noted the overall stakeholder support for the principles and practical proposals set out in the document, which were also received favourably by Parliament.

Against this background, the Commission pursued its reform programme, adopting:

- new guidelines for risk capital (²) and for research and development and innovation (³);

- a regulation concerning regional aid (⁴), exempting from the requirement to give prior notification to the Commission regional investment aid that complies with the approved regional aid map for each Member State for the period 2007–13; and

- a new regulation concerning *de minimis* aid (⁵), exempting from the requirement to give prior notification to the Commission State aid of less than EUR 200 000 (as against EUR 100 000 under the previous regulation).

The Commission twice updated the 'State aid scoreboard', on 27 March (⁶) with a focus on acceding and candidate countries, and on 11 December (⁷) with a chapter dedicated to rescue and restructuring aid. In addition, at the beginning of April the Commission published the conclusions of a study on the application at national level of the rules on State aid, which gives an overview of the role of national courts in both the protection of undertakings against the granting of illegal aid to their competitors, and Member States' implementation of their recovery decisions.

(¹) COM(2005) 107.
(²) OJ C 194, 18.8.2006.
(³) OJ C 323, 30.12.2006.
(⁴) Regulation (EC) No 1628/2006 (OJ L 302, 1.11.2006).
(⁵) Regulation (EC) No 1998/2006 (OJ L 379, 28.12.2006).
(⁶) COM(2006) 130.
(⁷) COM(2006) 761.

In the interests of greater transparency, at the beginning of the year the Commission launched the 'State aid weekly e-news' e-bulletin [1], which details its activities relating to State aid.

The statistics show that, at 921, the number of State aid notifications to the Commission was up in 2006 compared with a year earlier. The Commission also took 713 final decisions [2]. It approved aid in about 98 % of cases; in the remaining 2 % of cases, it took a negative decision after concluding that the measures did not comply with State aid rules and with the common market.

Competition and businesses

In its capacity as guardian of free competition between businesses, the Commission has focused on consolidating earlier reforms and improving the enforcement of Community competition law with the proposal and implementation of modifications to both the legislation and the texts which lay down the framework for the exercise of its own decision-making powers.

On 28 June the Commission adopted guidelines clarifying the method applied by the Commission when it sets the fines imposed for violation of the antitrust rules and increasing the deterrent effect of these fines [3].

On 25 September the Council extended the scope of the rules on competition applicable to maritime transport [4] to include cabotage and tramp vessel services [5].

On 28 September the Commission adopted a block exemption regulation, which abolished the exemption for International Air Transport Association (IATA) passenger tariff conferences for routes within the European Union [6] from 1 January 2007.

On 7 December the Commission adopted an amended version of the leniency notice, which rewards undertakings that report hardcore cartels [7]. The revised leniency notice clarifies the information an applicant needs to provide to the Commission to benefit from immunity or from a reduction of fines and introduces a marker system for immunity applicants.

---

[1] http://ec.europa.eu/comm/competition/state_aid/overview/newsletter.html.
[2] These covered sectors such as the coal industry, agriculture, fisheries and transport, and the manufacturing and service sector.
[3] OJ C 210, 1.9.2006.
[4] Regulation (EC) No 1/2003 (OJ L 91, 4.1.2003).
[5] Regulation (EC) No 1419/2006 (OJ L 269, 28.9.2006).
[6] Regulation (EC) No 1459/2006 (OJ L 272, 3.10.2006).
[7] IP/06/1705.

As regards cartels, the Commission imposed fines totalling around EUR 1.8 billion for cartels involving bleaching chemicals ([1]), acrylic glass ([2]), road pavement bitumen ([3]), copper fittings ([4]) and synthetic rubber ([5]).

Concerning the abuse of dominant positions, on 29 March the Commission imposed a fine of EUR 24 million on the Tomra group for having abused its dominant position on the market for the supply of machines for the collection of used drink containers by means of exclusivity agreements, quantity commitments and loyalty-inducing discounts. On 12 July the Commission imposed a penalty of EUR 280.5 million on Microsoft for persistent failure to comply with some of the obligations laid down in the Commission decision of 24 March 2004 to eliminate the abuse of a dominant position in the market for operating-system software.

The Commission adopted several decisions rendering commitments entered into by undertakings legally binding. Such decisions are taken under a new procedure introduced at the time of the 'modernisation' of the rules implementing the provisions on competition laid down in the EC Treaty which allows the Commission to accept legally binding commitments offered by an undertaking and thereby bring an investigation to a close. The Commission thus adopted decisions to accept undertakings' commitments on 22 February concerning the market in rough diamonds ([6]), on 22 March concerning the sale of media rights to the Premier League football competition ([7]), on 12 April concerning service stations in Spain ([8]) and on 4 October concerning central licensing agreements for music copyrights ([9]).

In the area of company mergers, the number of notifications to the Commission continued to increase compared with previous years. More than 90 % of notified mergers were approved, most within one month. In a few cases, however, the Commission opened an in-depth investigation. In particular, in the energy sector the Commission took steps to ensure that mergers would not have anti-competitive effects on the markets. Thus, on 14 March, the Commission authorised the Danish gas incumbent to acquire control of the regional electricity generation incumbents in Denmark and Danish electricity suppliers only subject to compliance with certain conditions and obligations ([10]). Similarly, on 14 November, after an in-depth investigation, the Commission authorised the merger of Gaz de France and Suez, subject to certain conditions. In the light of the corrective structural measures

---

([1]) IP/06/560.
([2]) IP/06/698.
([3]) IP/06/1179.
([4]) IP/06/1222.
([5]) IP/06/1647.
([6]) IP/06/204.
([7]) IP/06/356.
([8]) IP/06/495.
([9]) IP/06/1311.
([10]) IP/06/313.

proposed by the parties, the Commission concluded that the merger would not significantly impede competition ([1]).

Asserting a proactive policy

In line with the proactive competition policy promoted by the Commission, the first findings were drawn from the sectoral inquiries launched in 2005 in areas key to the success of the Lisbon strategy ([2]). The energy sector inquiry interim report confirmed the existence of serious problems with the operation of the gas and electricity markets, such as a lack of significant cross-border competition and a lack of transparency in the setting of prices, at the expense of potential new operators and consumers. Similarly, the interim report for the inquiry into payment cards revealed the existence of several barriers to market entry, such as practices by banks and networks that raise costs for entrants ([3]).

With regard to information, the European Competition Network, which brings together the Commission and the national competition authorities, opened a website ([4]) which provides businesses, their advisors and citizens with information on the application of competition law, including all the press releases and annual reports produced by these different bodies.

Implementation of the social agenda

Social services of general interest

On 26 April the Commission presented a communication entitled 'Implementing the Community Lisbon programme: Social services of general interest in the European Union' ([5]). This communication, which is a follow-up to the White Paper on services of general interest ([6]), is a first step in taking the specific nature of social services more systematically into account at European level. It is structured around three topics: social services — pillars of European society and the European economy; the application of the Community rules in the area of social services; and better monitoring of and support for social services of general interest in the European Union. This initiative was welcomed by the Committee of the Regions in an opinion of 7 December.

General references and other useful links

- Lisbon strategy:
  http://ec.europa.eu/growthandjobs/index.htm

([1]) IP/06/1558.
([2]) COM(2004) 293.
([3]) IP/06/496.
([4]) http://www.internationalcompetitionnetwork.org/.
([5]) COM(2006) 177.
([6]) COM(2004) 374.

- Sustainable development:
  http://ec.europa.eu/environment/eussd/
- Stability and convergence programmes:
  http://ec.europa.eu/economy_finance/about/activities/sgp/scp_en.htm
- Excessive deficits:
  http://ec.europa.eu/economy_finance/about/activities/sgp/edp_en.htm
- European Central Bank (ECB):
  http://www.ecb.eu/home/html/index.en.html
- Taxation:
  http://ec.europa.eu/taxation_customs/taxation/gen_info/tax_policy/index_en.htm
- Competition:
  http://ec.europa.eu/comm/competition/index_en.html
- Prohibited restrictive agreements:
  http://ec.europa.eu/comm/competition/antitrust/cases/
- State aid:
  http://ec.europa.eu/comm/competition/state_aid/overview/index_en.html
- International Competition Network:
  http://www.internationalcompetitionnetwork.org/

Section 2

Levers of prosperity

Innovation and enterprise policy

Innovation and competitiveness

On 24 October the European Parliament and the Council adopted the 'Competitiveness and innovation' framework programme ([1]), which the Commission had proposed establishing in April 2005 ([2]). Designed for the period 2007–13, this programme is intended to open up and facilitate action in the fields of entrepreneurship and innovation, the use of information and communication technologies (ICT), and renewable energy and environmental technologies.

On 13 September the Commission presented a communication entitled 'Putting knowledge into practice: a broad-based innovation strategy for the European Union' ([3]), in which it defines a framework for the promotion of innovation combining different policy areas that have a bearing on innovation and draws attention to the

([1]) Decision No 1639/2006/EC (OJ L 310, 9.11.2006).
([2]) COM(2005) 121.
([3]) COM(2006) 502.

modernisation of universities, the European Institute of Technology, technology exchanges between industry and universities, the development of 'clusters', encouraging innovation through public procurement, and the development of a strategy to make better use of intellectual property. Furthermore, it introduces a more targeted strategy to facilitate the creation and marketing of new or innovatory products and services in promising areas ('high-growth markets'). To implement this initiative, the Commission does not propose to create new structures, but builds on the existing framework of the revised Lisbon partnership for growth and employment, which has already established a political platform for partnership between the Member States and the Commission.

On 12 October, further to the communication of 13 September, and as part of the preparations for the European Council (informal meeting) on 20 October in Lahti (Finland), the Commission adopted a communication entitled 'An innovation-friendly, modern Europe' ([1]). Stressing that the success of the revised Lisbon strategy will depend mainly on the progress made with regard to innovation, it takes the view that Europe's capacity for innovation could be significantly boosted by means of the following measures: establishing European leadership in future strategic technologies (nanoelectronics, innovative medicines, aeronautics, etc.), in particular through 'joint technology initiatives' based on dedicated public–private partnerships; forging stronger links between universities, research and business; and improving the framework conditions for innovation (a genuinely integrated single market, in particular in the service sector; financing; intellectual property policy; faster setting of open and interoperable standards; and sector-specific conditions). At their meeting in Lahti, the Heads of State or Government agreed, on the basis of this analysis, on the need for the Union to have a comprehensive strategy to stimulate innovation and strengthen Europe's competitiveness on world markets.

At its meeting in December, the European Council recalled that innovation is vital to ensuring that Europe is able to respond effectively to globalisation and to benefit from it. It called on the Commission to present a full strategy with regard to intellectual property rights.

Promoting entrepreneurship

In close liaison with the implementation of the Community's Lisbon programme, the Commission adopted two communications on promoting entrepreneurship.

- The first communication, approved on 13 February, recommends fostering entrepreneurial mindsets through education and learning ([2]). The aim is to support Member States in formulating a more systematic strategy for entrepreneurship training through recommendations based on examples of good practice found in

---

[1] COM(2006) 589.
[2] COM(2006) 33.

Europe. The communication was endorsed by the European Economic and Social Committee at its July session ([1]).

- The second communication, approved on 14 March, concerns the transfer of businesses and is entitled 'Continuity through a new beginning' ([2]). Given the potential for the transfer of businesses over the next decade, the Commission calls on the Member States to improve the economic environment of such operations and to strengthen support measures, e.g. in terms of finance and taxation.

Small and medium-sized enterprises (SMEs)

At its spring meeting, the European Council, recognising the crucial role which SMEs play in increasing growth and creating better jobs in Europe, called for the development of comprehensive support policies for such enterprises and a regulatory framework that is simple, transparent and easy to apply. It considers that the 'think small first' principle should be systematically applied and become a guiding principle for all legislation, whether Community or national.

The communication presented by the Commission in November 2005 in conjunction with the implementation of the Community's Lisbon programme and entitled 'Modern SME policy for growth and employment' ([3]) was endorsed by the Council on 13 March, the Committee of the Regions on 15 June, and Parliament on 30 November ([4]).

On 29 June, with the same aim of implementing the Lisbon partnership for growth and employment, the Commission adopted a new communication on the financing of SMEs with the idea of promoting European added value ([5]). It wishes, in this way, to improve the policies and programmes supporting access for SMEs to finance, in particular through action to be taken at European level. The political activities thus envisaged supplement the financial instruments in the competitiveness and innovation framework programme referred to above and the 'Jeremie' instrument designed to facilitate access for SMEs and micro-enterprises to credit. The latter instrument was, moreover, welcomed by the European Economic and Social Committee at its March session ([6]).

Industrial policy

The Commission's thinking, as set out in its communication of 5 October 2005 ([7]) regarding the definition of a political framework to strengthen the European Union's manufacturing industry as part of a more integrated approach to industrial

---

([1]) OJ C 309, 16.12.2006.
([2]) COM(2006) 117.
([3]) COM(2005) 551.
([4]) OJ C 229, 22.9.2006.
([5]) COM(2006) 349.
([6]) OJ C 110, 9.5.2006.
([7]) COM(2005) 474.

policy, was the subject of encouraging positions defined by the European Economic and Social Committee on 20 April ([1]), the Council at its meeting on 29 and 30 May, the Committee of the Regions on 15 June and Parliament on 5 July ([2]). The Council in particular stressed the need to take rapid and coordinated action on both the horizontal and sectoral initiatives advocated by the Commission, inasmuch as these concern important elements for achieving the objectives of the Lisbon strategy.

Corporate social responsibility

In a communication of 22 March also linked to the implementation of the Lisbon partnership for growth and employment, the Commission proposes making Europe a pole of excellence on corporate social responsibility (CSR) ([3]). It accordingly supports the launch of a European alliance on CSR, which is a political umbrella for CSR initiatives by major companies and SMEs with the close involvement of these companies' other stakeholders, both internal (trade unions) and external (non-governmental organisations, investors, consumers, etc.). The aim is to help mainstream CSR among businesses and thereby optimise their contribution to sustainable development, growth and employment in Europe.

Standardisation

On 24 October the European Parliament and the Council adopted a decision on the financing of European standardisation ([4]), this process being necessary for the development of standards which are essential to support Community legislation and policies in areas such as the internal market, in particular the service sector, consumer and worker protection, and environmental protection and transport. The beneficiaries will be European standardisation bodies.

Tourism

On 17 March the Commission adopted a communication entitled 'A renewed European Union tourism policy: towards a stronger partnership for European tourism' ([5]). With a view to analysing the competitiveness of this industry and creating jobs through the sustainable growth of tourism in Europe and globally, it presents initiatives which it plans to adopt with regard to the development of policies in this area and the manner in which partnerships between the stakeholders concerned should develop. The Council approved this approach in its conclusions of 25 September. For its part, at its September session ([6]), the European Economic and Social Committee delivered an

---

([1]) OJ C 185, 8.8.2006.
([2]) OJ C 229, 22.9.2006.
([3]) COM(2006) 136.
([4]) Decision No 1673/2006/EC (OJ L 315, 15.11.2006).
([5]) COM(2006) 134.
([6]) OJ C 318, 23.12.2006.

opinion stressing the major importance of social tourism not only for the sector itself but also for the economy, employment, social cohesion and regional development.

Product policy

REACH

On 18 December ([1]) the European Parliament and the Council signed:

- Regulation (EC) No 1907/2006 concerning the registration, evaluation, authorisation and restriction of chemicals (REACH) and establishing a European Chemicals Agency; and

- Directive 2006/121/EC amending Directive 67/548/EEC to adapt it to the abovementioned regulation.

These legislative instruments, which were the product of a long legislative process following a proposal presented by the Commission in 2003 ([2]), are aimed at ensuring a high level of protection of human health and the environment and the freedom of movement of chemical substances in the internal market while boosting competitiveness and innovation. A European Chemicals Agency will be established in Helsinki in 2007 to manage the new databases.

Automotive industry

In 2006, several legislative acts were adopted in the automotive industry sector. Within the framework of the United Nations Economic Commission for Europe (UNECE), the European Union played a central role in the development and adoption of three global technical regulations concerning a new worldwide on-board diagnostic system for trucks and buses, worldwide test procedures for measuring emissions from trucks and buses and a test procedure concerning braking systems for motorcycles. In December the European Parliament and the Council concluded a first reading agreement for the adoption of the regulation on emissions from passenger and commercial vehicles (Euro 5 and Euro 6) and on access to vehicle repair information ([3]).

Pharmaceutical products

On 12 December the European Parliament and the Council adopted a regulation on medicinal products for paediatric use ([4]). This new proposal follows on from a Council resolution which invited the Commission to find solutions to the issue of inadequate medicines for children and which has three key objectives: to ensure high-quality research into and development of medicines for children; over time, to ensure that the

---

([1]) OJ L 396, 30.12.2006.
([2]) COM(2003) 644.
([3]) COM(2005) 683.
([4]) Regulation (EC) No 1901/2006 (OJ L 378, 27.12.2006).

majority of medicines used by children are specifically authorised for such use; and to ensure the availability of high-quality information about medicines used by children.

Construction products

Two studies on the competitiveness of the construction industry were completed in 2006 ('Comparative study of construction costs in the Member States' and 'Analysis and assessment of the aspects of certain Community policies which impact on the competitiveness of the construction industry'). Six Commission decisions on the construction products directive (CPD) (¹) have been adopted by the Commission. As part of the Commission's programme to simplify legislation (²), work has been undertaken to recast the CPD.

Competitiveness in the key sectors

In the context of international regulatory cooperation, the Agreement on Technical Barriers to Trade establishes a notification procedure which requires all members of the World Trade Organisation to inform other members, through the WTO Secretariat, of their proposed technical regulations and conformity assessment procedures.

By 1 December the Commission had received 699 notifications from WTO members and had issued 46 comments. It had also notified 103 technical regulations of the Community and Member States to the WTO. The Commission has systematically replied to comments from third countries.

Cosmetics

At the end of 2006 the Commission launched a comparative study of the macroeconomic and microeconomic characteristics of the cosmetics industry in Europe with particular emphasis on the key policy issues determining competitiveness in this sector. This study will be complementary to a study carried out for the Commission in 2004 which focused mainly on issues of regulation.

Medical devices

Following the study on competitiveness in the medical devices sector, it was decided to carry out a survey on the specific obstacles and barriers affecting competitiveness and innovation which companies face in the European business environment. The final results of the survey will be published in the first quarter of 2007.

(¹) Directive 89/106/EEC (OJ L 40, 11.2.1989).
(²) See Chapter I, Section 1, of this Report.

Pharmaceutical products

The Commission continued to support the discussions of the 'Pharmaceutical Forum', which consists of representatives of the Member States, Members of the European Parliament and other key players in the pharmaceutical sector. The forum deals with complex issues concerning the competitiveness of the European Union in the field of pharmaceuticals, such as the prices of medicinal products, their cost-effectiveness, and the sensitive issue of patient information. At the forum's first ministerial-level meeting, held on 29 September, the ministers established a work programme, focusing in particular on specific objectives such as improving access to medicinal products and increased recognition of the benefits of innovation. The forum's ultimate objective is to create the best possible conditions for pharmaceutical investment in Europe.

Forestry industries

On 20 September the Commission proposed repealing Directive 68/89/EEC on the classification of wood in the rough ([1]). In October and November it carried out a public consultation on innovative and sustainable forestry industries in the European Union.

Research and space policy

Seventh research framework programme

On 7 February the Commission adopted a proposal for a regulation ([2]) laying down the rules for the participation of undertakings, research centres and universities in actions under the seventh framework programme of the European Atomic Energy Community and for the dissemination of research results (2007–11). The rules proposed by the Commission have been drawn up with the twofold aim of (i) ensuring that the rules for participation and dissemination fit the characteristics of the programme and (ii) simplifying and streamlining the provisions of the sixth framework programme in order to make them clearer and easier to understand and thus make it easier for members of the research community to participate in the seventh framework programme. The following new features have therefore been introduced into the new rules: streamlining of the funding scheme; simplification of the procedures for the evaluation and selection of proposals for indirect action and for making awards; clarification of the financial provisions relating to the Community contribution; and introduction of provisions on intellectual property. The regulation was adopted by the Council on 18 December ([3]). The same day the European Parliament and the Council adopted the equivalent regulation for implementation of the seventh programme of the European Community for the period 2007–13 ([4]).

([1]) COM(2006) 557.
([2]) COM(2006) 42.
([3]) Regulation (Euratom) No 1908/2006 (OJ L 400, 30.12.2006).
([4]) Regulation (EC) No 1906/2006 (OJ L 391, 30.12.2006).

On 24 May, following the interinstitutional agreement of 17 May on the financial framework for 2007–13 ([1]), the Commission adopted a proposal for a decision of the European Parliament and of the Council concerning the seventh framework programme of the European Community for research, technological development and demonstration (2007–13), and a proposal for a Council decision concerning the seventh framework programme of the European Atomic Energy Community (Euratom) for nuclear research and training activities (2007–11) ([2]). These decisions were adopted on 18 December ([3]).

In addition to the specific programme to be implemented by means of direct actions by the Joint Research Centre under the seventh framework programme of the European Community for research, technological development and demonstration activities (2007–13) ([4]), various specific programmes proposed by the Commission in 2005 have been brought into line with the interinstitutional agreement on the financial framework for 2007–13. These concern:

- the 'Cooperation' programme ([5]) to support international cooperation projects across the European Union and beyond in a number of thematic areas (health; food, agriculture and biotechnology; information and communication technologies; nanosciences, nanotechnologies, materials and new production technologies; energy; environment, including climate change; transport, including aeronautics; socioeconomic sciences and the humanities; and space and security); these themes correspond to the major fields of progress in knowledge and technology where research must be strengthened to address European social, economic, public health, environmental and industrial challenges;

- the 'Ideas' programme ([6]) to promote scientific excellence throughout Europe; the programme proposes the creation of a European Research Council, which is both a significant new development in Community research and at the same time a logical progression of European research policy, fully coherent with the aims of the European research area and conferring on European 'frontier research' status and visibility which should attract talent and creativity to Europe;

- the 'People' programme ([7]) to encourage Europeans to embark upon and pursue research careers, to encourage researchers to stay in Europe and to attract the best brains to Europe;

([1]) See Chapter I of this Report.
([2]) COM(2005) 119.
([3]) Decision No 1982/2006/EC (OJ L 412, 30.12.2006) and Decision 2006/970/Euratom (OJ L 400, 30.12.2006).
([4]) COM(2005) 439.
([5]) COM(2005) 440.
([6]) COM(2005) 441.
([7]) COM(2005) 442.

- the 'Capacities' programme (¹) to enhance research and innovation capacity throughout the European Union (new research infrastructure, and support for small and medium-sized enterprises), the development of 'regions of knowledge', unlocking research potential in 'convergence' regions and outermost regions) and to give science a better place within society;

- the specific programme implementing the seventh Euratom framework programme for nuclear research and training (²); and

- the specific programme to be carried out by means of direct actions by the Joint Research Centre under the seventh Euratom framework programme (2007–11) for nuclear research and training (³).

Following the success of the interinstitutional negotiations on the programmes, the legislative acts implementing them were adopted by the Council on 18 and 19 December (⁴).

ITER (international thermonuclear experimental reactor)

Background

Nuclear fusion offers the prospect of an almost limitless supply of clean energy for the long term. Following successful developments in recent years, fusion energy research and development has reached the point where effective progress towards the demonstration of the generation of sustainable energy from nuclear fusion can be envisaged. The international thermonuclear experimental reactor, a major experimental facility which is aimed at demonstrating the scientific and technical feasibility of fusion power, is the crucial next step required to address the key objectives of the European fusion programme and other fusion programmes in the world.

On 1 April the representatives of the seven parties to the ITER negotiations adopted the final report on negotiations on the joint implementation of the ITER project (⁵), which confirms the completion of the negotiation process, refers to statements of the willingness of each party to proceed towards conclusion of the agreement, and records the common understandings shared among the parties at the conclusion of the negotiations and the draft arrangement on the provisional application of the agreement. On the same occasion, the final report of negotiations on the agreement on the privileges and immunities of the ITER International Fusion Energy Organisation for the joint implementation of the ITER project was adopted.

(¹) COM(2005) 443.
(²) COM(2005) 445.
(³) COM(2005) 444.
(⁴) Decisions 2006/971/EC, 2006/972/EC, 2006/973/EC, 2006/974/EC, 2006/975/EC, 2006/976/Euratom and 2006/977/Euratom (OJ L 400, 30.12.2006).
(⁵) China, South Korea, United States of America, India, Japan, Russia and the European Union.

On 19 May the Commission proposed to the Council the conclusion of the agreement on the establishment of the ITER international organisation (¹). On 14 August it adopted a proposal for a decision (²) establishing a joint undertaking for the ITER and the development of fusion energy. The joint undertaking's primary task will be to meet Europe's wide-ranging obligations towards the international thermonuclear experimental reactor by working with European industry and research organisations to supply the components for the construction of the ITER and to administer the European Union's financial contribution to the project, which will come mainly from the Community budget. The joint undertaking will progressively implement a programme of activities to prepare for the first demonstration fusion power reactors, building on the experience of the ITER. The joint undertaking will have a lean managerial structure, respecting accountability and transparency. Its activities will complement the other parts of the integrated European fusion energy research programme carried out in national fusion laboratories in the Member States and other associated European countries — Bulgaria and Romania, plus Switzerland since 1979 — under the Euratom umbrella.

On 21 November the representatives of six countries (China, South Korea, the USA, India, Japan and Russia) and the European Union signed an agreement in Paris on the official launching of the construction of the ITER. This international agreement represents the conclusion of several years of difficult international negotiations.

Space policy

Background

The two 'Space' Councils held in 2005 made it possible to lay the foundations for European space policy by defining the objectives, roles and responsibilities of the various institutional players, namely the European Union, the European Space Agency (ESA) and the national space agencies. The second 'Space' Council, in June 2005, called on the Commission and the ESA to develop, on the basis of the preliminary elements, a European space policy (ESP) in close collaboration with the Member States and a flexible and inclusive 'common European space programme'.

In 2006, intensive consultations with the Member States and industry led to significant progress being made in the development of this policy. The ESP document, which will be finalised in the spring of 2007, will explain the strategic objectives, establish the key elements of an industrial policy to boost the competitiveness of the European space industry and will raise the question of the future institutional framework for space and the international links. The ESP will also deal with links between the civilian space components and their possible synergy or use in the field of security.

(¹) COM(2006) 240.
(²) COM(2006) 458.

The 'Global monitoring for space and security' (GMSS) programme is, alongside Galileo, an important pillar in this landscape and has European and global ambitions at a time when climate change concerns are a priority.

Other international developments

An agreement has been concluded with Switzerland and a cooperation agreement signed with South Korea as part of the consolidation of the European research area, more specifically in the field of international cooperation. Progress has also been made in the negotiations on a cooperation agreement with Japan.

Joint Research Centre (JRC)

Throughout 2006, the JRC confirmed its position as an independent provider of scientific and technical support to European Union policies. Concrete measures to enhance food and feed safety were realised by the opening of four new Community reference laboratories. A system called 'Contraffic' was developed to combat fraud and increase global security. Rapid responses were provided to the Lebanon crisis, the Indonesian earthquake and to fires, drought and flooding in Europe. The directive to create the infrastructure for spatial information in Europe received agreement from Parliament and the Council, and measurable steps were taken to promote relations with the new Member States, candidate countries and the western Balkans.

Besides the policy-driven support it gives to the European Commission and the Member States, the JRC also fulfils, through its nuclear activities, the research and development obligations under the Euratom Treaty. These have as their objectives to develop and assemble knowledge in the field of nuclear energy and to provide crucial scientific and technical data to support safety, security and control of nuclear systems. To achieve these objectives the JRC 2006 nuclear programme dealt with a wide range of nuclear and development activities: basic actinide research, nuclear data and nuclear measurements, radiation monitoring and radio nuclides in the environment, health and nuclear medicine, management of spent fuel and waste, safety of reactors and fuel cycle and nuclear safeguards and non-proliferation of nuclear weapons.

The challenges posed by the threat of proliferation of weapons of mass destruction and the security of citizens in more general terms were at the centre of the celebrations marking the 25th anniversary of the collaboration between the JRC and the International Atomic Energy Agency (IAEA) in October 2006. This event provided the JRC with a major opportunity to communicate the wide technical and scientific support provided to the IAEA.

In May, the European Atomic Energy Community became a party to the Framework Agreement for International Collaboration on Research and Development of Generation IV Nuclear Energy Systems (GIF framework agreement). The 'Generation IV' initiative concerns concepts for nuclear energy systems that can be operated in a manner that will provide a competitive and reliable supply of energy, while satisfactorily addressing nuclear safety, waste, proliferation and public perception concerns. The JRC, with its strong international dimension, is the implementing agent for Euratom in the GIF.

Development of information and communications technologies

i2010 initiative

The Commission is convinced that intelligent car systems offer major potential for solving transport problems. On 15 February it identified targeted actions ([1]) for raising users' awareness, focusing this initiative on three pillars: the eSafety Forum, the information and communication technologies research programme and activities to raise awareness and ensure communication.

For its part, on 27 April the European Parliament deplored the delay in some Member States in promoting the introduction of the in-vehicle emergency call system ('eCall'). It urged Member States which had not yet done so to sign as soon as possible the 'Protocol on European conformity agreement', which is intended to ensure that the system can operate in any Member State.

On 20 March the Commission invited Member States to update their existing national broadband strategies and to set clear targets for the connectivity of stakeholders such as schools, public administrations and health centres ([2]). For its part, the Commission will, within the i2010 high-level group, monitor and organise discussions centred on these strategies and will continue to monitor the digital divide through its i2010 annual activity reports.

On 25 April, as announced in the context of the i2010 initiative ([3]), the Commission proposed an action plan for the deployment of online government services in Europe ([4]), providing indicators for Community programmes, initiatives and policies from 2006 to 2010 and practical means such as roadmaps and strategic control in identified priority areas: access for everybody, increased efficiency, online procurement, safe access to services throughout the Union, and strengthening of the democratic decision-making process.

The first annual report on the European information society was adopted by the Commission on 19 May ([5]). As the Commission sees it, the Member States need more ambitious implementation programmes to derive all the benefits from information

---

[1] COM(2006) 59 (OJ C 151, 29.6.2006).
[2] COM(2006) 129 (OJ C 151, 29.6.2006).
[3] COM(2005) 229, (OJ C 236, 24.9.2005).
[4] COM(2006) 173 (OJ C 176, 28.7.2006).
[5] COM(2006) 215 (OJ C 176, 28.7.2006).

and communications technologies (ICT). Although they support the wider adoption of ICT, the national reform programmes fail to give a fresh impetus to information society policies or to cover drivers of growth such as the convergence of digital networks, content and devices. To help get growth back on track, Member States need to step up their efforts to improve access to broadband Internet connections, facilitate the circulation of digital content throughout the European Union, free-up radio spectrum for new applications, integrate research and innovation and modernise public services. The report also calls for policy convergence in the ICT sector to combine regulatory instruments and the promotion of Community-wide research in the interests of growth and jobs in Europe.

The flagship 'i2010: digital libraries' initiative — launched by the Commission in September 2005 [1] — was, early on in 2006, the subject of a major online initiative which has helped the Commission define more clearly the priorities in this field. The European digital library, which is the result of collaboration between national libraries, will provide a multilingual access point to European digital resources.

A Commission recommendation on the digitisation and online accessibility of cultural material and digital preservation was adopted on 24 August [2]. The Commission recommends that the Member States put in place large-scale digital services to speed up the online availability of the European cultural heritage through the European digital library. Furthermore, it encourages the Member States to act in various areas, from editorial rights to the systematic conservation of digital content, in order to guarantee long-term access to digital library content. In the conclusions of the 13 November Council, the European ministers of culture supported the Commission proposals and agreed on a firm timetable for results to be achieved.

This should make it possible for all citizens to make better use of the European cultural heritage for their studies, work or leisure. It will also provide researchers, artists and entrepreneurs with essential raw material for their creative efforts. The 'digital libraries' initiative is also reflected in the financial contribution earmarked by the Commission in Community research programmes and the eContentplus programme for the digital libraries initiative. Europe's libraries, museums and archives now spearhead a series of projects launched to add to the foundations of the European digital library.

Legislative work continued with a view to the adoption of a recommendation of the European Parliament and of the Council on the protection of minors and human dignity and the right of reply in relation to the competitiveness of the European audiovisual and information services industry. This recommendation had been proposed by the Commission [3] in 2004 to continue responding to the challenges of technological developments which had arisen since the initial 1998 recommendation,

---

[1] COM(2005) 465.
[2] Recommendation 2006/585/EC (OJ L 236, 31.8.2006).
[3] COM(2004) 341.

which remains in force. The issues dealt with cover the following in particular: media education, the rating or classification of audiovisual content, the portrayal of the sexes in the media and advertising, and the right of reply in relation to online media. On 20 January the Commission amended its proposal ([1]). On 18 September the Council adopted a common position, and on 13 December the European Parliament gave its opinion at second reading and welcomed the common position, which sets out the main proposals defended by the political groups in Parliament. The recommendation was finally adopted on 20 December ([2]).

To explain and demonstrate more clearly to a wide audience the contribution of information and communication technologies to growth, employment and well-being, the Commission has implemented a communication strategy ([3]) based on making more intensive and better targeted use of the media, multiplier networks and audiovisual content and an increased presence on the Internet. It covers matters of public interest such as reducing the excessive costs of international roaming, 'intelligent' cars, and the new top-level Internet domain '.eu'.

Electronic communications — Regulatory framework

On 2 February the Commission adopted a communication on reviewing the interoperability of digital interactive television services ([4]). It takes account of market developments and considers it preferable for the market to continue to be based on non-binding standardisation initiatives emanating from businesses.

After public consultation, and in conformity with the requirements of the current directive ([5]), the Commission re-examined the scope of the universal service and on 7 April decided not to propose changing the scope of the universal service at that stage ([6]). It believes, however, that the contributions it has received on the longer-term issues constitute a good basis for pursuing policy discussion on universal service provision in the framework of the general regulatory review of electronic communications

On 6 February, moreover, two years after the entry into force of the regulatory framework for electronic communications ([7]), the Commission adopted its first activity report ([8]). The Commission welcomed the fact that the market analyses carried out by the Member States and the consultation provided for in Article 7 are boosting competition in the sector to the benefit of consumers. It also found that the regulatory

---

[1] COM(2006) 31.
[2] Recommendation 2006/952/EC (OJ L 378, 27.12.2006).
[3] See Chapter I, Section 2, of this Report.
[4] COM(2006) 37 (OJ C 67, 18.3.2006).
[5] Directive 2002/22/EC (universal service directive) (OJ L 108, 24.4.2002).
[6] COM(2006) 163 (OJ C 151, 29.6.2006).
[7] Directive 2002/21/EC (framework directive) (OJ L 108, 24.4.2002).
[8] COM(2006) 28 (OJ C 104, 3.5.2006).

framework for electronic communications, especially the Community consultation mechanism, has helped to bring about more consistency as regards the regulatory obligations imposed on operators and has enhanced transparency for market players.

On 20 February the Commission adopted its 'European electronic communications regulation and markets in 2005 (11th report)' ([1]). In what is in effect a snapshot of the situation in the electronic communications sector prior to the review of the regulatory framework, it looks at the latest market developments, mainly in the field of broadband, mobile and fixed services, as well as the regulatory framework and consumer interests. It stresses that some Member States have already adopted almost all the national laws and practices necessary to implement Community legislation on telecommunications, and that others have made substantial progress. While boosting competition provides advantages for consumers, the report also stresses the need to reduce the cost of using mobile telephones abroad ('international roaming'), to make the public aware of the single European emergency telephone number (112) and to avoid imposing an excessive regulatory burden on the new Internet telephone services.

On 15 March the Commission also reviewed ([2]) the operation of the Community framework for electronic signatures ([3]). Based partly on the results of an independent study carried out by external consultants and the results of informal consultations with the interested parties, the report points out that the directive has introduced legal certainty as regards the general admissibility of electronic signatures. The Commission therefore did not consider it necessary to review this framework.

On 31 May the Commission adopted a communication entitled 'A strategy for a secure information policy — "Dialogue, partnership and empowerment"' ([4]). It considers that businesses, individuals and public administrations in Europe underestimate the risks of insufficiently protecting networks and information. It therefore proposes a strategy for promoting greater awareness about security through an open and inclusive multi-stakeholder dialogue on specific actions to be carried out. The European Agency for Network and Information Security is invited to play an important role in implementing this strategy.

On 29 June the Commission adopted a communication on the review of the European Union's regulatory framework for electronic communications networks and services ([5]). In addition to simplifying procedures for market analysis, the Commission proposes a more flexible approach to the use of frequencies by introducing concepts regarding technological and service neutrality. It also wants to see modernisation of the regulatory framework and consolidation of the internal market and recommends

---

([1]) COM(2006) 68 (OJ C 104, 3.5.2006).
([2]) COM(2006) 120 (OJ C 104, 3.5.2006).
([3]) Directive 1999/93/EC (OJ L 13, 19.1.2000).
([4]) COM(2006) 251 (OJ C 176, 28.7.2006).
([5]) COM(2006) 334.

measures to improve consumer protection and to strengthen network security. Along with this review of the regulatory framework, the Commission plans to reduce the number of markets subject to *ex ante* regulation by developing effective competition in several of them.

On 15 November the Commission adopted a communication on fighting spam, spyware and malware ([1]). The communication takes stock of efforts made so far to fight these threats. The Commission notes that, while some Member States have taken initiatives, there is insufficient action to address the evolution and persistency of online threats. Building on the results so far the communication identifies further actions that need to be taken by the relevant stakeholders, including enforcement, cooperation on national and international level, industry initiatives and European Union legislative and research activities.

On 12 July the Commission adopted a proposal for a regulation on roaming on public mobile telephone networks within the Community and amending Directive 2002/21/EC on a common regulatory framework for electronic communications networks and services ([2]). The objective is to amend the existing regulatory framework for electronic communications to provide the necessary legal basis for effective and timely action to bring about substantial reductions in the level of mobile roaming charges across the Community in a harmonised manner. This is to be achieved by applying the approach that prices paid by users of public mobile networks for roaming services when travelling within the Community should not be unjustifiably higher than the charges payable when calling within their home country (the 'European home market approach').

.eu domain name

The creation of .eu was decided at the Lisbon Council in 2000 to stress the importance that Europe gives to the information society and to electronic commerce as a means of underpinning its competitiveness. Open to everyone since 7 April 2006, this domain has been very successful and more than 2 million names have already been registered since it came into service. Thanks to it, businesses will be able to enhance their Internet visibility within the single market and further afield, advertise their pan-European outlook and be provided with greater legal certainty.

Follow-up to the World Summit on the Information Society

In a communication of 27 April ([3]) the Commission, which wishes to remain a driving force behind this process, evaluated the main results of the World Summit on the Information Society (WSIS) following its Tunis phase in 2005. Noting the real influence

---

([1]) COM(2006) 688.
([2]) COM(2006) 382.
([3]) COM(2006) 181 (OJ C 176, 28.7.2006).

which the European Union had on the summit's results, the Commission spelt out future priorities and put forward proposals on how it can support the follow-up to the summit. It noted that in relations with international partners information society policies should be mainstreamed into the broader context of economic cooperation and development as a condition for the respect of human rights and fundamental freedoms, economic development and efforts to achieve the millennium development goals. It also found that the European Union should maintain the momentum of the multiple dialogues established with other governments, institutions and organisations. These dialogues have allowed the European Union to present a coherent position on sensitive issues such as Internet governance and financing the information society in developing countries.

Audiovisual media services

On 10 February the Commission adopted the fifth report on the application of the 'Television without frontiers' directive in 2003 and 2004 ([1]). Noting that the 'Television without frontiers' directive continues to function successfully in ensuring the freedom to provide television services in the European Union, the report confirms the validity of the joint European approach to audiovisual matters. However, it finds that there is a need to review the current European Union regulatory framework in view of market and technological developments. On 14 August the Commission adopted the seventh communication on the application of the 'Television without frontiers' directive, for the period 2003–04 ([2]), which essentially contains statistics. The 10 Member States which joined the European Union on 1 May 2004 are, for the first time, included in the report, for the period 1 May to 31 December 2004.

In 2006 further legislative work was carried out on the review of the 'Television without frontiers' directive proposed by the Commission in December 2005 ([3]). On 13 November the Council agreed on a general approach broadly in line with the Commission proposal, which in particular recommends making this text a directive on audiovisual media services. The European Parliament expressed its opinion at first reading on 13 December.

MEDIA 2007 programme

On 15 November the European Parliament and the Council adopted a new programme of support for the European audiovisual sector: MEDIA 2007 ([4]). This fourth generation of the MEDIA programme will have a budget of EUR 755 million over a seven-year period (2007–13).

([1]) COM(2006) 49 (OJ C 104, 3.5.2006).
([2]) COM(2006) 459.
([3]) COM(2005) 646.
([4]) Decision No 1718/2006/EC (OJ L 327, 24.11.2006).

Following on from earlier programmes, MEDIA 2007 activities will focus on the pre-production and post-production phases. Community action will henceforth come under a single programme. Furthermore, the impact of the digital revolution and the enlargement of the European Union on the balance on European audiovisual markets makes it essential to recast the priorities and structure of the future programme in overall terms. Firstly, MEDIA activities should be adapted in the light of technological and market development in order to respond to the changes brought about by digitisation. In addition, MEDIA 2007 should include measures to address the problems facing the professionals from the new Member States, as well as innovative and focused actions in respect of digitisation and measures for facilitating access to financing for SMEs.

Education and training

Background

As part of the relaunch of the Lisbon strategy, the spring 2005 European Council deemed human capital to be Europe's most important asset. It therefore called on the Member States to step up their efforts to raise the general standard of education and reduce the number of early school-leavers, in particular by continuing with the 'Education and training 2010' work programme designed to dovetail with the Lisbon strategy. The European Council also stressed that lifelong learning is a sine qua non *requirement for achieving the Lisbon objectives. For its part, the Commission paid particular attention to the modernisation of education and training systems, in particular those of European universities.*

General approach

At its spring 2006 meeting, the European Council again emphasised the importance of education and training as areas for priority action to be implemented by the end of 2007 in the context of the renewed partnership for growth and employment. These conclusions confirm the essential messages in the second joint interim report of the Council and the Commission on progress made under the 'Modernising education and training: a vital contribution to prosperity and social cohesion in Europe' work programme, which was adopted on 24 February. It stresses the dual socioeconomic role of education and training, and the need for greater effort with regard to reform in two areas: targeted investment and improved governance.

In a communication of 5 September the Commission described what it considers to be the key points needed to strengthen the effectiveness and equity of education and training systems in Europe. Taking the view that the social dimension of education is too often ignored, it recommends combining the objectives of efficiency and equity in order to optimise the potential of education and training policies and contribute to the inclusion of all people. In this respect, on 14 November the Council adopted conclusions setting out the main messages of the communication and emphasising the need to review the means by which European education systems are governed and funded in order to combine their efficiency and equity more effectively.

European Institute of Technology

Specific and major progress was made in 2006 as regards the building of a genuine knowledge-based society with the initiative to set up a European Institute of Technology (EIT), which would be a new centre of excellence in the field of higher education, research and innovation.

In the first communication, of 22 February ([1]), the Commission set out its initial ideas on the structure and funding of the future institute, which will have a triple objective: to attract the best talents in terms of students, researchers and staff; to offer new opportunities for marketing research results; and to strengthen two-way exchanges between the private and the public sectors.

In a new communication of 8 June ([2]) the Commission gave details of its action plan for the establishment of the EIT and paved the way for an official proposal to this end. It also set out in particular the findings of a consultation to clarify the proposed structure and operation of the future institute, which is designed to complement other Community actions to strengthen the innovation, research and teaching potential in Europe. The initiative also received strong support from the European Council during its June meeting and was welcomed by the Committee of the Regions in an opinion of 6 December.

On 18 October ([3]) the Commission put forward a proposal for a regulation of the European Parliament and of the Council establishing the EIT. It recommends basing the structure of the institute on the principle of integrated networks: on the one hand, there should be the EIT itself, managed by a governing board responsible for defining its overall strategic priorities; on the other hand, there should be 'knowledge and innovation communities' (KICs), which are defined as joint ventures of partner organisations involving universities, research organisations and businesses which will be responsible for implementing the innovation, research and teaching activities and which will join forces to form an integrated partnership to respond to calls for proposals from the EIT. The aim moreover is to make the EIT operational by 2008.

European Training Foundation

On the basis of a recent external evaluation, on 19 December ([4]) the Commission adopted a communication in which it considers the changes to the role, the geographic cover and the activities of the European Training Foundation since the previous external evaluation in 2002.

([1]) COM(2006) 77.
([2]) COM(2006) 276.
([3]) COM(2006) 604.
([4]) COM(2006) 832.

Higher education

On 15 February the European Parliament and the Council adopted a recommendation ([1]) on further European cooperation in quality assurance in higher education, encouraging the Member States to create a 'European register of quality assurance and accreditation agencies' to be chosen from among their higher education establishments.

On 10 May, in response to a request made by the European Union Heads of State or Government at the Hampton Court Informal Summit in October 2005, the Commission presented a communication entitled 'Delivering on the modernisation agenda for universities: education, research and innovation' ([2]). Convinced that universities are an immense reservoir of knowledge, talent and energy, the Commission singles out the areas in which changes should be made to provide them with a framework enabling them, in the age of globalisation, to boost their weight in society and the knowledge-based economy. The Commission's proposals consist, for example, in: increasing the number of graduates who spend a term abroad or in industry; structuring university courses so that they directly increase graduate employability; creating incentives for structure partnerships with the business world; facilitating and accelerating the procedures for the recognition of university qualifications and bringing them into line with those which apply to professional qualifications and making European degrees more easily recognised outside the European Union; allocating at least 2 % of gross national product (GNP) (public and private funding) to a modernised higher education system; and putting in place new systems of funding for universities, based more on results, and increasing the responsibility of universities for their long-term financial sustainability, in particular in the field of research.

At its meeting in June the European Council asked for action to be taken on this Commission communication.

Lifelong education and training

On 15 November, on the basis of a revised proposal presented by the Commission on 24 May ([3]), the European Parliament and the Council established an action programme in the field of lifelong education and training ([4]), covering the period 2007–13. The programme aims in particular to foster interchange, cooperation and mobility between education and training systems within the Community. It comprises: the four previous sectoral programmes (Comenius, Erasmus, Leonardo da Vinci and Gundtvig); a transversal programme; and the Jean Monnet programme to support establishments and activities relating to European integration.

---

[1] Recommendation 2006/143/EC (OJ L 64, 4.3.2006).
[2] COM(2006) 208.
[3] COM(2006) 236.
[4] Decision No 1720/2006/EC (OJ L 327, 24.11.2006).

In a resolution adopted on 18 May the Council recommended adapting the European system established in 2004 (^{1}) to improve the transparency and comparability of skills and qualifications in the European Union so that the system also takes account of young people's 'informal' skills.

On 5 September the Commission proposed establishing a European qualifications framework (EQF) for lifelong learning (^{2}), which businesses and individuals can use as a reference tool for comparing qualification levels in different education and training systems.

On 23 October the Commission adopted a communication entitled 'Adult learning: it is never too late to learn' (^{3}) to promote adult learning as a vital component of lifelong learning and to show its vital contribution to achieving the Lisbon objectives.

For its part, in an own-initiative opinion of 13 September, the European Economic and Social Committee pleaded for more intensive use to be made of information technology to support lifelong learning (^{4}), in particular through job-based education and training.

On 14 November the Council approved a recommendation of the European Parliament and the Council on key competences regarding lifelong learning. The recommendation provides a European reference framework for the key competences which all young people should develop by the end of their initial education and training and which adults should have the opportunity to acquire, maintain and update as part of lifelong learning.

On 5 December, on the basis of the Council's conclusions of 14 November, the ministers responsible for vocational education and training in the Member States, the candidate countries and the European Free Trade Association(EFTA)/European Economic Area (EEA) countries and the European social partners adopted the 'Helsinki communiqué on enhanced European cooperation in vocational education and training (VET)'. The communiqué enhances this cooperation (the Copenhagen process) which was put in place in 2004 and the priorities it set; the tools and initiatives already launched need to be supplemented and put into practice to improve the attractiveness and quality of VET, in particular by developing a European credit system for vocational education and training (ECVET).

With regard to mobility within the Community for education and training purposes, the proposal for a recommendation of the European Parliament and of the Council

---

(^{1}) Decision No 2241/2004/EC (OJ L 390, 31.12.2004).
(^{2}) COM(2006) 479.
(^{3}) COM(2006) 614.
(^{4}) OJ C 318, 23.12.2006.

on a 'European quality charter for mobility' put forward by the Commission in 2005 (¹) was approved by Parliament on 26 September and the Council on 18 December (²).

Multilingualism

In a resolution adopted on 27 April the European Parliament endorsed the proposal put forward by the Commission in its communication of 1 August 2005 to establish a European indicator of language competence (³). The Council also commented on the proposal in its conclusions of 19 May, although there was some disagreement between Member States on the ideal age at which to test pupils.

The communication presented by the Commission on 22 November 2005 advocating a new framework strategy for multilingualism (⁴) was the subject of opinions delivered by the Committee of the Regions on 14 June (⁵), the European Economic and Social Committee on 26 October (⁶) and Parliament on 15 November.

International cooperation

On 21 June the European Community and the United States signed an agreement in Vienna renewing for the period 2006–13 their cooperation programme in the field of higher education and vocational training (⁷), formerly covered by a first agreement for the period 2001–05. A similar agreement is currently being renewed with Canada (⁸).

Transport

Strategic approach

New guidelines for Europe's transport policy in the next few years were adopted by the Commission on 22 June as part of its review of the 2001 White Paper on transport, in the form of a communication entitled 'Keep Europe moving — Sustainable mobility for our continent — Mid-term review of the European Commission's 2001 transport White Paper' (⁹).

The Council discussed the guidelines at its 12 October session. The Finnish Presidency summed up the discussions, which revealed widespread support from the Member States for the new guidelines. The European Parliament began discussions in November and is expected to complete them in 2007.

(¹) COM(2005) 450.
(²) Recommendation 2006/961/EC (OJ L 394, 30.12.2006).
(³) COM(2005) 356.
(⁴) COM(2005) 596.
(⁵) OJ C 229, 22.9.2006.
(⁶) OJ C 324, 30.12.2006.
(⁷) OJ L 346, 9.12.2006.
(⁸) Decision 2006/964/EC (OJ L 397, 30.12.2006).
(⁹) COM(2006) 314.

The new guidelines are the fruit of a technical and economic analysis and exchanges of information with those concerned in the different consultations held by the Commission. They constitute only a basis on which to carry out further work, however, and will have to be fleshed out with new measures prepared in cooperation with all interested parties in the public and private sectors, and be backed up by impact assessments. An ongoing dialogue with stakeholders will be crucial to the success of the policy.

The new guidelines follow on from earlier policies — opening up and connecting markets and sustainable development of mobility — focusing on the need to ensure the competitiveness of European industries and the prosperity of our societies. Their key objectives are to promote efficient mobility and to protect the environment and citizens. To allow these goals to be achieved, the communication proposes a wider range of implementing measures, in line with the Lisbon strategy and the strategy on sustainable development. These measures must to a large extent be inspired by the concepts of innovation, efficiency and the intelligent use of modes of transport, and be debated by the interested parties.

In this context, the Commission intends in the coming years to launch a range of action plans on key transport policy issues such as urban transport, logistics, green propulsion and a common European maritime space. Following the approval of the new road-charging directive [1], it is also planned to draft a report on the impact of the internalisation of external costs by 2008. The Commission will also continue to develop intelligent transport systems (Galileo, SESAR, ERTMS) and pursue its efforts in the fields of innovation and research.

Rail transport

On 3 May the Commission adopted a report on the implementation of the first railway package [2]. It found that on 1 January 2006 all the Member States except Luxembourg had formally adopted the package transposing the directives into their national legislation, but not at the same pace. The resulting delays affected the ability of the actors to assert themselves on the European stage. Nevertheless, the Commission saw the implementation of the first railway package as being well under way. In addition to making a number of recommendations to the Member States, the Commission indicated that it would keep a close watch on the market situation and take all action necessary to correct unwanted situations.

On 13 December the Commission adopted a communication entitled 'Facilitating the movement of locomotives across the European Union' [3], together with a proposal

---

[1] Directive 2006/38/EC (OJ L 157, 9.6.2006).
[2] COM(2006) 189.
[3] COM(2006) 782.

to recast the directives on the interoperability of the Community rail system [1], a proposal for a directive on safety on the Community's railways [2] and a proposal for a regulation amending the regulation establishing a European Railway Agency [3]. The aim of these proposals is to facilitate the free movement of trains by simplifying the procedure for approving locomotives. According to manufacturers and railway companies, this procedure is still in many cases very long and costly, thus constituting a major barrier to the development of international rail traffic at a point when the opening up of the rail freight markets offers a real chance to revitalise it.

Land transport

The following were signed by the European Parliament and the Council:

- on 18 January, Directive 2006/1/EC on the use of vehicles hired without drivers for the carriage of goods by road [4] and consolidating Directive 84/647/EEC [5];

- on 15 March, Directive 2006/22/EC [6] on minimum conditions for the implementation of social legislation relating to road transport activities, which relates to road checks on drivers of coaches and heavy goods vehicles;

- on 17 May, Directive 2006/38/EC [7] amending Directive 1999/62/EC [8] on the charging of heavy goods vehicles for the use of certain infrastructures in order to reduce the differences between Member States in this field; and

- on 12 December, Directive 2006/94/EC [9] on the establishment of common rules for certain types of carriage of goods by road.

On 1 August the Commission adopted a proposal for a regulation on the elimination of controls performed at the frontiers of Member States in the field of road and inland waterway transport [10], consolidating Regulation (EEC) No 4060/89 [11].

Transport over waterways

On 7 January the Commission adopted an integrated European action programme for inland waterway transport [12], which aims to anchor inland waterway transport more firmly in the common transport policy. This is a medium and long-term plan

---

[1] COM(2006) 783.
[2] COM(2006) 784.
[3] COM(2006) 785.
[4] OJ L 33, 4.2.2006.
[5] OJ L 335, 22.12.1984.
[6] OJ L 102, 11.4.2006.
[7] OJ L 157, 9.6.2006.
[8] OJ L 187, 20.7.1999.
[9] OJ L 374, 27.12.2006.
[10] COM(2006) 432.
[11] OJ L 390, 30.12.1989.
[12] COM(2006) 6.

(2006–13) incorporating measures corresponding to five objectives which are essential to the development of inland navigation: creating favourable conditions for services; stimulating fleet modernisation and innovation; promoting employment and professional qualification; improving the image and perception of inland waterway transport; and providing adequate infrastructure.

On 24 October the Commission proposed the adoption of a directive allowing the rapid entry into force of new technical requirements for inland waterway vessels ([1]). The European Parliament and the Council signed the directive on 18 December ([2]).

Shipping

The European Parliament and the Council signed the following:

- on 18 January, Decision No 167/2006/EC concerning the activities of certain third countries in the field of cargo shipping ([3]) and codifying Decision 78/774/EEC ([4]);

- on 15 February, Regulation (EC) No 336/2006 on the implementation of the International Safety Management Code within the Community ([5]), which improves safety management, the safe operation of ships and pollution prevention in the case of vessels flying the flag of a Member State and all ro-ro passenger ferries operating on a regular service to and from ports of the Member States;

- on 24 October, Regulation (EC) No 1692/2006 establishing the second Marco Polo programme for the granting of Community financial assistance to improve the environmental performance of the freight transport system (Marco Polo II) ([6]); and

- on 18 December, a regulation on multiannual funding for the action of the European Maritime Safety Agency in the field of response to pollution caused by ships and amending Regulation (EC) No 1406/2002 ([7]); the reference amount for the period 2007–13 has been fixed at EUR 154 million.

For its part, the Commission adopted:

- on 15 June, a communication under Article 138(2) of the EC Treaty on the strengthening of maritime labour standards ([8]);

---

[1] COM(2006) 646.
[2] Directive 2006/137/EC amending Directive 2006/87/EC (OJ L 389, 30.12.2006).
[3] OJ L 33, 4.2.2006.
[4] OJ L 258, 21.9.1978.
[5] OJ L 64, 4.3.2006.
[6] OJ L 328, 24.11.2006.
[7] Regulation (EC) No 1891/2006 (OJ L 394, 30.12.2006).
[8] COM(2006) 287.

- on 11 May, a communication updating and rectifying the communication on the interpretation of Regulation (EEC) No 3577/92 applying the principle of freedom to provide services to maritime transport within Member States [1]; and

- on 13 July, a communication entitled 'Mid-term review of the programme for the promotion of short sea shipping' [2], in which it emphasises that such shipping has maintained its position as the only mode of transport able to challenge the fast growth of road transport, and that the work on the 14 actions introduced by the original promotion programme should be continued, although some need to be supplemented or refocused.

Air transport

On 17 January the European Parliament expressed its support for the communication from the Commission entitled 'Developing the agenda for the Community's external aviation policy' [3]. On 5 April the European Parliament and the Council signed Directive 2006/23/EC, which aims to harmonise the requirements governing training and the issuance of licences for Community air traffic controllers [4].

On 5 July the European Parliament and the Council signed Regulation (EC) No 1107/2006 concerning the rights of disabled persons and persons with reduced mobility when travelling by air [5], to protect them against discrimination and to ensure that they receive assistance.

On 18 July the Commission adopted a proposal for a regulation [6] which seeks to revise, simplify and consolidate the legislation on the operation of air transport services in the Community. On 12 December Parliament and the Council signed a directive [7] codifying regulation of the operation of aeroplanes in line with international rules.

Intermodal approach

Galileo

The Commission adopted a range of proposals on the Galileo project:

- on 24 May, an amended proposal for a regulation on the implementation of the deployment and commercial operating phases of the European programme of satellite radio navigation [8], following the agreement of 17 May on the financial

[1] COM(2006) 196.
[2] COM(2006) 380.
[3] COM(2005) 79.
[4] OJ L 114, 27.4.2006.
[5] OJ L 204, 26.7.2006.
[6] COM(2006) 396.
[7] Directive 2006/93/EC (OJ L 374, 27.12.2006).
[8] COM(2004) 477.

framework 2007–13 (¹); in it, the Commission clarifies that it is the European GNSS Supervisory Authority which manages and monitors the use of funds from the Community contribution allocated to the programme;

- on 2 June, a proposal for a regulation on the establishment of structures for the management of the European satellite radio navigation programmes (²), which amends Regulation (EC) No 1321/2004 (³), to enable the European GNSS Supervisory Authority to complete the development phase of the Galileo programme after the Galileo joint undertaking is wound up; the regulation was adopted by the Council on 12 December (⁴); and

- on 29 June, a proposal for a regulation amending the statutes of the Galileo joint undertaking (⁵); the regulation was adopted by the Council on 12 December (⁶).

Moreover, on 7 June the Commission drew up a communication entitled 'Taking stock of the Galileo programme' (⁷), which sets out the recent key developments in the programme.

Other developments

In addition, on 8 December the Commission adopted a Green Paper on satellite navigation applications (⁸), which gives an overview of the possibilities offered by this technology and is intended to open public debate in the first quarter of 2007. On the same day, it adopted a recommendation to the Council authorising the Commission to begin negotiations with third countries with a view to concluding agreements on their status of associate member in order to cooperate with the European GNSS Supervisory Authority. On 12 December a cooperation agreement was signed with Morocco.

Logistics

On June 28 the Commission adopted a communication entitled 'Freight transport logistics in Europe — The key to sustainable mobility' (⁹), which advocates an overall approach to the improvement of transport logistics and rehearses the issues in preparation for an action plan in 2007 to promote them. According to the Commission, transport logistics makes it possible to optimise flows of goods. Logistics is thus an essential tool for meeting the challenges of growing mobility and competitiveness. It is

---

(¹) See Chapter I of this Report.
(²) COM(2006) 261.
(³) OJ L 246, 20.7.2004.
(⁴) Regulation (EC) No 1942/2006 (OJ L 367, 22.12.2006).
(⁵) COM(2006) 351.
(⁶) Regulation (EC) No 1943/2006 (OJ L 367, 22.12.2006).
(⁷) COM(2006) 272.
(⁸) COM(2006) 769.
(⁹) COM(2006) 336.

also a means of reducing the adverse effects of mobility, such as pollution, congestion and energy dependence.

International developments

In the field of international cooperation between the European Union and its partners in the field of aviation, the Commission successfully continued implementing the roadmap adopted by the Council in 2005 and centred on three pillars:

- the creation, before 2010, of a European common aviation area (ECAA): in this connection, 2006 saw the signing of an ECAA agreement with seven western Balkan partners, and a Euro-Mediterranean agreement with Morocco; on 12 December the Commission was given a mandate to negotiate a comprehensive agreement with Ukraine;

- negotiating comprehensive agreements with the European Union's key partners in the field of aviation: in 2006 negotiations continued in this field with the United States; in March the Commission was given a mandate to negotiate with Russia on overflying Siberia; the subsequent negotiations led to an agreement with Russia which was signed on 24 November; and

- achieving legal compliance of existing bilateral agreements for air services: 430 agreements have already been amended so as to recognise the principle of a Community air carrier, 342 by means of 'horizontal' agreements with the Community; in 2006 the Commission signed horizontal agreements with Moldova, Georgia, Albania, Bosnia and Herzegovina, Bulgaria, Croatia, Romania, Serbia, Montenegro, the former Yugoslav Republic of Macedonia, New Zealand, Lebanon, the Maldives and Uruguay respectively; it also initialled horizontal agreements with Paraguay and Vietnam; in 2006 the Commission took decisions on 86 bilateral agreements on the basis of Regulation (EC) No 847/2004.

As regards Galileo, negotiations continued with a view to allowing South Korea and Morocco to join the system.

Trans-European transport networks (TEN-T)

On 11 December the Council reached political agreement with a view to adopting the amended proposal of the European Parliament and of the Council laying down the general rules for the granting of Community financial aid in the field of trans-European transport (TEN-T) and energy (TEN-E) networks and amending Council Regulation (EC) No 2236/95. This adaptation follows from the agreement of 17 May 2006 on the financial framework for 2007–13 (¹). Final adoption of the regulation will take place in 2007.

(¹) See Chapter I of this Report.

Energy

Strategic approach

On 8 March the Commission adopted a Green Paper entitled 'A European strategy for sustainable, competitive and secure energy' ([1]), in which it defines the bases for a European energy policy and three main objectives: sustainability, competitiveness and security of supply. It accordingly launched a debate in six priority areas: completing the internal market; security of supply, which it hopes will be based on solidarity between Member States; a more sustainable, efficient and diverse energy mix; combating climate change; a strategic energy technology plan; and a common external energy policy. For the latter, it is proposing, in particular, identifying priorities for infrastructure necessary for the security of European Union energy supplies, establishing a 'common regulatory space' with neighbouring countries with a view to creating a pan-European energy Community, and strengthening dialogue with countries which are energy providers and with other consumers. Parliament focused on the external energy policy in a resolution of 23 March. It urged the Union to speak with one voice in the international arena and underlines the need to connect energy policy with foreign and security policies. Moreover, following the spring European Council, which adopted a list of actions to be undertaken on both internal and external aspects of energy policy, the Commission, acting jointly with the Secretary-General of the Council and Union High Representative for the Common Foreign and Security Policy, presented a document entitled 'An external policy to serve Europe's energy interests'. Work is in progress with a view to presenting a strategic analysis of the European energy policy early on in 2007.

On 4 July the Commission presented a document entitled 'Comments of the Commission on the conclusions and recommendations of the mid-term evaluation of the "Intelligent Energy — Europe" programme (2003–06)' ([2]).

On 1 July the Energy Community Treaty entered into force, creating the largest internal energy market in the world, bringing together the 25 Member States of the European Union and nine close European States and territories into a single trading block (the two new Member States of the European Union from 1 January 2007: Bulgaria and Romania; the countries of the western Balkans: Albania, the former Yugoslav Republic of Macedonia, Bosnia and Herzegovina, Croatia, Montenegro, Serbia and the United Nations Interim Administration Mission in Kosovo). With the entry into force of this Treaty, participating States have to allow free movement of electricity and gas across their borders in return for the assurance of minimum environmental and commercial standards.

The Energy Community allows the European Union to achieve several strategic goals: it establishes direct connections to countries that themselves border on the substantial

---

([1]) COM(2006) 105.
([2]) COM(2006) 357.

reserves of the Caspian Sea and the Middle East; it extends environmental standards to neighbours of the European Union; and it provides a solid basis for macroeconomic reform by providing sustainable and secure energy supplies to businesses and consumers.

On 20 December the European Union and the United States signed a new agreement to continue the Energy Star programme for office equipment for a further five years. The agreement proposes innovative and demanding energy efficiency criteria for computers, photocopiers, printers and monitors. The programme is part of the Commission's strategy to better manage energy demand, contribute to the security of energy supply and mitigate climate change.

Energy efficiency

In an opinion [1] delivered in February on the June 2005 Green Paper on energy efficiency [2], the Economic and Social Committee supported the Commission's plan to reduce energy consumption by 20 % and found that, as the two sectors with the largest energy consumption, the transport and construction industries should be the focus of intense efforts and the search for innovation. The Committee hoped that the European Union and the Member States would become strongly involved in convergent policies aimed at promoting energy efficiency, the exchange of best practices, the distribution of the best technologies and information and incentive campaigns for households and consumers. For its part, the Committee of the Regions welcomed the Green Paper at its February session [3], but rejected the setting of absolute efficiency increase targets. It pointed out that information and training was needed which should not be restricted to energy-sector professionals. The Committee also called on the Commission to adopt various measures aimed at reducing final consumer prices for energy-efficient equipment and renewable-energy technologies.

On 5 April the European Parliament and the Council signed Directive 2006/32/EC on energy end-use efficiency and energy services [4].

On 19 October the Commission adopted an action plan for energy efficiency [5]. This aims to exploit the energy efficiency improvement potential of more than 18 % which, it is said, still exists today in the European Union as a result of market barriers which prevent the satisfactory spread of energy-efficient technology and the efficient use of energy. The Commission proposes measures to enhance the integration of energy efficiency into other Community non-energy policy and programme areas, such as regional and urban policy, taxation and tariff policy, and research and technology. It

---

[1] OJ C 88, 11.4.2006.
[2] COM(2005) 265.
[3] OJ C 192, 16.8.2006.
[4] OJ L 114, 27.4.2006.
[5] COM(2006) 545.

also proposes redirecting Community measures which have already produced good results, as well as new joint and coordinated actions and measures.

Renewable energy

On 8 February the Commission proposed a European Union strategy for biofuels ([1]), with three main objectives: promoting biofuels in the European Union and developing countries, while ensuring that their production and use is globally positive for the environment and that they contribute to the objectives of the Lisbon strategy; preparing for the large-scale use of biofuels by improving their cost-competitiveness through the optimised cultivation of dedicated feedstocks; and undertaking studies exploring the opportunities for developing countries for the production of biofuels.

Trans-European energy networks

On 7 August the Commission adopted a report on the implementation of the guidelines for trans-European energy networks in the period 2002–04 ([2]). In it, it emphasised that the objective of focusing the support on priority projects was being implemented and that the need for political support by means of the 'TEN-E label' was becoming more and more essential for public acceptance and for accelerating the authorisation procedure. This idea has been integrated into the new guidelines adopted on 6 September for the TEN-E ([3]): these identify 42 projects of European interest with a view to providing priority Community support, both political and financial. The draft priority interconnection plan for the TEN-E, which aims to accelerate the actual implementation of projects of European interest, follows the same lines. This plan, which is to be submitted to the Council early in January 2007, proposes five measures: targeting Community action; improving coordination; proposing a regional approach; accelerating authorisation procedures; and mobilising financial resources, in particular from the European Investment Bank. The Commission considers that the European Investment Bank is well suited to playing a major role in better integrating the European Union gas and electricity markets.

Nuclear energy

On 20 November the Council adopted a directive laying down a Community system of supervision and control of transboundary shipments of radioactive waste and spent fuel ([4]), so as to guarantee adequate protection. The directive amends and repeals Council Directive 92/3/Euratom, clarifying and adding concepts and definitions, addressing situations that had been omitted in the past, and simplifying the procedure for the shipment of radioactive waste between Member States. It also ensures consistency with other Community and international provisions, in particular

---

[1] COM(2006) 34.
[2] COM(2006) 443.
[3] Decision No 1364/2006/EC (OJ L 262, 22.9.2006).
[4] Directive 2006/117/Euratom (OJ L 337, 5.12.2006).

with the Joint Convention on the Safety of Spent Fuel Management and on the Safety of Radioactive Waste Management, to which the Community acceded on 2 January.

The regulation on on additional financial assistance (2007–13) for the decommissioning of the Ignalina (Lithuania) nuclear power plant was adopted on 21 December ([1]). It provides for an overall contribution of EUR 837 million, thus ensuring that all the legal instruments will be available in time for the actual launch of the programme in January 2007.

International developments

Signed on 28 April 2005, the agreement between the European Atomic Energy Community and the Cabinet of Ministers of Ukraine for cooperation in the peaceful uses of nuclear energy ([2]) entered into force on 1 September 2006.

On 27 February the Council reached an agreement with Japan on cooperation in the peaceful uses of nuclear energy, under which the two sides are to cooperate to promote and facilitate trade, research and development in the civil nuclear sector. The agreement entered into force on 20 December.

Following the deposit of the instruments of accession, on 14 December Euratom became a party to two International Atomic Energy Agency (IAEA) conventions:

- the Convention on Early Notification of a Nuclear Accident, which aims to strengthen international cooperation by requiring information on nuclear accidents to be communicated as rapidly as possible to the States which are or may be physically affected, so that the transboundary radiological consequences can be kept to a minimum; and

- the Convention on Assistance in the Case of a Nuclear Accident or Radiological Emergency, which sets out a framework for cooperation between the States parties and with the IAEA to facilitate prompt assistance and support in the event of nuclear accidents or radiological emergencies in order to reduce as much as possible the consequences thereof.

On 7 November the European Union and Azerbaijan signed a memorandum of understanding aimed at the establishment of an energy partnership. Implementation of the memorandum will bring about a better integration of Azerbaijan into European energy markets, strengthen European Union energy security and develop more efficient energy demand management in Azerbaijan.

At the Energy Charter Conference on 20 November the Commission represented the Community and contributed to the conclusion of several decisions, including the

---

[1] Regulation (EC) No 1990/2006 (OJ L 411, 30.12.2006).
[2] OJ L 261, 22.9.2006.

appointment of the new chairman of the conference, Ambassador Kawamura, as well as to the invitation to Pakistan to accede to the Energy Charter Treaty.

On 30 November the ministerial conference on energy within the framework of the 'Baku initiative', which brings together the European Union Member States and the governments of the Caspian and Black Sea countries, was held in Astana, Kazakhstan. The conference adopted an energy roadmap. Its implementation will pave the way for a comprehensive legal and regulatory framework governing an integrated common energy market between the European Union and the regions concerned based on the body of European Union law.

On 4 December the European Union and Kazakhstan signed a memorandum of understanding which establishes the basis for enhanced cooperation in the field of energy. It provides a basis for enhancing energy supply security and industrial cooperation. The two parties also signed an agreement on cooperation in the peaceful uses of nuclear energy.

On 16 March ([1]) the Commission recommended enhancing the status of the European Atomic Energy Community at the International Atomic Energy Agency, noting that its status of observer limited its influence and visibility and was not commensurate with the Community's competence in the Agency's field of activities.

On 28 April the Commission adopted a draft interinstitutional agreement on interinstitutional cooperation in the framework of international conventions to which the European Atomic Energy Community and its Member States are parties ([2]). This sets out general principles for interinstitutional coordination between the Member States represented in the Council, and the Commission.

Labour mobility

The year 2006 was designated European Year of Workers' Mobility. Detailed information on the implementation of this initiative is given under 'Mobility of workers and coordination of social security schemes' in Chapter III, Section 1, of this Report.

Progress of the internal market

Background

The internal market is an important part of the Lisbon strategy, as relaunched in 2005. The main actions in this area at Community level are included in the Lisbon programme, which

---

([1]) COM(2006) 121.
([2]) COM(2006) 179.

> means that it is the responsibility of each Member State to implement them correctly. It is also essential to act at both Community and national levels in order to create and maintain a smooth running internal market in all sectors of the economy, take full advantage of its potential contribution towards creating more growth and jobs and offer more tangible benefits to all citizens, be they consumers or entrepreneurs. In the light of this, the emphasis the European Union puts on the need for better regulation (¹) is particularly pertinent.
>
> Moreover, following the wide-ranging consultation launched in 2005 on monitoring the action plan for financial services, the Commission has chosen to make targeting implementation of the consultation a key objective of its internal market policy until 2010.
>
> On the legislative front, one of the key subjects remains the effort made to successfully complete the proposal for a directive on services.

Directive on services in the internal market: decisive progress made in 2006

In its opinion delivered at first reading on 16 February the European Parliament made significant changes to the Commission proposal for a services directive (²). It replaced the principle of the country of origin with that of the freedom to provide services, with the result that the Member States will be obliged to respect the right of service providers to operate in a Member State other than that in which they are established, and that the State of destination will have to ensure freedom of access to services and the freedom to provide services in its territory. Moreover, Member States may restrict the freedom to provide services originating in other Member States only through national measures which are non-discriminatory, proportional and justified on grounds of public policy, public safety, public health or environmental protection. Parliament also excluded a number of services of general interest from the scope of the proposal, in particular health and audiovisual services, and some social services, services provided by notaries, private security services and services provided by temporary employment agencies.

On 4 April the Commission adopted an amended proposal (³) reflecting the compromise reached in Parliament. At its meeting of 29 and 30 May the Council reached a political agreement on the basis of a compromise text similar to Parliament's opinion at first reading. On 24 July it adopted a common position reflecting this political agreement.

The European Parliament's vote at second reading was held on 15 November. Parliament did not change the substance of the Council's common position. Only three amendments were adopted, reflecting the new regulatory committee procedure with scrutiny. The directive was finally adopted on 12 December (⁴).

(¹) See Chapter I, Section 1, of this Report.
(²) COM(2004) 2.
(³) COM(2006) 160.
(⁴) Directive 2006/123/EC (OJ L 376, 27.12.2006).

Services of general interest

In an opinion delivered on 6 July ([1]) the European Economic and Social Committee called for the adoption of a framework directive laying down the common basic principles which should apply to all services of general interest. It also recommended creating an observatory made up of political representatives and representatives of organised civil society in order to evaluate economic and non-economic services of general interest.

In a European Parliament resolution of 27 September in response to its White Paper on services of general interest ([2]), the Commission was asked to clarify the distinction between services of general interest (SGI) and services of general economic interest (SGEI).

On 2 February, further to the Commission report of 23 March 2005 ([3]) on the application of the postal directive ([4]), the European Parliament adopted a resolution stating that the reform and developments on the market had until then had a positive impact and asking the Commission to place particular emphasis, when preparing a prospective study, on several aspects linked to universal service.

On 18 October the Commission adopted a proposal for a directive on opening the European Union's postal services to competition in 2009 ([5]). The proposal still contains an obligation on Member States to provide a universal quality service and, at the same time, strengthens consumers' rights, in particular in terms of complaint procedures, and the independence and the role of national regulatory authorities. It also set out a non-exhaustive list of financing measures in the event of an additional cost linked to the provision of universal service. The proposal is accompanied by an impact assessment, a prospective study on opening the market on universal service and the third report on the application of the postal directive ([6]).

Financial services

On 18 January the European Parliament set up a committee of inquiry to look into the financial debacle of the Equitable Life Assurance Society. Its role is to investigate allegations of infringements of Community law, and it is to submit its final report in early 2007. On 4 July the European Parliament adopted an interim report by the committee of inquiry and extended the latter's mandate until April 2007.

([1]) OJ C 309, 16.12.2006.
([2]) COM(2004) 374.
([3]) COM(2005) 102.
([4]) Directive 97/67/EC (OJ L 15, 21.1.1998), as last amended by Directive 2002/39/EC (OJ L 176, 5.7.2002).
([5]) COM(2006) 594.
([6]) COM(2006) 595.

On 5 April the European Parliament and the Council adopted a directive (^{1}) postponing from 30 April 2006 until 31 January 2007 the deadline for transposal by the Member States into national law of the directive on markets in financial instruments (^{2}).

On 14 June the European Parliament and the Council adopted two directives, the first on the taking up and pursuit of the business of credit institutions (^{3}) and the second on the capital adequacy of investment firms and credit institutions (^{4}). These two directives establish new capital adequacy requirements for banks and investment firms and form part of the European Union's action plan for financial services.

On 15 November the European Parliament and the Council adopted a regulation on information on the payer accompanying transfers of funds (^{5}). This regulation transposes Special Recommendation VII of the financial action task force into Community legislation. It aims to ensure the complete traceability of transfers of funds to help prevent, investigate and detect money-laundering services and the funding of terrorism.

In a resolution adopted on 4 July the European Parliament asked the institutions of the European Union to launch a debate on the structure of the prudential supervision of European financial markets.

On 12 September the Commission adopted a proposal for a directive on procedural rules and evaluation criteria for the prudential assessment of acquisitions and increase of shareholdings in the financial sector (^{6}). It recommends measures to improve the approval process by the supervisory authorities in the event of mergers and acquisitions with, in particular, stricter procedures for evaluating mergers and acquisitions in the banking, insurance and securities sectors.

In a resolution on asset management adopted on 27 April the European Parliament stressed the importance of strengthening the competencies of the investor, particularly as regards new investment products. It also asked the Commission to identify and remove obstacles to a true internal market, in particular those affecting the handling of cross-border mergers.

At its plenary session of 15 and 16 March the European Economic and Social Committee delivered an opinion (^{7}) on the Commission Green Paper on the enhancement of the European Union framework for investment funds (^{8}). In particular it suggested using

---

(^{1}) Directive 2006/31/EC (OJ L 114, 27.4.2006).
(^{2}) Directive 2004/39/EC (OJ L 145, 30.4.2004).
(^{3}) Directive 2006/48/EC (OJ L 177, 30.6.2006).
(^{4}) Directive 2006/49/EC (OJ L 177, 30.6.2006).
(^{5}) Regulation (EC) No 1781/2006 (OJ L 345, 8.12.2006).
(^{6}) COM(2006) 507.
(^{7}) OJ C 110, 9.5.2006.
(^{8}) COM(2005) 314.

the current debate to examine carefully the development of 'responsible social finance', a concept which sacrifices neither social development nor environmental protection to profit. On 15 November the Commission adopted a White Paper on enhancing the single market framework for investment funds ([1]). It defines a set of measures to simplify the operating environment of this major pillar of the European financial system. To this end it recommends overhauling cumbersome notification procedures and slimming down the simplified prospectus. The Commission also identifies the need to give investors better tools for taking decisions on the basis of reliable information and to ensure that they receive objective and impartial assistance from fund distributors. Furthermore, it proposes examining in detail issues linked to recent innovations in investment techniques and products, in order to allow an appropriate policy debate on the regulatory framework at European level.

On 12 December the Commission presented a communication entitled 'Investment research and financial analysts' ([2]), in which it reviews relevant measures in recent European legislation and provides practical guidelines for the parties concerned.

In an opinion adopted on 5 July ([3]) on the Commission White Paper 'Financial services policy 2005–10' ([4]), the European Economic and Social Committee welcomed the Commission proposal to devote the next five years to the dynamic consolidation of the financial services industry, but pointed out the need to take account of the social impact of the consolidation processes. The Council also addressed the White Paper in its conclusions of 5 May.

On 1 August the Commission adopted a directive ([5]) adding to Community legislation on preventing the use of the financial system for money-laundering and funding terrorism.

On 7 November a European code of conduct for the clearing and settlement industry was signed by all members of the main associations in the sector (the Federation of European Securities Exchanges, the European Association of Central Counterparty Clearing Houses, and the European Central Securities Depositories Association). This initiative comes in response to the Commission's wish to have an approach steered by businesses rather than a directive to overcome the last barriers to integrating the market in post-negotiation operations. The measures set out in the code concern mainly the transparency of prices and services, access and interoperability, the unbundling of services, and accounting separation. The Council also welcomed this initiative in its conclusions of 28 November.

---

[1] COM(2006) 686.
[2] COM(2006) 789.
[3] OJ C 309, 16.12.2006.
[4] COM(2005) 629.
[5] Directive 2006/70/EC (OJ L 214, 4.8.2006).

On 27 November the Commission adopted a communication concerning the review of Directive 94/19/EC on deposit guarantee schemes (¹).

Free movement of capital

On 10 October the Council adopted conclusions on the single euro payments area (SEPA). The aim of the SEPA project is to remove all distinctions between national and cross-border payments made in euro within the European Union.

Free movement of goods

The Commission has continued to scrutinise Member States' national legislation in accordance with Article 28 of the EC Treaty and the principle of mutual recognition. As at 1 December 2006 it had recorded a total of 27 new complaints and own-initiative cases and had closed the file on 75 cases. As at the same date and as part of the preliminary assessment of draft national technical rules under Directive 98/34/EC, the Member States had notified 625 measures and the Commission had issued 44 detailed opinions.

On 2 March the Commission adopted a proposal for a directive amending Council Directive 91/477/EEC on control of the acquisition and possession of weapons (²). This proposal was prompted by the accession of the European Community to the Protocol annexed to the United Nations Convention against Transnational Organised Crime.

On 20 September the Commission adopted a proposal for a regulation on the export of cultural goods (³).

On 14 September the Commission adopted the third report (⁴) on the application between 2001 and the first quarter of 2006 of the directive concerning liability for defective products (⁵). The Commission concludes that it is not necessary to amend the directive but does not rule out taking steps to that effect if the application of the text differs significantly between Member States.

The year 2006 also marks the end of the preparatory work for a Commission proposal to review the 'new approach' legislative technique. The Commission is proposing a two-tiered strategy based on:

- a decision of the European Parliament and of the Council, the purpose of which is to ensure coherence between the various technical instruments already in use in existing legislation aimed at improving the free marketing of products (in particular

---

(¹) COM(2006) 729.
(²) COM(2006) 93.
(³) COM(2006) 513.
(⁴) COM(2006) 496.
(⁵) Directive 85/374/EEC (OJ L 210, 7.8.1985), as last amended by Directive 1999/34/EC (OJ L 141, 4.6.1999).

the criteria for bodies assessing conformity, harmonised conformity assessment procedures and the obligations on economic operators); and

- a regulation to supplement the various instruments at the public authorities' disposal both at national and European levels to simplify and harmonise the conditions for correctly implementing Community legislation; it also contains a proposal to clarify the meaning of the 'CE' mark and the responsibilities linked to its use.

Preparatory work was also carried out with regard to a legislative proposal on mutual recognition. This instrument will set out the rights and obligations of the national authorities as well as companies which wish to sell in one Member State products manufactured or already sold in another. It will also specify on whom the burden of proof will fall at various stages of the mutual recognition procedure, improve the organisation of administrative cooperation and establish 'product' points of contact in the Member States.

In addition, an interpretative communication from the Commission on vehicle registration has been drafted to update the 1996 communication on this subject and integrate subsequent developments in the case-law of the Court of Justice of the European Communities.

For further information on the free movement of goods please see 'Product policy' discussed above.

Company law and corporate governance

On 5 January the Commission adopted a proposal for a directive on the exercise of voting rights by shareholders of companies having their registered office in a Member State ([1]). This proposal sets out the measures to be taken to enable shareholders in a company to vote without being present at the general meeting. It provides, in particular, for removing legal obstacles to electronic participation in general meetings.

On 14 June the European Parliament and the Council adopted a directive ([2]) amending Directive 78/660/EEC on the annual accounts of certain types of companies, Directive 83/349/EEC on consolidated accounts, Directive 86/635/EEC on the annual accounts and consolidated accounts of banks and other financial institutions and Directive 91/674/EEC on the annual accounts and consolidated accounts of insurance undertakings. The collective liability of administrators serves to introduce a declaration on company management as part of the annual report of companies listed on the European capital markets and improve the transparency of transactions with connected parties, as

---

([1]) COM(2005) 685.
([2]) Directive 2006/49/EC (OJ L 224, 16.8.2006).

well as a declaration on the use of off-balance-sheet transactions. However, in order to avoid adding to the administrative burden on small firms, the directive increases the scope of exemptions provided that they satisfy certain criteria relating to their statement of accounts, net turnover and number of employees.

On 17 May the European Parliament and the Council adopted a directive on statutory audits of annual accounts and consolidated accounts, amending Council Directives 78/660/EEC and 83/349/EEC and repealing Council Directive 84/253/EEC [1]. The purpose of the new directive is to amend European rules on audits of annual accounts and consolidated accounts. The directive also introduces an obligation on the Member States to set up a public oversight system for auditors and audit boards as well as a quality assurance system. It also lays the foundations for effective and balanced cooperation between European Union regulators and those in third countries.

In a resolution adopted on 4 July the European Parliament called upon the Commission to look into the options for simplifying the statutes for a European company and to draw up a proposal on the European private company in order to respond to the needs of small and medium-sized enterprises.

On 6 September the European Parliament and the Council amended the current system as regards the formation of public limited liability companies and the maintenance and alteration of their capital [2].

Intellectual property

On 17 May the European Parliament and the Council adopted a regulation on compulsory licensing of patents relating to the manufacture of pharmaceutical products for export to countries with public health problems [3]. The regulation implements at Community level the decision taken by the World Trade Organisation to grant compulsory licences to companies which manufacture generic medicines intended for export to the least developed countries.

In May the Commission adopted two proposals for directives codifying copyright rules: the first on rental right and lending right and on certain rights related to copyright in the field of intellectual property [4], and the second on the term of protection of copyright and certain related rights [5].

In a resolution adopted on 12 October the European Parliament again pointed out that an effective and competitive patent system is a key requirement of the Lisbon strategy. It strongly urged the Commission to explore all avenues with a view to improving the

---

[1] Directive 2006/43/EC (OJ L 157, 9.6.2006).
[2] Directive 2006/68/EC (OJ L 264, 25.9.2006).
[3] Regulation (EC) No 816/2006 (OJ L 157, 9.6.2006).
[4] COM(2006) 226.
[5] COM(2006) 219.

system of patents and resolving patent-related disputes in the European Union, in particular participation in the European Patent Litigation Agreement. This agreement provides for establishing a network of national courts linked to a European court of appeal whose role would be to interpret the law in this area.

Data protection

Concerned about the increasing lack of respect for private life and data protection, Parliament referred, in a resolution adopted on 6 July, to the United States Anti-Terrorism Assistance Programme, which allows all financial data held by the Swift company to be transmitted to the American authorities. Parliament pointed out that all transfers of data within the European Union intended to be handled outside the Union must comply with the directive on the protection of data (¹). It called on the Commission to assess all European Union anti-terrorist legislation in terms of effectiveness, necessity, proportionality and respect for human rights.

On 6 October, following the judgment of the Court of Justice of the European Communities annulling the previous agreement on the communication of the personal data of air passengers to the American authorities (²), the European Union and the United States concluded a provisional agreement, signed by the Council on 16 October (³), which aims to prevent and combat terrorism while ensuring a high level of protection for this type of personal data.

Public procurement

On 4 May the Commission adopted a proposal for a directive aimed at improving the effectiveness of review procedures concerning the award of public contracts (⁴). The aim of this proposal is to encourage companies from one Member State to submit tenders in the other Member States by guaranteeing an effective appeal system under the same conditions irrespective of the Member State concerned.

On 1 August, in order to help contracting authorities comply with the standards established by the Court, the Commission adopted an interpretative communication on the Community law applicable to contract awards which are not subject or not fully subject to the provisions of the public procurement directives (⁵).

On 12 October the Committee of the Regions gave its opinion on the Commission communication on public–private partnerships and Community law on public procurement and concessions (⁶). As the Committee sees it, there is little point in

---

(¹) Directive 95/46/EC (OJ L 281, 23.11.1995).
(²) *European Parliament* v *Council* (joined cases C-317/04 and C-318/04) (OJ C 178, 29.7.2006).
(³) OJ L 298, 27.10.2006. See also 'Transatlantic relations' in Chapter V, Section 2, of of this Report.
(⁴) COM(2006) 195.
(⁵) OJ C 179, 1.8.2006.
(⁶) COM(2005) 569.

proposing new legislation on the principles for awarding concessions for work and services. It also takes the view that service concessions should not be subject to the Community directive on public procurement, as they require a more flexible procedure. On 26 October the European Parliament asked the Commission to clarify the application of public contract law to the creation of public–private companies within the framework of the awarding of contracts or tenders. Parliament spoke in favour of a legislative initiative as regards tenders. It felt, moreover, that the Commission should shed light on the legal uncertainty regarding cooperation between public authorities.

On 30 November, as part of the simplification of the body of Community law, the Commission proposed (¹) repealing Directive 71/304/EEC (²), given that it had become obsolete. The directive is in two parts, one concerning public procurement procedure, currently dealt with by Directives 2004/18/EC and 2004/17/EC, and the other on non-discriminatory access to works in general, aimed directly at the application of Articles 43 and 49 of the EC Treaty, and comes into play upstream or downstream of the call for tender procedure. The latter part is superseded by the Court's case-law on the free movement of goods. As a result, Directive 71/304/EEC has become redundant and can therefore be repealed without in any way adversely affecting the rights of economic operators.

On 7 December the Commission adopted an interpretative communication on the application of Article 296 of the Treaty in the field of defence procurement (³). Its purpose is to reinforce the application of Community law on all military supply services which are not specifically excluded by the Treaty in accordance with very strict conditions linked to the Member States' essential security interests.

Accountancy and auditing

On 11 July the Commission established criteria which must be taken into account when reviewing the system for funding the International Accounting Standards Board, which expires at the end of 2007.

General references and other useful links

- Enterprises:
  http://ec.europa.eu/enterprise/index_en.htm

- Innovation scoreboard:
  http://trendchart.cordis.lu/

- Directorate-General for Research:
  http://ec.europa.eu/research/index_en.cfm

- ITER:
  http://www.iter.org/index.htm

(¹) COM(2006) 748.
(²) OJ L 185, 16.8.1971.
(³) COM(2006) 779.

- Joint Research Centre:
  http://www.jrc.ec.europa.eu/

- Space:
  http://ec.europa.eu/enterprise/space/index_en.html

- Directorate-General for Information Society and Media:
  http://ec.europa.eu/dgs/information_society/index_en.htm

- Education:
  http://ec.europa.eu/education/index_en.html

- Directorate-General for Energy and Transport:
  http://ec.europa.eu/dgs/energy_transport/index_en.html

- Internal market:
  http://ec.europa.eu/internal_market/index_en.htm

Chapter III

Solidarity

Consolidating economic and social cohesion

Regional dimension

Implementation of the Lisbon objectives

With the relaunch of the Lisbon strategy, cohesion policy has been recognised as the primary instrument at Community level for implementing the growth and jobs strategy.

The fourth progress report on cohesion, 'The growth and jobs strategy and the reform of European cohesion policy' ([1]), was adopted by the Commission on 12 June. It describes the current situation, looking at trends in, and disparities between, the Member States and regions, before going on to outline the key developments in the policy framework, including the agreement reached at the European Council in December 2005 on the resources to be devoted to cohesion policy. Strategies designed at local and regional levels must now form an integral part of the effort to promote growth and rank alongside innovation as key drivers of growth. The nature of the growth, jobs and competitiveness agenda, which emphasises the role of small and medium-sized businesses, the importance of clusters and the need for local innovation centres, is such that in many cases it has to be built from the bottom up, starting at the regional and local levels. Moreover, this applies not only to the economic agenda but also to the broader effort to involve citizens, who, through the partnership and multilevel governance arrangements through which cohesion policy is managed, have the opportunity to become involved directly in the Union's growth and jobs strategy. The report also underlines that, over the past year, the Commission has been developing new instruments to assist Member States and the regions to improve the

---

([1]) COM(2006) 281.

quality of projects while, at the same time, making Community financial resources work harder by increasing the leverage effect of cohesion policy. Accordingly, for the new programmes, specific initiatives have been developed to promote financial engineering for start-ups and micro-enterprises, combining technical assistance and grants with non-grant instruments such as loans, equity, venture capital or guarantees. These actions will be undertaken through enhanced cooperation between the Commission and the European Investment Bank and other international financial institutions on financial engineering. The added value produced by cooperation in this area could take various forms, such as additional loan resources for business creation and for development in the regions of the Union or the adoption of strong incentives for successful implementation by beneficiaries by combining grants with loans.

A further step forward was the adoption by the Commission on 13 July of a communication entitled 'Cohesion policy and cities: the urban contribution to growth and jobs in the regions' (¹). In this communication, the Commission offers tools for an integrated urban policy, on the basis of the needs of cities, urban areas and regions. It is designed to help national, regional and city authorities in the preparation of the new round of cohesion policy programmes. Its main purpose is to amplify and complete the Community strategic guidelines by expanding and strengthening the urban dimension. The Commission notes that there is more than one path to sustainable urban development, depending on the particular characteristics and needs of urban areas. Its suggestions include making cities more attractive and increasing networking between them, reinforcing the role of cities as poles of growth, promoting entrepreneurship, innovation and the knowledge economy, supporting small and medium-sized businesses; decreasing disparities between neighbourhoods and social groups, and tackling crime and the fear of crime.

Also on 13 July the Commission adopted a proposal for a Council decision on Community strategic guidelines on cohesion (²). In line with the renewed Lisbon strategy, it recommends that programmes co-financed through the cohesion policy target resources on the following three priorities: improving the attractiveness of Member States, regions and cities by improving accessibility, ensuring an adequate quality and level of services and preserving their environmental potential; encouraging innovation, entrepreneurship and the growth of the knowledge economy by promoting research and innovation, including new information and communication technologies; and creating more and better jobs by attracting more people into employment or entrepreneurial activity, improving the adaptability of workers and enterprises and increasing investment in human capital.

On 8 November the Commission adopted a communication 'Regions for economic change' (³), in which it describes its plans to focus interregional cooperation and

---

(¹) COM(2006) 385.
(²) COM(2006) 386.
(³) COM(2006) 675.

the urban development network programme on testing best practice for economic modernisation and increased competitiveness.

Establishing a new regulatory framework

Several regulations were adopted on 5 July. These concerned the European Regional Development Fund [1], the European Social Fund [2] and a European grouping of territorial cooperation [3]. A further regulation adopted on 11 July established the Cohesion Fund [4].

Also on 11 July the Council adopted general provisions on the European Regional Development Fund, the European Social Fund and the Cohesion Fund [5].

On 8 December the Commission laid down the detailed rules for implementing these basic regulations.

On 4 August and 31 October the Commission adopted a series of decisions [6] defining the Member States and regions eligible for funding under the cohesion policy and the allocation by Member States of the appropriations available for cohesion policy as laid down by the European Council of December 2005.

Outermost regions

On 30 January the Council adopted specific measures for agriculture in the outermost regions of the Union [7]. The regulation provides for specific supply arrangements, measures to assist local agricultural products, targeted support measures and financial provisions. In view of the difficulties of these regions and in order to boost trade, imports of certain agricultural products will be exempt from customs duty. Aid will also be granted for the supply of products of Community origin to the outermost regions.

On 30 November the Commission adopted a proposal for a regulation introducing a scheme to compensate for the additional costs incurred in the marketing of certain fishery products from the Azores, Madeira, the Canary Islands, and the French departments of Guiana and Réunion [8].

---

[1] Regulation (EC) No 1080/2006 (OJ L 210, 31.7.2006).
[2] Regulation (EC) No 1081/2006 (OJ L 210, 31.7.2006).
[3] Regulation (EC) No 1082/2006 (OJ L 210, 31.7.2006).
[4] Regulation (EC) No 1084/2006 (OJ L 210, 31.7.2006).
[5] Regulation (EC) No 1083/2006 (OJ L 210, 31.7.2006).
[6] Decisions 2006/593/EC, 2006/594/EC, 2006/595/EC, 2006/596/EC, 2006/597/EC (OJ L 243, 6.9.2006), 2006/609/EC (OJ L 247, 9.9.2006) and 2006/769/EC (OJ L 312, 11.11.2006).
[7] Regulation (EC) No 247/2006 (OJ L 42, 14.2.2006).
[8] COM(2006) 740. See also 'Outermost regions' in Section 2 of this chapter.

Social dimension

General approach

Following the interinstitutional agreement of 17 May concerning the financial perspective (¹), the Commission adopted an amended proposal seeking to establish a Community programme for employment and social solidarity ('Progress'). This was adopted by the European Parliament and by the Council on 24 October (²). Designed to support financially the implementation of the objectives of the European Union in the fields of employment and social affairs, the programme takes the form of a single, streamlined financial instrument divided into five sections: employment, social protection and inclusion, working conditions, anti-discrimination and diversity, and gender equality.

On 14 July the Commission issued a proposal (³) for simplifying and rationalising the provisions of the Community directives on the health and safety of workers at work. The proposal includes harmonising the frequency of the national reports on practical implementation of the directives, and requiring only a single report covering all the directives.

On 24 May, as part of the follow-up to the United Nations Millennium Declaration, the Commission adopted a communication entitled 'Promoting decent work for all' (⁴), which identifies the possible lines of action to be developed in the context of enlargement, neighbourhood policy, regional, bilateral and multilateral relations and external trade. It lays particular emphasis on the role of corporate social responsibility in this approach. The issue of decent work for all was also addressed in Council conclusions adopted on 1 December.

On 22 November the Commission adopted a Green Paper entitled 'Modernising labour law to meet the challenges of the 21st century' (⁵). This document seeks to launch a public debate on how labour law can evolve to support the Lisbon strategy's objectives for creating more and better jobs.

Employment

The spring European Council (23 and 24 March) considered that the Union should give top priority to increasing employment rates in Europe, once again laying particular emphasis on increasing the labour market participation of women, young people, older workers, persons with disabilities, legal migrants and minorities. It saw close cooperation with the social partners as an important factor in achieving this objective. It also called upon Member States to adopt a life-cycle approach to work.

(¹) See Chapter I of this Report.
(²) Decision No 1672/2006/EC (OJ L 315, 15.11.2006).
(³) COM(2006) 390.
(⁴) COM(2006) 249.
(⁵) COM(2006) 708.

The European Council also took note of the Commission proposal to establish a European Globalisation Adjustment Fund ([1]), the aim of which would be to provide additional support for workers made redundant as a result of major structural changes in world trade patterns. It would complement the efforts of the Member States by financing one-off personalised support services tailored to meet the specific needs of individuals facing immediate and serious social difficulties as a result of unforeseen serious economic disruption. The new Fund was established by the European Parliament and the Council on 20 December ([2]).

On 18 July the Council adopted a decision on guidelines for the employment policies of the Member States ([3]). The decision points out that, while the reform of the Lisbon strategy in 2005 placed the emphasis on growth and jobs, the employment guidelines of the European employment strategy and the broad economic policy guidelines were adopted as an integrated package, thereby making the employment strategy a driving force in the implementation of the employment and labour market objectives of the Lisbon strategy. The guidelines adopted in 2005, which targeted full employment, quality and productivity at work and social cohesion, were maintained for 2006. On 12 December the Commission put forward a proposal to maintain them again for 2007 ([4]).

Social protection and social inclusion

On 13 February the Commission adopted its draft 'Joint report on social protection and social inclusion' ([5]). As regards social integration, the report stresses the role of education and training in breaking the cycle of poverty transmission from generation to generation. It also sets out the main conclusions drawn from the analyses conducted on pensions, healthcare in general and long-term care in particular and social protection systems, and puts forward options for improving them. It sees it as vital to ensure that the open method of coordination interacts effectively with the revised Lisbon process.

In June the Commission worked together with the Austrian Presidency and the Latvian government to organise a ministerial conference in Riga, at which 34 ministerial delegations approved a declaration setting the priorities and identifying the action needed to establish a barrier-free information society. The aim is to use information technologies to combat all forms of exclusion while ensuring that information technologies do not in themselves become an exclusion factor. This conference was the starting point for preparing the e-Inclusion 2008 event, which had been announced in the Commission communication 'i2010 — A European information society for growth and employment' ([6]).

([1]) COM(2006) 91.
([2]) Regulation (EC) No 1927/2006 (OJ L 406, 30.12.2006).
([3]) Decision 2006/544/EC (OJ L 215, 5.8.2006).
([4]) COM(2006) 815.
([5]) COM(2006) 62.
([6]) COM(2005) 229.

Workers' mobility and coordination of social security schemes

The year 2006 was designated European Year for Workers' Mobility, with the objective of familiarising European citizens with their rights when taking up residence in another European Union Member State. A further aim of the European Year was to demonstrate that removing obstacles to and enhancing mobility by appropriate means is instrumental in establishing a real European labour market. The new EURES website for employment ([1]) has been launched, marking its opening with the posting online of almost a million job vacancies throughout the European Union.

Having announced its intention to delete the articles concerning the posting of workers in the amended proposal for a directive on services in the internal market ([2]), on 4 April the Commission presented guidelines for the Member States ([3]) to ensure that they complied with the Community *acquis* as interpreted by the European Court of Justice with reference to Article 49 of the EC Treaty.

The EU-15 Member States were asked to notify the Commission of their intentions for the second phase (2006–09) of the transitional arrangements applying to the free movement of workers from the new Member States. In a report adopted on 8 February ([4]), the Commission indicated that migratory flows within the Union since enlargement to 25 Member States had not been large enough to affect the European labour market in general. Spain, Portugal, Finland, Greece and, in July, Italy announced that they would follow the example of the United Kingdom, Ireland and Sweden in not applying restrictions.

In January the Commission presented two proposals to continue the process of simplifying and modernising the legislation on the coordination of social security systems ([5]). The proposals aim to simplify the legislation and administrative procedures applied by the European and national authorities. To this end, they provide for special provisions for implementing the legislation of individual Member States while taking into account the particularities of their respective social security systems. They also define the measures and procedures which will allow the coordination principles to be applied uniformly in practice.

In addition, on 5 April the European Parliament and the Council amended the regulations on the application of social security schemes to employed persons, to self-employed persons and to members of their families moving within the Community ([6]), in order both to take account of changes in the legislation of the Member States, in particular in the new Member States since the end of the accession negotiations, and

---

([1]) http://ec.europa.eu/eures/.
([2]) See Chapter II, Section 2, of this Report.
([3]) COM(2006) 159.
([4]) COM(2006) 48.
([5]) COM(2006) 7 and COM(2006) 16.
([6]) Regulation (EC) No 629/2006 (OJ L 114, 27.4.2006).

to complete the process of simplifying the procedures applicable to medical care received abroad. A further amendment was made on 18 December (^{1}).

Health and safety at work

On 7 February the Commission adopted a directive (^{2}) establishing a second list of indicative occupational exposure limit values in implementation of Council Directive 98/24/EC (^{3}). The new directive sets the indicative limit values for 33 substances in the light of the evaluation of the latest available scientific data by the Scientific Committee for Occupational Exposure Limits to Chemical Agents.

Fourteen years after an initiative on protecting workers against the risks of exposure to physical agents was first launched by the Commission, the European Parliament and the Council finally adopted, on 5 April, the directive on the minimum health and safety requirements regarding the exposure of workers to risks arising from physical agents (artificial optical radiation) (^{4}), the last of the four parts of the Commission's initial proposal (^{5}). The directive imposes a number of obligations on employers, including risk assessment, reduction of exposure, health surveillance and information and training for workers exposed to risks from artificial optical radiation at work.

Combating discrimination

On 17 May the European Parliament and the Council designated 2007 as the European Year of Equal Opportunities for All (^{6}). The general objective of this initiative is to increase the participation in society of groups that are victims of discrimination, in particular by supporting the Member States and other countries concerned (accession countries, EEA/EFTA States, countries of the western Balkans) in implementing the Community legislation on equal treatment and non-discrimination.

Equality between women and men

On 22 February the Commission adopted its annual report on equality between women and men (^{7}), in which it notes that, despite some progress, a significant gender gap persists in many areas. It also stresses the contribution of equality policy to the new Lisbon strategy.

(^{1}) Regulation (EC) No 1992/2006 (OJ L 392, 30.12.2006).
(^{2}) Directive 2006/15/EC (OJ L 38, 9.2.2006).
(^{3}) OJ L 131, 5.5.1998.
(^{4}) Directive 2006/25/EC (OJ L 114, 27.4.2006).
(^{5}) The three earlier directives concerned the following risks: vibration (Directive 2002/44/EC — OJ L 177, 6.7.2002), noise (Directive 2003/10/EC — OJ L 42, 15.2.2003) and electromagnetic fields (Directive 2004/40/EC — OJ L 184, 24.5.2004).
(^{6}) Decision No 771/2006/EC (OJ L 146, 31.5.2006).
(^{7}) COM(2006) 71.

In its 'Roadmap for equality between women and men 2006–10' (¹), adopted on 1 March, the Commission outlines the priority areas for European Union action over that period and identifies the priority objectives and key actions for each area. With an eye to better governance, it plans to participate in setting up the new European Institute for Gender Equality, which was set up by the European Parliament and the Council on 20 December (²). The institute, which has its headquarters in Vilnius (Lithuania), will serve as a centre of excellence in equality issues at European level and provide technical support to the Community institutions and the Member States. Its management board will include a representative of each Member State.

At its spring meeting the European Council adopted a 'European pact for gender equality' to encourage the Member States and the Union to take action in various areas to achieve the equality objective.

On 5 July the European Parliament and the Council signed the directive on the implementation of the principle of equal opportunities and equal treatment of men and women in matters of employment and occupation (³), the aim of which is to simplify, modernise and improve Community legislation on equal treatment between men and women by bringing together in a single text the relevant passages of the directives on this subject to make the provisions clearer and more practical for all citizens.

Demographic challenges

Background

Demographic ageing, i.e. the increase in the proportion of older people, is above all the result of significant economic, social and medical progress that gives Europeans the opportunity to live a long life in unprecedented comfort and security. However, as was stressed by the Heads of State or Government at the Hampton Court Informal Summit in October 2005, it is also one of the main challenges that the European Union will have to face in the years to come.

In 2005 the Commission took the first steps to launch a discussion on this issue with two initiatives: the publication in March of a Green Paper entitled 'Confronting demographic change: a new solidarity between the generations' (⁴) and, in November, the presentation to the European Council of a communication on 'European values in the globalised world' (⁵).

In 2006 the Commission extended the discussion started in 2005 by adopting, on 12 October, a new communication entitled 'The demographic future of Europe —

(¹) COM(2006) 92.
(²) Regulation (EC) No 1922/2006 (OJ L 403, 30.12.2006).
(³) Directive 2006/54/EC (OJ L 204, 26.7.2006).
(⁴) COM(2005) 94.
(⁵) COM(2005) 525.

from challenge to opportunity' (¹). After analysing the trends that play a major role in demographic ageing and its impact on the labour market, productivity, economic growth, social security and public finances, the Commission put forward five areas for a constructive response to the demographic challenge:

- promoting demographic renewal in Europe through family policies;

- promoting employment in Europe, in particular by raising employment rates for workers aged over 55 to over 50 %;

- a more productive and competitive Europe, through the structural reforms generated by the revised Lisbon strategy;

- receiving and integrating migrants in Europe; and

- sustainable public finances in Europe, guaranteeing adequate social security and equity between the generations. At the same time as this communication, the Commission also adopted a report on the long-term sustainability of public finances (²).

General references and other useful links

- Structural measures:
  http://ec.europa.eu/regional_policy/funds/prord/sf_en.htm

- European Social Fund:
  http://ec.europa.eu/employment_social/esf2000/index_en.html

- Social policy agenda:
  http://ec.europa.eu/employment_social/social_policy_agenda/social_pol_ag_en.html

- Joint report:
  http://ec.europa.eu/employment_social/employment_strategy/employ_en.htm

- Coordination of social security schemes:
  http://ec.europa.eu/employment_social/social_security_schemes/index_en.htm

- Free movement of workers:
  http://ec.europa.eu/employment_social/free_movement/index_en.htm

---

(¹) COM(2006) 571.
(²) See 'The macroeconomic framework' in Chapter II, Section 1, of this Report.

Section 2

Solidarity with future generations and management of natural resources

Environment

On 16 February the Commission adopted a communication '2005 environment policy review' ([1]) in which it identifies the salient points of 2005, namely: the links between the economy and the environment; the sustainable development and Lisbon strategies ([2]); and progress on climate change, chemicals and the new thematic strategies. It also puts forward its priorities for 2006, building on the impetus generated in 2005 as regards climate change, biodiversity, eco-innovation, improvement of the legislative process and the implementation of legislation.

Emissions trading and climate change

On 8 February the Commission adopted ([3]) the fourth national communication from the European Community under the United Nations Framework Convention on Climate Change, in which it describes the wide range of policies on climate change, provides projections for greenhouse gas emissions and outlines the effect of European Community policies and measures on such gases. It also highlights the numerous climate change impact, adaptation and mitigation projects which have received European Union support in the field of development.

On 17 May the European Parliament and the Council signed Regulation (EC) No 842/2006 on certain fluorinated greenhouse gases ([4]), and Directive 2006/40/EC relating to emissions from air conditioning systems in motor vehicles ([5]) and amending Council Directive 70/156/EEC ([6]).

On 24 August the Commission adopted a communication 'Implementing the Community strategy to reduce CO_2 emissions from cars: sixth annual communication on the effectiveness of the strategy' ([7]), which covers monitoring in 2004 and the studies launched that year.

([1]) COM(2006) 70.
([2]) The sustainable development strategy and the Lisbon strategy are discussed in detail in Chapter II, Section 1, of this Report.
([3]) COM(2006) 40.
([4]) OJ L 161, 14.6.2006.
([5]) OJ L 161, 14.6.2006
([6]) OJ L 42, 23.2.1970.
([7]) COM(2006) 463.

On 13 November the Commission adopted a communication entitled 'Building a global carbon market' ([1]). Drawn up pursuant to Article 30 of Directive 2003/87/EC concerning the establishment of a scheme for greenhouse gas emission allowance trading in the Community ([2]), this report underlines the key importance of the scheme in tackling climate change, and lists a number of strategic aspects to be re-examined, such as the drawing up of guidelines for controlling its application.

On 11 December the Commission adopted a proposal for a directive to include aviation activities in the scheme for greenhouse gas emission allowance trading within the Community from 2011 ([3]).

Biodiversity and nature

On 22 May the Commission adopted a communication entitled 'Halting the loss of biodiversity by 2010 — and beyond: Sustaining ecosystem services for human well-being' ([4]), in which it defines a policy strategy and identifies four key policy fields: biodiversity in the European Union; the European Union and global biodiversity; biodiversity and climate change; and strengthening the knowledge base. Priority objectives are put forward in respect of each policy field, in particular the safeguarding of the most important habitats and species and the adoption of measures regarding the wider European Union countryside and marine environment.

On 22 September the Commission adopted a communication entitled 'Thematic strategy for soil protection' ([5]) and accompanied by a proposal for a directive ([6]). Soil protection is for the first time dealt with by the Commission as part of a detailed comprehensive strategy, describing individually the gravest threats to the integrity of what is a vital and non-renewable asset. The proposal for a directive supplements the communication with a number of specific initiatives and measures aimed at safeguarding it.

On 9 March the Commission adopted a report on the implementation of national measures on the coexistence of genetically modified crops with conventional and organic farming ([7]). In what is a factual analysis, national coexistence measures are evaluated in relation to the principles set out in Commission Recommendation 2003/556/EC ([8]) on the guidelines concerned.

([1]) COM(2006) 676.
([2]) OJ L 275, 25.10.2003.
([3]) COM(2006) 818.
([4]) COM(2006) 216.
([5]) COM(2006) 231.
([6]) COM(2006) 232.
([7]) COM(2006) 104.
([8]) OJ L 189, 29.7.2003.

On 14 June the Commission adopted a proposal for a directive on the contained use of genetically modified micro-organisms (¹), codifying Council Directive 90/219/EEC (²). Moreover, in accordance with Directive 2001/18/EC of the European Parliament and of the Council (³), it adopted decisions or presented to the Council proposals for decisions on the placing on the market of certain genetically modified products (maize, oilseed rape and carnations) or, where applicable, on a temporary ban on the sale and use of such products (maize).

LIFE

On 24 May the Commission adopted an amended proposal for a regulation concerning the financial instrument for the environment (LIFE+) (⁴). It did so in the wake of the interinstitutional agreement of 17 May on the 2007–13 financial framework (⁵), which provided the basis for the subsequent legislative work.

Environment and health and quality of life

On 12 July the Commission adopted a communication entitled 'A thematic strategy on the sustainable use of pesticides' (⁶) and a proposal for a directive establishing a framework for Community action to that effect (⁷). The Commission's aim is to reduce the impact of pesticides on human health and the environment and, more generally, to bring about a more sustainable use of pesticides, with an appreciable reduction in such use and in the risks concerned, while allowing for the need to protect crops. The Commission proposes that a number of measures be undertaken by the Member States in order to achieve these goals.

On 18 January the European Parliament and the Council signed Regulation (EC) No 166/2006 concerning the establishment of a European Pollutant Release and Transfer Register (⁸), the aim of which is to facilitate public access to environmental information.

On 18 July, within the framework of the implementation of the Stockholm Convention and the Protocol to the 1979 Convention on Long-Range Transboundary Air Pollution, Parliament and the Council amended (⁹) the provisions applicable to persistent organic pollutants.

(¹) COM(2006) 286.
(²) OJ L 117, 8.5.1990.
(³) OJ L 106, 17.4.2001.
(⁴) COM(2006) 239.
(⁵) See Chapter I of this Report.
(⁶) COM(2006) 372.
(⁷) COM(2006) 373.
(⁸) OJ L 33, 4.2.2006.
(⁹) Regulation (EC) No 1195/2006 (OJ L 217, 8.8.2006).

On 21 February the Commission adopted a proposal for a directive ([1]) amending Directive 76/769/EEC relating to restrictions on the marketing of certain measuring devices containing mercury ([2]). The purpose of the proposed directive is to establish uniform rules for the movement of such devices within the internal market.

On 26 October the Commission adopted a proposal for a regulation on the banning of exports and the safe storage of metallic mercury ([3]).

On 30 May the Commission presented to the Council a proposal to approve the Rotterdam Convention on the Prior Informed Consent Procedure for certain hazardous chemicals and pesticides in international trade ([4]).

On 30 November the Commission adopted a report on the operation of Regulation (EC) No 304/2003 concerning the export and import of dangerous chemicals ([5]) and a proposal for a regulation on the same subject ([6]).

On 11 December the Commission adopted a proposal for a regulation concerning statistics on plant protection products ([7]). The data concerned will be of fundamental importance in assessing the risks which the use of such products poses to human health and the environment.

On 23 October, following a vote in Parliament at first reading, the Council reached a political agreement on the proposal for a directive on air quality ([8]).

In regard to water protection, 15 February saw the signing by Parliament and the Council of:

- Directive 2006/7/EC concerning the management of bathing water quality ([9]); this updates the legislation in force with a view to reducing health risks to bathers by focusing on the most relevant analytical parameters, in particular intestinal enterococci and *Escherichia coli;* and

- Directive 2006/11/EC on pollution caused by certain dangerous substances discharged into the aquatic environment of the Community ([9]), which codifies and replaces, but does not make any substantive changes to, Directive 76/464/EEC ([10]).

([1]) OJ L 262, 27.9.1976.
([2]) COM(2006) 69.
([3]) COM(2006) 636.
([4]) COM(2006) 250.
([5]) COM(2006) 747.
([6]) COM(2006) 745.
([7]) COM(2006) 778.
([8]) COM(2005) 447.
([9]) OJ L 64, 4.3.2006.
([10]) OJ L 129, 18.5.1976.

For its part, on 12 May, the Commission adopted a proposal for a directive on the quality required of shellfish waters (¹), which is aimed at codifying Directive 79/923/EEC (²). The directive was adopted by the European Parliament and the Council on 12 December (³). On 17 July it adopted:

- a proposal for a directive on environmental quality standards in the field of water policy (⁴) and amending Directive 2000/60/EC (⁵), aimed at improving prevention and reducing or even eliminating sources of chemical pollution brought about by human activities (farming, industry, incineration and/or dumping of waste at sea); and

- a communication entitled 'Integrated prevention and control of chemical pollution of surface waters in the European Union' (⁶); the Commission is seeking to set environmental quality standards in the field of water policy and accordingly defines clear, ambitious and sustainable objectives for priority substances in surface waters.

The proposal for a directive on the protection of groundwater against pollution, as amended by the Commission in 2005 (⁷), led to a conciliation committee agreement between the European Parliament and the Council on a joint text on 17 October. The text was then formally adopted by the Council on 11 December and by Parliament a day later. The directive thus adopted (⁸) is aimed at providing greater protection for groundwater by laying down evaluation criteria and setting maximum limits for pollutants while balancing the prerogatives of Community and national authorities in the light of the subsidiarity principle.

Marine pollution

On 22 December the Commission presented a communication on cooperation in the field of accidental or deliberate marine pollution after 2007 (⁹).

REACH

The registration, evaluation and authorisation of chemicals and the restrictions thereto (REACH) are discussed under 'Product policy' in Chapter II, Section 2, of this Report.

(¹) COM(2006) 205.
(²) OJ L 281, 10.11.1979.
(³) Directive 2006/113/EC (OJ L 376, 27.12.2006).
(⁴) COM(2006) 397.
(⁵) OJ L 327, 22.12.2000.
(⁶) COM(2006) 398.
(⁷) COM(2005) 282.
(⁸) Directive 2006/118/EC (OJ L 372, 27.12.2006).
(⁹) COM(2006) 863.

Natural resources and waste

On 25 January, under the financial perspective for 2007–13, the Commission adopted a communication entitled 'External action: thematic programme for environment and sustainable management of natural resources including energy' (¹). The aim is to highlight, by means of a single programme for external action, the environmental dimension both of development and of the other external policies and to promote the European Union's environmental and energy policies abroad.

On 15 March the European Parliament and the Council signed Directive 2006/21/EC on the management of waste from extractive industries (²), which is aimed at ensuring that the said management is friendly both to the environment and to human health. On 5 April they adopted Directive 2006/12/EC on waste (³), which codifies Directive 75/442/EEC (⁴). For its part, on 19 July, in the report on the implementation of the Community legislation on waste for the period 2001–03 (⁵), the Commission noted that while, on the whole, further progress had been made, implementation of the legislation concerned still could not be regarded as satisfactory.

On 14 June the European Parliament and the Council signed Regulation (EC) No 1013/2006 on shipments of waste (⁶), which is aimed at strengthening, simplifying and clarifying the control procedures currently applicable to shipments of waste and is set to replace Regulation (EEC) No 259/93 (⁷) from 12 July 2007.

On 6 September the European Parliament and the Council adopted Directive 2006/66/EC on batteries and accumulators and waste batteries and accumulators and repealing Directive 91/157/EEC (⁸). The directive is aimed at reducing to a minimum the adverse effects of batteries and accumulators on the environment while laying down a number of requirements designed to ensure the correct operation of the internal market in that respect.

On 27 June the Council adopted conclusions relating to the communication from the Commission on the thematic strategy on the prevention and recycling of waste (⁹).

On 23 October the Council adopted conclusions relating to the communication from the Commission on the thematic strategy on the sustainable use of natural resources (¹⁰).

(¹) COM(2006) 20.
(²) OJ L 102, 11.4.2006.
(³) OJ L 114, 27.4.2006.
(⁴) OJ L 78, 26.3.1991.
(⁵) COM(2006) 406.
(⁶) OJ L 190, 12.7.2006.
(⁷) OJ L 30, 6.2.1993.
(⁸) OJ L 266, 26.9.2006.
(⁹) COM(2005) 666.
(¹⁰) COM(2005) 670.

On 6 December the Commission adopted a report on the implementation of Directive 94/62/EC on packaging and packaging waste and its impacts on the environment, as well as on the functioning of the internal market ([1]). The report concludes that the recovery/recycling targets are appropriate and should at this stage be left unchanged, having regard in particular to the lengthy transition periods (which in some cases do not expire until 2015) applicable to some Member States.

Civil protection and disaster response

These are discussed in Chapter IV, Section 2, of this Report.

Global environment and the international dimension

On 4 September the Commission adopted a communication entitled 'Establishing an environment strategy for the Mediterranean' ([2]), in which it sets out the guidelines for cooperation with the European Union's Mediterranean partners and introduces the initiative for depollution of the Mediteranean (Horizon 2020).

In 2006 the Commission played a pivotal role in the launch of the strategic approach to international chemicals management (SAICM), drawn up and finally adopted in February in Dubai by the Governing Council of the United Nations Environment Programme. The SAICM is aimed at ensuring that chemicals management is, throughout the world, effected in a manner that will help reach the target set at the 2002 World Summit on Sustainable Development, namely that 'by 2020, chemicals are used and produced in ways that lead to a minimisation of significant adverse effects on human health and the environment'. The European Union firmly supports the SAICM and intends to contribute actively to the implementation of the global plan of action and the nearly 300 different activities which are provided for to help countries reach the objective laid down. The Community's new regulation on chemicals (REACH), which is in the process of being adopted, will help the European Union to achieve the SAICM goals.

Access to information and public participation

On 26 June the Commission proposed the conclusion, on behalf of the European Community, of an amendment ([3]) to the Aarhus Convention on access to information, public participation in decision-making and access to justice in environmental matters. The purpose of the amendment is to specify the obligations on contracting parties with regard to the participation of the public in decision-making on genetically modified organisms. The Convention, which was signed in 1998, had been approved by the Community early on in 2005. On 6 September the European Parliament and the

---

([1]) COM(2006) 767.
([2]) COM(2006) 475.
([3]) COM(2006) 338.

Council signed Regulation (EC) No 1367/2006 on the application of the provisions of the Aarhus Convention to Community institutions and bodies (¹) from 28 June 2007.

The proposal for a directive establishing an infrastructure for spatial information in the Community ('Inspire') (²) led to a conciliation committee agreement on a joint text on 21 November between Parliament and the Council. Inspire is intended to act as a key geographical and environmental information and control instrument in accordance with the sixth action programme for the environment.

Agriculture and rural development

Content of the common agricultural policy (CAP)

On 24 May, in keeping with the consensus on the financial perspective for 2007–13 which emerged from the European Council in December 2005 and was embodied in the interinstitutional agreement of 17 May (³), the Commission presented a proposal for a regulation (⁴) laying down rules for voluntary modulation of direct payments provided for in Regulation (EC) No 1782/2003. In the proposal, the Commission spells out the arrangements applicable to voluntary modulation and to the use of the funds for rural development. It would then be for the Member States to notify the Commission of the rates of voluntary modulation they wish to apply in 2007–12.

On 30 January the Council adopted a regulation laying down specific measures for agriculture in the outermost regions of the Union (⁵). The regulation provides for a reform of the POSEI scheme, requiring each of the Member States concerned to present a general programme featuring supply estimates and support measures for local production in its outermost regions.

On 18 September the Council adopted a regulation laying down specific measures for agriculture in favour of the smaller Aegean islands (⁶). The measures are designed to palliate the difficulties faced by those islands as a result of their remoteness and insularity.

In a report (⁷) it sent to the Council on 22 September, the Commission proposed extending the aid for energy crops to all the new Member States. It takes the view that the scheme needs to be simplified in order to make it more attractive to farmers. The proposal for a regulation which accompanies the report further provides for

---

(¹) OJ L 264, 25.9.2006.
(²) COM(2004) 516.
(³) See Chapter I of this Report.
(⁴) COM(2006) 241.
(⁵) Regulation (EC) No 247/2006 (OJ L 42, 14.2.2006). See also 'Outermost regions' in Section 1 of this chapter.
(⁶) Regulation (EC) No 1405/2006 (OJ L 265, 26.9.2006).
(⁷) COM(2006) 500.

simplifying the single payment scheme and extending until 2010 the optional period of application by the new Member States of the single area payment scheme (simplified direct aid scheme).

Food aid to the poorest

In its resolution of 4 April Parliament drew the Commission's attention to the consequences of the reform of the common agricultural policy as regards the supply of foodstuffs to charities. It expressed concern about the future of the arrangements concerned since, in view of a sustained decline in physical public intervention stocks, the European programme of aid to the poorest stands to lose its legal basis. Parliament asked that the European food aid programme be placed on a permanent footing, allocated an overall multiannual budget and opened up to new sectors such as pigmeat, poultry and eggs.

Rural development

On 19 June, in accordance with the financial perspective for 2007–13 and the interinstitutional agreement on budgetary discipline and sound financial management (¹), the Council set the amount of Community support for rural development from the European Agricultural Fund for Rural Development for the period 1 January 2007 to 31 December 2013 at EUR 69.75 billion, broken down annually. An initial Council decision set at EUR 27.699 billion the minimum amount to be concentrated in regions eligible under the convergence objective (²). The regime was supplemented by two new regulations adopted by the Council on 19 December (³).

The Community strategic guidelines for rural development (2007–13) (⁴), which were set on 20 February, focus on three key areas: the agri-food economy, the environment and the broader rural economy and population. The new generation of rural development strategies and programmes are to be built around four axes, namely:

- axis 1, on improving the competitiveness of the agricultural and forestry sector;

- axis 2, on improving the environment and the countryside;

- axis 3, on the quality of life in rural areas and diversification of the rural economy; and

- axis 4, on Leader.

On 19 June the Council concluded, on behalf of the European Community, the Mountain Farming Protocol to the Alpine Convention (⁵). Thanks to the Convention

---

(¹) See Chapter I of this Report.
(²) Decision 2006/493/EC (OJ L 195, 15.7.2006).
(³) Regulations (EC) No 1944/2006 (OJ L 367, 22.12.2006) and (EC) No 2012/2006 (OJ L 384, 29.12.2006).
(⁴) Decision 2006/144/EC (OJ L 55, 25.2.2006).
(⁵) Alpine Convention, ratified by the Community on 26 February 1996.

and its Protocol the Community can, within a single framework, formulate a cross-border approach to maintaining a type of farming that is environmentally friendly and adapted to the Alpine region.

Common market organisations

On 20 September the Commission put forward a proposal for a regulation introducing a comprehensive reform of the market organisation for bananas ([1]). The reform has three main aims:

- to contribute to ensuring a fair standard of living for the agricultural community concerned while stabilising public expenditure;

- to align the regime with the main principles of the CAP and with World Trade Organisation rules; and

- to take adequately into account the particularities of producer regions.

The principal changes proposed include an in-depth reform of the aid scheme, in the shape of a budgetary transfer to the programme of options specific to remote and insular regions (POSEI). The aim would be to make POSEI the principal instrument for providing aid to banana producers in the outermost regions. The overall annual POSEI budget for these regions would be increased by EUR 278.8 million. Banana-growing areas not situated in the outermost regions would come under the single payment scheme and would be allocated EUR 1.2 million. Cyprus would receive an additional budget of EUR 3.4 million, adjusted in accordance with the schedule of increments applied for the new Member States. The regulation was adopted by the Council on 19 December ([2]).

Cases of avian influenza had a major adverse effect on the consumption of poultrymeat in the European Union. Accordingly, 25 April saw the adoption of an amendment ([3]) to the legislation governing the market organisation for eggs and poultrymeat, the aim being to allow the introduction, at the request of the Member States, of exceptional market support measures where, as a direct result of a loss in consumer confidence caused by public health or animal health risks, there is serious disturbance on the market.

On 19 June the Council adopted a regulation simplifying the marketing standards for eggs ([4]). The regulation provides for two classes of eggs: class A, fresh eggs intended for direct human consumption; and class B, eggs used by the food and non-food industry.

([1]) COM(2006) 489.
([2]) Regulation (EC) No 2013/2006 (OJ L 384, 29.12.2006).
([3]) Regulation (EC) No 679/2006 (OJ L 119, 4.5.2006).
([4]) Regulation (EC) No 1028/2006 (OJ L 186, 7.7.2006).

A major reform of the market organisation for sugar (^{1}) was approved on 20 February. It provides for an overall reduction of 36 % in the price of sugar between 2006/07 and 2009/10 and direct aid to producers which is designed to offset 60 % of the reduction from 2006/07. In order to encourage restructuring in the sector, aid will be granted to sugar factories whose owners opt to cease production in the course of the four marketing years concerned. A safeguard measure (suspension or temporary withdrawal of trade concessions) will be applied if, from 2008/09, sugar imports from a non-member country eligible under the 'Everything but arms' initiative (^{2}) increase by more than 25 % compared with the preceding year. Moreover it has been foreseen in 2006 to grant financial compensation totalling EUR 40 million in favour of the 18 ACP (African, Caribbean and Pacific) countries that export sugar to the European Union (^{3}). On 13 November the Council concluded a protocol to the stabilisation and association agreement with Croatia with a view to amending the preferential agreements on sugar (^{4}).

The Commission carried out an assessment of the common organisation of the market in wine in the light of the actual conditions on European and international markets. The assessment, which on 22 June was the subject of a communication (^{5}), had as its aim formally to initiate discussions with all the parties concerned and the European institutions and to draw up legislative proposals with a view in particular to:

- strengthening the competitiveness of growers in the European Union, underpinning the reputation enjoyed by quality wines from the European Union as the world's best, reconquering former markets and capturing new ones in the European Union and throughout the world;

- creating a wine regime that operates through clear, simple and effective rules that balance supply and demand; and

- establishing a wine regime that preserves the best traditions of European Union wine production, reinforces the social fabric of many rural areas, and ensures that all production respects the environment.

In the course of their December sessions, both the Committee of the Regions and the European Economic and Social Committee delivered an opinion on the communication from the Commission.

On 18 December the Commission proposed revising the existing 21 regulations on sector-specific common market organisations and combining them into a comprehensive single regulation, with a view to streamlining and simplifying the legal framework without changing the underlying policies (^{6}).

(^{1}) Regulations (EC) No 318/2006, (EC) No 319/2006 and (EC) No 320/2006 (OJ L 58, 28.2.2006).
(^{2}) Regulation (EC) No 416/2001 (OJ L 60, 1.3.2001).
(^{3}) Regulation (EC) No 266/2006 (OJ L 50, 21.2.2006).
(^{4}) Decision 2006/882/EC (OJ L 341, 7.12.2006).
(^{5}) COM(2006) 319.
(^{6}) COM(2006) 822.

Product quality

On 20 March the rules on quality agricultural products were amended in order to improve the arrangements for registration, simplify procedures and clarify the role of the Member States (¹).

Moreover the Commission is, in a great many proposals emanating from Parliament, the Member States and other quarters, being urged to undertake a review of the policy on product quality.

Forestry strategy

On 15 June the Commission presented a European Union forest action plan for 2007–11 (²). The plan provides for a total of 18 key actions to be carried out jointly with the Member States and built around four objectives:

- improving long-term competitiveness;

- improving and protecting the environment;

- contributing to the quality of life; and

- fostering coordination and communication.

When the Council met on 19 June the delegations representing the Member States were overwhelmingly in favour of those objectives and the actions proposed.

Agri-environmental indicators

In its communication of 15 September entitled 'Development of agri-environmental indicators for monitoring the integration of environmental concerns into the common agricultural policy' (³), the Commission describes the progress made towards developing those indicators and identifies key challenges and actions for the future. It proposes:

- consolidating a limited set of indicators by updating the databases concerned and extending their coverage to include the new Member States;

- overcoming the limitations that currently restrict the information potential of certain indicators; and

- establishing over the long term and in close cooperation with the Member States a permanent and stable arrangement for the functioning of the indicator system under the aegis of Eurostat.

(¹) Regulation (EC) No 509/2006 (OJ L 93, 31.3.2006).
(²) COM(2006) 302.
(³) COM(2006) 508.

Organic farming

A regulation on organic production and the labelling of organic products imported into the Community was adopted by the Council on 21 December (¹). It amends Article 11 of Regulation (EEC) No 2092/91, allowing the importation into the European Union of organic products from non-member countries whose rules in this respect are recognised as equivalent (continued application of the provision concerned), or organic products from operators in non-member countries who are subject to controls by specially recognised inspection bodies (new provision). The new regulation provides, in addition to the principle of equivalence, for direct access to the European market for producers and processors of organic produce who comply fully with the rules laid down in Regulation (EEC) No 2092/91.

Fisheries and maritime strategy

Content of the common fisheries policy

In a communication adopted on 9 March and entitled 'Improving the economic situation in the fishing industry' (²), the Commission looks into the reasons for the economic difficulties experienced by a number of European fishing fleets, sets out a series of measures for tackling that situation, and indicates the type of rescue and restructuring aid which can be awarded by Member States to help companies experiencing difficulties adapt and go forward on a sounder financial footing. It also looks into the long-term measures needed to encourage a return to lasting profitability for the European fisheries industry as a whole.

On 22 May the Council adopted a regulation establishing Community financial measures for the implementation of the common fisheries policy and in the area of the law of the sea (³). The measures provided for in that respect concern the following areas in particular: control and enforcement, conservation measures, data collection and improvement of scientific advice, governance, international relations and the law of the sea.

On 24 May the Commission adopted a communication entitled 'Improving consultation on Community fisheries management' (⁴), setting out a possible new working method for the annual preparation and adoption of fishing opportunities in the European Community. The aim would be to improve the consultation of stakeholders, thereby enabling the Commission to put forward proposals for certain stocks earlier on in the year and initiating earlier the discussions on other stocks.

(¹) Regulation (EC) No 1991/2006 (OJ L 411, 30.12.2006).
(²) COM(2006) 103.
(³) Regulation (EC) No 861/2006 (OJ L 160, 14.6.2006).
(⁴) COM(2006) 246 (OJ C 176, 28.7.2006).

On 22 June the Commission adopted a regulation on the application of Articles 87 and 88 of the EC Treaty to *de minimis* aid in the fisheries sector and amending Regulation (EC) No 1860/2004 ([1]). Experience has shown that the current ceiling on *de minimis* aid in the fisheries sector is too low, in particular because the average turnover of fishing undertakings in the European Union is higher than that of farms, added to the fact that the fisheries sector, unlike some parts of the farming industry covered by the common agricultural policy, does not receive any direct income aid.

On 4 July, in its communication entitled 'Implementing sustainability in European Union fisheries through maximum sustainable yield', the Commission proposed, as a new approach towards fisheries management in the Community, focusing on obtaining the best return from the productive potential of Europe's living marine resources, without compromising its use by future generations ([2]). As the Commission sees it, this is fully consistent with the broader objective of the common fisheries policy, which is to ensure that the exploitation of living aquatic resources takes place under sustainable economic, environmental and social conditions.

On 14 July the Commission adopted a communication entitled 'Reports from Member States on behaviours which seriously infringed the rules of the common fisheries policy in 2004' ([3]) and covering, for the first time, the new Member States. It emerges from the reports that 9 660 serious infringements were notified by the Member States in 2004, a slight increase on the preceding year (9 502). The most frequent 'serious infringements' relate to (i) unauthorised fishing and (ii) storing, processing, placing for sale and transporting fishery products that do not meet the marketing standards applicable.

On 27 November, in a proposal for a Council decision ([4]) amending Decision 2004/585/ EC establishing regional advisory councils under the common fisheries policy, the Commission advocated increasing the financial aid from the Community to these councils and accordingly proposed that they be defined as bodies pursuing an aim of general European interest. The amendment would thus strengthen the councils and provide them with a stable annual contribution from the Community budget.

European Fisheries Fund

On 27 July the Council adopted a regulation establishing the European Fisheries Fund (EFF) for 2007–13 ([5]). The purpose of this instrument, which is set to replace the existing Financial Instrument for Fisheries Guidance (FIFG) ([6]), is to facilitate the implementation of measures to ensure sustainable fishing and the diversification of

---

([1]) OJ C 276, 14.11.2006.
([2]) COM(2006) 360.
([3]) COM(2006) 387.
([4]) COM(2006) 732.
([5]) Regulation (EC) No 1198/2006 (OJ L 223, 15.8.2006).
([6]) Regulations (EEC) No 2080/93 (OJ L 193, 31.7.1993) and (EC) No 1263/1999 (OJ L 161, 26.6.1999).

economic activities in fishing areas. The aim is to reduce fishing pressure, thus allowing stocks to recover, and to encourage the use of equipment and practices in fisheries and aquaculture which are both environment friendly and supportive in terms of the processing and marketing of fisheries products. Provision is also made for assisting the regions hardest hit by job losses in the fisheries industry. The overall financial allocation to the EFF for the period concerned has been set at EUR 3.85 billion (at 2004 prices).

Market organisations

On 28 November the Council amended Regulation (EC) No 104/2000 on the common organisation of the markets in fishery and aquaculture products. The new regulation ([1]) allows the newly created European Agricultural Guarantee Fund to be applied as regards the funding of expenditure on fisheries markets.

On 19 December the Council set the guide prices and Community producer prices for certain fishery products for the 2007 fishing year.

Conservation and management of resources

The Commission put forward numerous proposals in this field in 2006 with a view to protecting natural resources through multiannual programmes. Accordingly, on 8 March, it adopted a proposal for a regulation laying down technical measures for the conservation of certain stocks of highly migratory species ([2]), followed, on 24 July, by a proposal for a regulation establishing a multiannual plan for the cod stocks in the Baltic Sea and the fisheries exploiting those stocks ([3]); and, on 24 August, a proposal for a regulation as regards fishing opportunities and associated conditions for certain fish stocks ([4]). This last regulation was adopted by the Council on 20 November ([5]).

On 23 February the Council also adopted a regulation establishing a multiannual plan for the sustainable exploitation of the stock of sole in the Bay of Biscay ([6]), followed, on 1 June, by a regulation concerning blue whiting and herring ([7]).

On 19 December the Council adopted a regulation fixing for 2007 and 2008 the fishing opportunities for Community fishing vessels for certain deep-sea fish stocks ([8]). On 21 December it adopted a regulation on the use of electronic log books and the remote sensing of fishing vessels ([9]).

([1]) Regulation (EC) No 1759/2006 (OJ L 335, 1.12.2006).
([2]) COM(2006) 100.
([3]) COM(2006) 411.
([4]) COM(2006) 461.
([5]) Regulation (EC) No 1782/2006 (OJ L 345, 8.12.2006).
([6]) Regulation (EC) No 388/2006 (OJ L 65, 7.3.2006).
([7]) Regulation (EC) No 941/2006 (OJ L 173, 27.6. 2006).
([8]) Regulation (EC) No 2015/2006 (OJ L 384, 29.12.2006).
([9]) Regulation (EC) No 1966/2006 (OJ L 409, 30.12.2006).

Outermost regions

On 7 November the Council adopted a regulation ([1]) amending Regulation (EC) No 639/2004 on the management of fishing fleets registered in the Community outermost regions. The particular structural, social and economic situation in the fisheries sector in the outermost regions of the Community and the difficulty of regularising what is a large informal sector in some of those regions together account for the fact that the adoption of the Council regulation on the European Fisheries Fund (see above) was accompanied by a joint statement by the Council and the Commission on the fleets of the regions concerned, and for the need to amend the rules applicable, in particular by extending the period of validity of some of the exemptions for which these regions qualify.

On 30 November the Commission put forward a proposal for a Council regulation introducing a scheme to compensate for the additional costs incurred in the marketing of certain fishery products from the Azores, Madeira, the Canary Islands, and the French departments of Guiana and Réunion from 2007 to 2013 ([2]). This would extend the period of validity of a scheme first introduced in 1992, allow the outermost regions to continue to receive financial aid to offset the additional costs of transporting their fisheries products, and enable the economic operators concerned to plan their activities more effectively, thus contributing decisively to stability within the sector.

Fisheries agreements with third countries

In 2006 the Commission embarked on the renegotiation of fisheries agreements and protocols with a number of third countries. The new partnership agreements, which provide the best means of ensuring the sustainable exploitation of resources in the interests of all those concerned, are aimed at ensuring greater consistency between the various Community policies. The countries with which such agreements have been concluded include the Seychelles, São Tomé and Príncipe, Mauritania, Peru, the Solomon Islands and Guinea-Bissau. Initialled on 22 July, the fisheries agreement negotiated with Mauritania is the biggest one ever concluded between the European Union and a non-member country both in financial terms (the European Union is to provide EUR 516 million in aid over the six years covered by the agreement) and as regards the fishing opportunities for Community vessels.

Maritime policy

On 7 June the Commission adopted a Green Paper entitled 'Towards a future maritime policy for the Union: a European vision for the oceans and seas' ([3]). This in effect launched one of the largest consultation exercises ever conducted in the European

---

[1] Regulation (EC) No 1646/2006 (OJ L 309, 9.11.2006).
[2] COM(2006) 740.
[3] COM(2006) 275.

Union, asking citizens how they wish to see oceans and seas managed. The findings will help the Commission define a new vision for an integrated maritime policy. The key questions posed in the Green Paper are whether Europe can afford to manage its seas and oceans in a sectoral, unconnected way, or whether the time has come to establish a truly integrated maritime policy that will release untapped potential in terms of growth and jobs while strengthening the protection of the marine environment and, if so, how this should be done. The Green Paper seeks to highlight the extent to which the various domains are linked and interdependent; this being an aspect which is often not taken into account under existing procedures.

General references and other useful links

- Directorate-General for Environment:
  http://ec.europa.eu/environment/index_en.htm

- Sustainable development:
  http://ec.europa.eu/environment/eussd/

- Climate change:
  http://europa.eu/press_room/presspacks/climate/index_en.htm
  http://ec.europa.eu/environment/climat/home_en.htm

- Kyoto Protocol:
  http://ec.europa.eu/environment/climat/kyoto.htm

- Directorate-General for Agriculture and Rural Development:
  http://ec.europa.eu/agriculture/index_en.htm

- Directorate-General for Fisheries and Maritime Affairs:
  http://ec.europa.eu/dgs/fisheries/index_en.htm

Section 3

Promoting common values within the European Union

Protecting fundamental rights and combating discrimination

Consular protection

On 28 November the Commission adopted a Green Paper entitled 'Diplomatic and consular protection of Union citizens in third countries' (¹). The objective is to launch broad public debate on the lines of action for reinforcing the right of Union citizens to diplomatic and consular protection enshrined in Article 20 of the EC Treaty and

---

(¹) COM(2006) 712.

included in the European Union's Charter of Fundamental Rights. According to this right, if citizens of the Union are in a non-member country in which the Member State of which they are a national is not represented, they are entitled to protection by the diplomatic and consular authorities of any Member State on the same conditions as nationals of that State. The Commission will adopt specific initiatives based on the results of this public consultation in 2007.

Agency for Fundamental Rights

In 2006 legislative work continued on the proposal which the Commission had presented on 30 June 2005 (1) with a view to creating, within the European Union, a genuine Agency for Fundamental Rights to replace the European Monitoring Centre on Racism and Xenophobia established in 1997. On 14 February the European Economic and Social Committee gave its opinion, recommending in particular that it should be possible for one or other institution to ask the Agency to assess the compatibility between the European Union's Charter of Fundamental Rights, adopted in 2000, and any new proposal for legislation or Community policy. On 12 October the European Parliament also issued a favourable opinion, with a few amendments, one of which also concerned examining European legislation and its implementation from the point of view of observing fundamental rights. Discussions in the Council led to a political agreement on 4 December.

Combating discrimination

In a resolution adopted on 18 January the European Parliament called for fresh measures at both European Union and Member State levels to eradicate homophobia (2). In a resolution adopted on 15 June it again condemned the rise in racist and homophobic violence in Europe, referring to various criminal acts in recent times. In an opinion delivered the same date, the Committee of the Regions argued in favour of strengthening the protection of minorities and anti-discrimination policies in an enlarged Europe (3).

Protection of women and children

On 2 February the European Parliament recommended that the Commission and the Member States consider violence against women an infringement of human rights, reflecting the unequal power relationship between the sexes, and that they should adopt a general policy to combat it. At its March session, the European Economic and Social Committee also stressed the need for a pan-European strategy on domestic violence against women (4). In a resolution adopted on 1 June the European Parliament

---

(1) COM(2005) 280.
(2) OJ C 287 E, 24.11.2006.
(3) OJ C 229, 22.9.2006.
(4) OJ C 110, 9.5.2006.

also expressed its concern about allegations of serious infringements of the rights of Roma women in the Union.

On 17 January the European Parliament recommended that the Union support child helplines as an essential part of the child protection system and that such lines should have a common toll-free telephone number throughout the Union ([1]).

European Group on Ethics in Science and New Technologies (EGE)

The EGE continued working on an opinion on the ethical aspects of nanomedicine, to be published at the beginning of 2007. A round table was held in March, followed by the publication of its minutes, in order to raise the profile of the group's work and to increase the participation of civil society. The group's future work will include drafting an opinion on the identification of measures to be carried out during the ethical review of embryonic stem cell research projects financed by the European Union and an opinion on modern agricultural techniques, with special attention to sustainable farming.

Culture

'Culture 2007' programme

Legislative work continued with a view to drawing up the 'Culture 2007' programme, following the conclusion of discussions on the new financial framework for the European Union for the period 2007–13 ([2]). On 19 May the Council was therefore able to come to a political agreement on this programme, which has three objectives: promoting transnational mobility for workers in the cultural sector, free transnational movement of works of art and cultural products, and improving intercultural dialogue. On 24 October the European Parliament made a few minor amendments to the common position which the Council had formalised on 18 July. Approved by the Council at second reading the programme was finally adopted by Parliament and the Council on 12 December ([3]).

European capitals of culture

On 24 October the European Parliament and the Council adopted a decision establishing a Community action for the European Capital of Culture event for the years 2007 to 2019 ([4]). The new scheme aims to improve the process by which a city is designated as 'capital' of culture by increasing competition and developing the 'European added value' of its programme.

([1]) OJ C 287 E, 24.11.2006.
([2]) See 'Financial perspective for 2007–13' in Chapter I of this Report.
([3]) Decision No 1855/2006/EC (OJ L 372, 27.12.2006).
([4]) Decision No 1622/2006/EC (OJ L 304, 3.11.2006).

On 13 November the Council designated Essen (Germany), Pécs (Hungary) and Istanbul (Turkey) as European capitals of culture for 2010 ([1]).

Cultural diversity

On 18 December the Community and certain Member States jointly ratified the Convention on the Protection and Promotion of the Diversity of Cultural Expressions, which the United Nations Educational, Scientific and Cultural Organisation (Unesco) adopted in 2005.

Certain aspects of cultural diversity related to multilingualism are dealt with under 'Education and training' in Chapter II of this Report.

Youth, active citizenship and sport

Youth policy

On 24 May, following the interinstitutional agreement reached on the new financial framework of the European Union for 2007–13 ([2]), the Commission adopted an amended proposal to establish a 'Youth in Action' programme to be implemented in the same period ([3]). Legislative work then proceeded on the basis of the amended proposal. This led to a joint decision signed by the European Parliament and the Council on 15 November ([4]). The programme, which has a budget of EUR 885 million and is simpler and more flexible than its predecessor, is to finance projects in five fields: youth for Europe, European voluntary service, youth in the world, socio-educational instructors, and support for policy cooperation in the youth field. Open to young people aged between 13 and 30, it will also be accessible to a wider number of partner countries than in the past.

The approach advocated by the Commission in May 2005 ([5]) for implementing the European Youth Pact adopted by the European Council in spring 2005 was welcomed by the Committee of the Regions at its February session ([6]). However, it recommended that the Member States ensure the participation of local and regional authorities in the design, implementation and monitoring of policies at national level and that the Council guarantee their participation at European Union level. In its conclusions of 23 February the Council noted that, for the first time, implementation of the pact had been dealt with in the Member States' national reform programmes, in particular by strengthening the role of youth in the revised Lisbon strategy. It asked the European Council of spring 2006 to promote further progress along these lines.

---

[1] Decision 2006/796/EC (OJ L 324, 23.11.2006).
[2] See 'Financial perspective for 2007–13' in Chapter I, Section 3, of this Report.
[3] COM(2006) 228.
[4] Decision No 1719/2006/EC (OJ L 327, 24.11.2006).
[5] COM(2005) 206.
[6] OJ C 192, 16.8.2006.

In a communication of 20 July (¹) on the follow-up to the 2001 White Paper entitled 'A new impetus for European youth' (²), the Commission presented the results of an analysis based on Member States' national reports, which confirmed common objectives regarding the participation of young people and information on youth issues. Drawing on recent initiatives such as Plan D (³), the Commission also proposed structuring dialogue with young people in a way which would increase their involvement in the development of the Union at a decisive moment in the debate on its future.

In an information report adopted on 14 September the European Economic and Social Committee gave an opinion on the educational, social and cultural support to be provided for young people under the European neighbourhood policy, in particular in the European partner countries.

For the fourth consecutive year, from 21 March to 9 May, the network of ministers for education organised, in cooperation with the Commission, the 'Spring Day in Europe' event, which is designed to raise the awareness of young people about European issues. Activities were held simultaneously in educational establishments in the Member States, acceding countries and other European countries such as Norway and Switzerland.

As regards taking young people into account in other policies, in 2006 priority was again given to combating discrimination, in particular racism and xenophobia. Priority was given to youth not only in calls for projects under the youth programme, but also in two campaigns: the Commission campaign 'For diversity — Against discrimination', which made young people one of the two main objectives of the initiative, and the Council of Europe's campaign 'All different/all equal', which is supported by the Commission under the partnership for youth.

Active citizenship

In 2006 legislative work continued on the proposal submitted by the Commission in April 2005 to establish the Citizens for Europe programme for the period 2007–13, the aim of which is to promote active citizenship (⁴). On 18 May the Council reached a political agreement which was formalised as a common position on 25 September. On 24 October the European Parliament made four amendments at second reading, mainly concerning the breakdown of the budget between the various measures included in the programme. The Council approved the proposal at second reading on 11 December. The Decision was finally adopted by Parliament and the Council on 12 December (⁵).

(¹) COM(2006) 417.
(²) COM(2001) 681.
(³) See 'Plan D' in Chapter I, Section 3, of this Report.
(⁴) COM(2005) 116.
(⁵) Decision No 1904/2006/EC (OJ L 378, 27.12.2006).

In an exploratory opinion adopted at its December session, the European Economic and Social Committee stressed the importance and role of voluntary activities in European society and the need for all those involved to promote such activities at all levels (European, national, regional and local). In particular, the Union could develop an appropriate structure and encourage the exchange of good practice.

On 12 December the Commission presented a report on the participation of European citizens in the 2004 European elections ([1]) on the basis of which it is proposing the adoption of a directive amending some of the detailed arrangements for the exercise of the right to vote and stand as a candidate in elections to the European Parliament for citizens of the Union residing in a Member State of which they are not nationals ([2]).

Sport

In a declaration on 14 March the European Parliament strongly condemned all forms of racism at football matches. In a resolution on 15 March it also expressed its concern about forced prostitution at international sporting events.

Central library

The Commission's central library, for the use of the officials of the institutions and external researchers, continued to develop the services offered, particularly as regards online access to publications. New software incorporating all the library's management activities into one system and providing an online catalogue was installed in 2006.

General references and other useful links

- Human rights:
  http://europa.eu/pol/rights/index_en.htm
- European Group on Ethics in Science and New Technologies:
  http://ec.europa.eu/european_group_ethics/index_en.htm
- Youth:
  http://ec.europa.eu/youth/index_en.html
- Active citizenship:
  http://ec.europa.eu/dgs/education_culture/activecitizenship/index_en.htm
- Town twinning:
  http://ec.europa.eu/towntwinning/index_en.html
- Sport:
  http://ec.europa.eu/sport/index_en.html
- Culture:
  http://ec.europa.eu/culture/eac/index_en.html

[1] COM(2006) 790.
[2] COM(2006) 791.

Chapter IV

Security and freedom

Section 1

European area of freedom, security and justice

Implementation of the Hague programme

Background

The Hague programme

In recent years the European Union has played an increased role in establishing police, judicial and customs cooperation and in implementing a coordinated policy on asylum, immigration and external border controls. The issue of the security of the Union and its Member States is even more acute in the aftermath of the terrorist attacks in the United States in 2001, in Madrid in 2004 and in London in 2005.

Ever since the Tampere European Council in 1999, the Union's policy on justice and home affairs has been conducted in a general context. Tampere established the first five-year programme.

In November 2004, following this initial five-year programme, the European Council adopted a new programme for the Union, the Hague programme, to run from 2005 to 2009. It covers all aspects of policies in the area of freedom, security and justice, including the external dimension, in particular fundamental rights and citizenship, asylum and immigration, border management, integration, the fight against terrorism and organised crime, judicial and police cooperation, and civil law. The Hague programme is accompanied by a strategy on drugs adopted by the European Council in December 2004.

In 2005 a joint Council and Commission action plan set the specific priorities on which efforts under the Hague programme were to focus in the years ahead. A strategy on the external dimension of the area of freedom, security and justice was also established.

In June the Commission presented a series of communications on the implementation of the Hague programme and on the evaluation of European Union policies on freedom, security and justice (^{1}), designed to prompt discussion on new policy initiatives and to suggest avenues to be explored to improve the operation of existing policies.

It also analysed the shortcomings in the decision-making arrangements in the area of police and judicial cooperation, where unanimity among the Member States is required. It accordingly proposed that the Council and Parliament use the 'passerelle' clause in Article 42 of the Treaty on European Union to transfer action in areas covered by Title VI to Title IV of the Treaty, where simple majority voting in co-decision with the European Parliament applies.

The progress made in implementing the Hague programme was examined by the Council on 4 December and by the European Council at its December meeting.

European law-enforcement area

Civil and commercial justice

On 19 March 2004 the Commission had adopted a proposal for a regulation creating a European order for payment procedure to simplify, speed up and reduce the costs of litigation in cross-border cases concerning uncontested pecuniary claims and to permit the free circulation of these European orders for payment throughout all Member States (^{2}). To this end it advocated the introduction of minimum standards whose observance would render unnecessary the bringing of any intermediate proceedings in the Member State of enforcement prior to recognition and enforcement. The Commission adopted an amended proposal on 7 February 2006 (^{3}) following the vote in the European Parliament. Parliament gave its second reading on 25 October. The Council accepted all Parliament's amendments and approved the regulation at second reading on 11 December. The regulation was signed by Parliament and the Council on 12 December (^{4}).

On 16 May the Commission adopted a report on the European Judicial Network in civil and commercial matters (^{5}), in which it concludes that the network has helped to improve judicial cooperation between Member States in general terms but that it is still far from having developed its full potential, chiefly because it does not yet have all the resources needed to perform its tasks. The Commission is planning to present a legislative proposal in 2007 amending the decision establishing the network in order to solve these problems. The report stresses the importance of the network as an essential tool for establishing a genuine European law-enforcement area.

(^{1}) COM(2006) 331, COM(2006) 332 and COM(2006) 333.
(^{2}) COM(2004) 173.
(^{3}) COM(2006) 57.
(^{4}) Regulation (EC) No 1896/2006 (OJ L 399, 30.12.2006).
(^{5}) COM(2006) 203.

On 29 June the Commission presented a communication on judicial training in the European Union, in both civil and criminal matters ([1]). The report analyses judicial training schemes in the Member States and makes proposals for the future, asserting its political will to mobilise substantial resources in various forms to support training for professionals in the administration of justice. The Commission feels that action should focus on three targets: increasing the familiarity of legal practitioners with the Union's legal instruments; improving mutual knowledge of the judicial systems of the Member States; and improving language training.

On 17 July, following extensive public consultation, the Commission adopted a proposal for a Council regulation amending Regulation (EC) No 2201/2003 concerning jurisdiction and introducing rules concerning applicable law in matrimonial matters ([2]). The objective is to increase legal certainty, predictability and flexibility for the growing number of international couples who divorce each year in the European Union. Among other things the proposal introduces a limited possibility for such couples to choose the applicable law and the court having jurisdiction in divorce and separation proceedings. Also on 17 July, the Commission adopted a Green Paper on conflict of laws in matters concerning matrimonial property regimes, including the question of jurisdiction and mutual recognition. The object of the exercise is to launch consultations on the subject, given the numerous difficulties facing European citizens due to the disparity in the substantive rules currently applicable in the Member States and in the relevant conflict rules ([3]).

On 24 October the Commission adopted a Green Paper on improving the efficiency of the enforcement of judgments in the European Union and the attachment of bank accounts ([4]). Its purpose is to launch a broad consultation among interested parties on how to improve the enforcement of monetary claims in Europe. The Green Paper describes the problems involved in the current legal situation and proposes the creation of a European system for the attachment of bank accounts as a possible solution. The consultation period expires on 31 March 2007.

On 1 December the Commission presented a proposal ([5]) amending its proposal of 7 July 2005 for a regulation amending Council Regulation (EC) No 1348/2000 of 29 May 2000 on the service in the Member States of judicial and extrajudicial documents in civil or commercial matters. The objective of the proposal is to further improve and accelerate the transmission and service of documents, simplify the application of certain provisions of the regulation and increase legal certainty for both the requesting and the requested parties.

([1]) COM(2006) 356.
([2]) COM(2006) 399.
([3]) COM(2006) 400.
([4]) COM(2006) 618.
([5]) COM(2006) 751.

Criminal justice

On 24 January the Commission presented a report on the European arrest warrant and the surrender procedures between Member States ([1]). It finds that the European arrest warrant is now being implemented by all the Member States following the enactment of the Italian transposal legislation in April 2005.

On 26 April the Commission presented a Green Paper on the presumption of innocence ([2]) to ascertain whether the concept is comparable in all the Member States and what rights are enjoyed as a result. If consultations suggest that there is a need, the Commission will consider including the rights enjoyed as a result of the presumption of innocence in a proposal for a framework decision.

Also on 26 April, the Commission adopted an amended proposal for a directive on criminal measures aimed at ensuring the enforcement of intellectual property rights ([3]). It incorporates in the original proposal ([4]) virtually all the provisions of the proposal for a framework decision to strengthen the criminal law framework to combat intellectual property offences, adopted at the same time. The amended proposal gives effect to the Commission communication of 23 November 2005 ([5]) on the implications of the judgment of the Court of Justice of 13 September 2005 ([6]), in which it held that the provisions of criminal law required for the effective implementation of Community law are a matter for Community law.

On 29 August the Commission presented a proposal for a Council framework decision on the European supervision order in pre-trial procedures between Member States of the European Union ([7]). The chief objective is to allow a judicial authority in the Member State where an offence has been committed to transfer pre-trial judicial supervisory measures to the Member State where the accused is habitually resident, thus obviating the need for pre-trial detention in a foreign country.

On 6 October the Council adopted a framework decision on the application of the principle of mutual recognition to confiscation orders ([8]). The aim is to facilitate cooperation between the Member States and the general principle is to require the competent authorities of a Member State to recognise and execute in its territory confiscation orders issued in accordance with the rules set out in the framework decision, without any other formality being necessary, and to take the necessary measures to comply.

([1]) COM(2006) 8.
([2]) COM(2006) 174.
([3]) COM(2006) 168.
([4]) COM(2005) 276.
([5]) COM(2005) 583.
([6]) Case C 176/03 *Commission* v *Council*.
([7]) COM(2006) 468.
([8]) Framework Decision 2006/783/JHA (OJ L 328, 24.11.2006).

Legislative work continued on a framework decision on taking account of convictions in the Member States in the course of new criminal proceedings ([1]). The purpose of this framework decision is to determine the conditions in which prior convictions handed down in another Member State for different facts are to be taken into consideration in new proceedings against the same person.

Police and customs cooperation

On 27 April the Council approved a recommendation on the drawing up of agreements between police, customs and other specialised law enforcement services in relation to the prevention and combating of crime. The purpose of such formal agreements or other arrangements at national level between the competent authorities is to secure a high degree of cooperation and multidisciplinary common action.

On 18 December the Council adopted a framework decision on simplifying the exchange of intelligence between law enforcement authorities of the Member States of the Union ([2]).

Europol and CEPOL

On 1 June the Council approved cooperation agreements between the European Police College (CEPOL) and the Icelandic National Police College, the Norwegian Police University College and the Swiss Police Institute. The purpose of these agreements is to improve the efficiency of police forces in the fight against crime, particularly cross-border crime in Europe, by organising joint training for senior police officers.

On 20 December the Commission proposed replacing the Europol Convention by a Council decision which would be easier to adapt ([3]).

Data protection and exchange of information

On 21 April the Commission adopted a report ([4]) on the operation of the Council common position requiring the Member States to ensure that their competent authorities exchange data on issued and blank passports that are stolen, lost or misappropriated, formatted for integration in a specific information system, whilst at the same time ensuring that the fundamental rights of data subjects are respected ([5]). In its report the Commission observes that, while the Member States have largely abided by the spirit of the common position, a more proactive and comprehensive effort is still required to bring about the kind of operation that will offer all of the Member States maximum return from their participation in the exchange of information with Interpol.

([1]) COM(2005) 91.
([2]) Framework Decision 2006/960/JHA (OJ L 386, 29.12.2006).
([3]) COM(2006) 817.
([4]) COM(2006) 167.
([5]) Common Position 2005/69/JHA (OJ L 27, 29.1.2005).

Fight against terrorism, crime and drugs

Fight against terrorism

On 1 September the Commission adopted a Green Paper on detection technologies in the work of law enforcement, customs and other security authorities ([1]). The aim of this initiative is to provide basic input for dialogue on the subject of detection technologies and to define what role the European Union might play in encouraging their development in support of security for the general public. The Council updated the list of persons, groups and entities to which the European Union applies anti-terrorism and asset-freezing measures ([2]).

On 12 December the Commission presented a package of measures to improve the protection of critical infrastructure in Europe ([3]). They consist of a communication on a European programme for critical infrastructure protection and a proposal for a directive on the identification and designation of European critical infrastructure and the assessment of the need to improve its protection. The aim of this initiative is to ensure that any disruption or manipulation of critical infrastructure is as brief, infrequent, manageable, geographically isolated and minimally detrimental as possible.

Fight against crime

On 21 February the Commission presented a communication on disqualifications arising from criminal convictions in the European Union ([4]). It seeks to clarify the concept of disqualification, to assess the legislation applicable at European level and to outline the approach likely to be followed in this regard. While a number of measures have already been taken to improve information exchange mechanisms, lack of harmonisation still constitutes a barrier to mutual recognition.

On 2 March the Commission proposed that the Council conclude the United Nations Convention against Corruption ([5]). The Convention aims inter alia to promote: measures to prevent and combat corruption more efficiently and effectively; international cooperation and technical assistance; and integrity, accountability and proper management of public affairs and public property.

On 15 March the European Parliament and the Council adopted a directive on the retention of data generated or processed in connection with the provision of publicly available electronic communications services or of public communications networks

---

([1]) COM(2006) 474.
([2]) Common Positions 2006/231/CFSP (OJ L 82, 21.3.2006) and 2006/1011/CFSP (OJ L 379, 28.12.2006).
([3]) COM(2006) 786.
([4]) COM(2006) 73.
([5]) COM(2006) 82.

services (¹). The aim is to ensure that such data are available for the purpose of the investigation, detection and prosecution of serious crime, as defined by each Member State in its national law.

On 7 August the Commission adopted a communication on developing a comprehensive and coherent European Union strategy to measure crime and criminal justice (²). The communication describes the coordinated activities to be undertaken by the Commission and by Eurostat, their expert groups (³) and other relevant bodies under a five-year plan of action (2006–10) to develop quantitative measurements of crime and criminal justice in the European Union. The recommended strategy aims to define and develop common minimum standards and data-collection methods throughout the Union. In the longer term, the development of statistics in the European Union will make it possible to compare the structure, levels and trends of crime and criminal justice measures in the Member States and their regions. In September the European Economic and Social Committee considered how civil society could be involved in combating organised crime and terrorism.

Fight against human trafficking

The fight against trafficking in human beings was a major item on the Council agenda for its meeting on 27 and 28 April. In particular the Council considered the role that Europol might play in this area. It also took stock of progress in implementation of the action plan adopted in 2005 and reaffirmed its determination to prevent and combat what it regards as one of the most serious human rights violations. On 2 May the Commission presented a report on trafficking in human beings (⁴), which finds that the Member States generally respect the requirements established by the Council (⁵) either by applying existing national legislation or by introducing new specific measures.

On 24 July the Council approved two additional protocols to the United Nations Convention against Transnational Organised Crime: the first concerns the smuggling of migrants by land, sea and air; the aim of the other is to prevent, suppress and punish trafficking in persons, especially women and children.

Drugs

On 1 June the Commission put a proposal to the Council (⁶) that, even before their accession, Bulgaria, Romania and Turkey should be involved in the work of the European Monitoring Centre for Drugs and Drug Addiction, whose role is to supply the European Union and its Member States with objective, reliable and comparable

---

(¹) Directive 2006/24/EC (OJ L 105, 13.4.2006).
(²) COM(2006) 437.
(³) Decision 2006/581/EC (OJ L 234, 29.8.2006).
(⁴) COM(2006) 187.
(⁵) Framework Decision 2002/629/JHA (OJ L 203, 1.8.2002).
(⁶) COM(2006) 255, COM(2006) 256 and COM(2006) 257.

information on drugs and drug addiction. In July the Council authorised the Commission to open negotiations with Croatia for the same purpose.

On 12 December the European Parliament and the Council revised the regulation establishing the Centre (¹) with a view to further legislative simplification in that area (²).

On 26 June the Commission adopted a Green Paper on the role of civil society in drugs policy in the European Union (³). The object of the Green Paper is to explore the scope for bringing those most directly concerned by the drugs problem closer to the policy process on drugs at Union level. To this end, it launches a wide-ranging consultation on how to organise a structured and continuous dialogue on this issue between the Commission and civil society. The Commission is also looking at ways in which civil society could provide added value by giving constructive advice and placing its specific expertise at the disposal of the European Union policymaking process in a practical and sustainable form. The principal objective at this stage is to realise such input in relation to the European Union action plans on drugs.

Border management and immigration

Migration flows, asylum and immigration

On 25 January the Commission adopted a communication on a thematic programme for cooperation with third countries in the areas of migration and asylum (⁴). The general objective of the programme is to provide specific, complementary assistance for third countries to support them in their efforts to ensure better management of migratory flows in all their dimensions. There are five strands: fostering the links between migration and development; promoting well-managed labour migration; fighting illegal immigration and facilitating the readmission of illegal immigrants; protecting migrants against exploitation and exclusion; and promoting asylum and international protection. This programme continues the activities launched under the Aeneas programme (⁵), which expired in 2006.

On 17 February the Commission presented a communication on strengthened practical cooperation entitled 'New structures, new approaches: improving the quality of decision-making in the common European asylum system' (⁶). It explains how practical cooperation between Member States can provide the basis for achievement of the goals set at Tampere and in the Hague programme: a Union-wide single procedure; joint collections, assessment and application of country of origin information; and

---

(¹) Regulation (EEC) No 302/93 (OJ L 36, 12.2.1993).
(²) Regulation (EC) No 1920/2006 (OJ L 376, 27.12.2006).
(³) COM(2006) 316.
(⁴) COM(2006) 26.
(⁵) Regulation (EC) No 491/2004 (OJ L 80, 18.3.2004).
(⁶) COM(2006) 67.

improved cooperation between Member States in addressing particular pressures on asylum systems resulting from factors such as geographic location. The main goal of greater convergence in decision-making by Member States within the framework of the rules set by the Community asylum legislation is to improve quality across all aspects of asylum management in Member States.

On 19 July the Commission adopted a communication on policy priorities in the fight against illegal immigration of third-country nationals ([1]). Advocating a multi-faceted approach that targets all stages of the migration process, the Commission considers measures ranging from cooperation with third countries to improving the exchange of information between Member States. It proposes focusing on three main questions: tougher security measures at external borders, regularisations, and illegal employment of third-country nationals residing illegally.

On 30 November the Commission presented two communications on migration.

- The first, 'The global approach to migration one year on: towards a comprehensive European migration policy' ([2]), sums up the substantial work accomplished in the course of the year with African countries and regional organisations. This approach is geographically limited to Africa as it responds to the mandate given to the Commission by the European Council. However, the communication suggests how similar measures could be extended, where relevant, to other regions such as eastern Europe, Latin America and Asia. It also proposes ways and means of strengthening dialogue and cooperation with Africa on all aspects of migration: legal and illegal migration, better protection for refugees, and promotion of the migration and development agenda.

- The second, 'Reinforcing the management of the European Union's southern maritime borders' ([3]), focuses on operational activities undertaken in support of the Union's migration policy. It addresses maritime border management in the face of the steadily increasing pressure of illegal migration. This communication considers how to maximise the capacity of the European Agency for the Management of Operational Cooperation at the External Borders of the Member States of the European Union (Frontex). It outlines a number of new tools to improve integrated border management, including a coastal patrol network, a European surveillance system and operational assistance to improve the capacity of Member States to deal with mixed flows of illegal immigrants. Finally, the Commission proposes establishing a pool of experts from Member States' administrations who could be deployed rapidly to help Member States with the initial profiling of asylum seekers through the provision in particular of interpretation services or country of origin expertise.

([1]) COM(2006) 402.
([2]) COM(2006) 735.
([3]) COM(2006) 733.

In July the European Parliament passed a resolution on strategies and means for the integration of immigrants in the European Union. It welcomed the Commission proposal to establish the European Fund for the Integration of Third-Country Nationals (¹), urged the Council to adopt a comprehensive framework directive on legal migration, and called on Member States to encourage the political participation of immigrants and discourage their political and social isolation.

In September Parliament passed a resolution on the European Union's common immigration policy in which it expressed its firm belief that Member States must respect their international obligations despite the increasing pressure on immigration and asylum systems. It also stressed that any comprehensive approach to immigration cannot ignore the 'push factors' that lead people to leave their countries and that the European Union needs to come up with clear plans for development and investment in the countries of origin and transit.

In July the Council adopted conclusions recognising the growing importance of migration-related issues as an integral part of European Union external relations in the framework of a balanced and comprehensive approach to migration. It expressed concern regarding the increasing illegal migratory flows in the Mediterranean and Atlantic areas and underlined the need to address all aspects of this serious situation through measures including operational cooperation with a view to developing surveillance capacities at maritime borders.

On 5 October the Council adopted a decision establishing a mutual information mechanism concerning Member States' measures in the area of asylum and immigration (²). It requires Member States to transmit information on measures they intend to take, or have recently taken, in the areas of asylum and immigration which are likely to have an impact on the other Member States as soon as possible and at the latest when this information becomes publicly available. The information is to be communicated through a web-based network run by the Commission. Specific national measures notified through the system may give rise to exchanges of views between experts from the Member States and the Commission. In addition to such technical discussions, the Commission will prepare a report each year summarising the most relevant information posted by the Member States. This report will be transmitted to the European Parliament and to the Council and will serve as a basis for ministerial debate on national asylum and immigration policies.

Visas, crossing of borders and internal movement

On 10 January the Commission presented a report on visa waiver reciprocity with certain third countries (³), noting considerable improvement in the situation since

---

(¹) COM(2005) 123.
(²) Decision 2006/688/EC (OJ L 283, 14.10.2006).
(³) COM(2006) 3.

the last round of enlargement in 2004. The Council welcomed the report but noted the lack of progress in extending the visa waivers given by Australia, Canada and the United States to all Union citizens, and asked the Commission to continue monitoring developments with regard to these countries. On 3 October the Commission presented a second report (¹) informing the Member States that full reciprocity is now in place with Uruguay, Costa Rica and Paraguay. It plans to consider what measures should be taken to reach reciprocity with other non-member countries where progress has so far proved insufficient.

At the EU–Russia Summit held in Sochi on 25 May, agreement was reached on visa facilitation for citizens of the European Union and Russia. A readmission agreement was also concluded establishing, again on a reciprocity basis, rapid and effective procedures for the identification and return of persons who do not meet the conditions for entry to or presence in Russia or the European Union.

On 31 May the Commission adopted a proposal for a regulation amending the common consular instructions on visas for diplomatic missions and consular posts in relation to the introduction of biometrics, including provisions on the organisation of the reception and processing of visa applications (²). The proposal is intended to create the legal basis for Member States to take mandatory biometric identifiers from visa applicants and to provide a legal framework for the organisation of Member States' consular offices with a view to implementing the visa information system. Common application centres will help to reinforce and rationalise local consular cooperation and cut costs for Member States by pooling and sharing resources.

On 1 June the Council adopted a decision on the fees to be charged corresponding to the administrative costs of processing visa applications (³). It provides for increased fees to cover the implementation of the visa information system and the collection of biometric data from visa applicants. In June the European Parliament and the Council also established a simplified regime for the control of persons at external borders based on the unilateral recognition by the Member States of certain residence permits issued by Switzerland and Liechtenstein for the purpose of transit through their territory (⁴).

On 13 July the Commission adopted a proposal for a regulation amending the list of third countries whose nationals must be in possession of visas when crossing the external borders of Member States and those whose nationals are exempt from that requirement (⁵). The amendment was adopted by the Council on 21 December (⁶).

(¹) COM(2006) 568.
(²) COM(2006) 269.
(³) Decision 2006/440/EC (OJ L 175, 29.6.2006).
(⁴) Decision No 896/2006/EC (OJ L 167, 20.6.2006).
(⁵) COM(2006) 84.
(⁶) Regulation (EC) No 1932/2006 (OJ L 405, 30.12.2006).

On 19 July the Commission presented a proposal for a regulation establishing a mechanism for the creation of rapid border intervention teams [1] whereby Member States facing extreme difficulties in controlling their external borders would be able to make use of the expertise and manpower of border guards of other Member States on a temporary basis, in particular at maritime borders.

On 20 December the European Parliament and the Council adopted a regulation laying down rules on local border traffic at the external land borders of the Member States [2].

Migration was a key item on the agenda of the European Council of 14 and 15 December. The Commission was tasked with producing proposals on a number of specific matters, including legal migration and illegal immigration, border controls and solidarity mechanisms. The European Council also stressed the importance of cooperation and dialogue with countries of origin and transit and the integration of migration issues into foreign policy in general and development policy in particular.

Schengen information system

On 15 March the European Parliament and the Council adopted a regulation establishing a Community code on the rules governing the movement of persons across borders (Schengen Borders Code) [3]. This code lays down rules governing border controls on persons crossing the external borders and provides for the absence of such controls at internal borders between the Member States. On 19 July the Commission adopted a proposal for a regulation establishing a Community code on visas [4]. Within the closer Schengen cooperation, a common visa policy has been identified as a fundamental component of the creation of a common area without internal border controls. The proposal incorporates all legal instruments governing visa-related decisions into one code on visas, builds on certain parts of current legislation in order to take account of recent developments, and enhances transparency and legal certainty.

On 12 July the Commission adopted a proposal for a regulation and a proposal for a decision [5] deferring until 31 December 2007 the original deadline for developing the second-generation Schengen information system (SIS II) and providing for allocation of the requisite budget. It is also recommended that the system be located in France and Austria during the development phase. The acts concerned were adopted by the Council on 20 December [6]. On the same day the European Parliament and the Council adopted regulations on the establishment, operation and use of SIS II [7] , and

---

[1] COM(2006) 401.
[2] Regulation (EC) No 1931/2006 (OJ L 405, 30.12.2006).
[3] Regulation (EC) No 562/2006 (OJ L 105, 13.4.2006).
[4] COM(2006) 403.
[5] COM(2006) 383.
[6] Regulation (EC) No 1988/2006 and Decision 2006/1007/JHA (OJ L 411, 30.12.2006).
[7] Regulation (EC) No 1987/2006 (OJ L 381, 28.12.2006).

on access to SIS II by the services in the Member States responsible for issuing vehicle registration certificates (¹).

General references and other useful links

- Area of freedom, security and justice:
  http://ec.europa.eu/justice_home/index_en.htm

- Eurojust:
  http://eurojust.europa.eu/

- Europol:
  http://www.europol.europa.eu/

- European Police College (CEPOL):
  http://www.cepol.net/KIM/

Section 2

Risk management

Public health

Health determinants

On 11 September the Commission published the results of the contributions to the Green Paper entitled 'Promoting healthy diets and physical activity: a European dimension for the prevention of overweight, obesity and chronic diseases' (²), which was adopted in December 2005. On this basis, it will propose a European Union strategy for nutrition and physical activity by the end of the first quarter of 2007.

On 24 October the Commission adopted a communication on the European Union strategy to support Member States in reducing alcohol-related harm (³). The communication lists the measures already taken at Union level, summarises the provisions and good practice applied in the Member States and identifies several areas of cooperation where Community action would complement and support national policy for combating the harmful effects of alcohol.

In November the Commission published the conclusions following the Green Paper entitled 'Improving the mental health of the population — Towards a strategy on

---

(¹) Regulation (EC) No 1986/2006 (OJ L 381, 28.12.2006).
(²) COM(2005) 637.
(³) COM(2006) 625.

mental health for the European Union' (¹), which will be used as the basis for drawing up a strategy on the issue by the end of the first quarter of 2007.

Health services

On 26 September the Commission launched a public consultation exercise concerning Community action on health services in order to draw up specific proposals during 2007.

Information on health-related issues

On 10 May the Commission and the Member States launched the new site 'Health-EU' (²) — the public health portal of the European Union, which is an easy-to-use, single point of access to reliable information on health-related issues. It is aimed at citizens, patients, health professionals, scientists, policymakers and administrators.

Blood donations

On 19 June the Commission adopted a first report (³) on the application of the blood directive (⁴). This report summarises the measures taken by the Member States to encourage voluntary and unpaid blood donations and presents those the Commission intends to adopt in order to promote the European Community's self-sufficiency on the basis of such donations.

Human tissues and cells

On 8 February the Commission adopted a directive concerning the technical rules on the donation and collection of, and experiments on, cells and tissue (⁵). These rules were drawn up to support the implementation of European Union law on the standards of quality and safety for tissue and cells, which were due to be transposed by the Member States before April 2006. A second set of implementing rules for the coding, processing, preservation, storage and distribution of human tissues and cells was adopted on 24 October (⁶).

Promotion of safety

On 23 June the Commission adopted a communication on 'Actions for a safer Europe' and a proposal for a Council recommendation on the prevention of injury and the promotion of safety (⁷).

(¹) COM(2005) 484.
(²) http://ec.europa.eu/health-eu/index_en.htm.
(³) COM(2006) 313 (OJ C 184, 8.8.2006).
(⁴) Directive 2002/98/EC (OJ L 33, 8.2.2003).
(⁵) Directive 2006/17/EC (OJ L 38, 9.2.2006).
(⁶) Directive 2006/86/EC (OJ L 294, 25.10.2006).
(⁷) COM(2006) 328 and COM(2006) 329 (OJ C 184, 8.8.2006).

On 26 September the Commission adopted a communication on the International Health Regulations (IHR), which had been revised in 2005 (^{1}). The IHR is an instrument which aims to prevent and control the spread of disease throughout the world, whilst avoiding unnecessary restrictions on trade and passenger traffic.

Influenza pandemic

On 30 March the Commission published the evaluation report on the Union-wide exercise on an influenza pandemic. The 'tabletop' simulation was carried out on 23 and 24 November 2005 and aimed to test the preparedness of the Member States and their capacity to act in a coordinated fashion, and also to assess the effectiveness of communication between the Commission, national authorities, European Union agencies, international organisations and the pharmaceutical industry.

Tobacco control

In February 2006 the Commission took part in the first conference of the parties to the Framework Convention on Tobacco Control, adopted by the World Health Assembly in 2003. In particular, this conference established a secretariat and four working groups: two groups to develop protocols in the area of cross-border advertising and illicit trade, and two groups to develop guidelines on smoke-free zones and on testing for tobacco ingredients and emissions.

The Commission has also completed its library of colour photographs for health warnings on tobacco products. These photographs can now be used on a voluntary basis by the Member States.

Consumer protection

On 4 May the Commission published a report on the implementation of Community action in support of consumer policy 2004–05 (^{2}), which gives an overview of the implementation of Decision No 20/2004/EC over that period and summarises the expenditure committed for each of the objectives and actions.

On 11 May the Commission adopted Decision 2006/502/EC (^{3}) prohibiting the sale of lighters which are not child-resistant and of lighters resembling objects particularly appealing to children (toy, food, mobile telephone).

On 24 May the Commission adopted amended proposals (^{4}) for decisions establishing programmes of Community action in the field of health and consumer protection

---

(^{1}) COM(2006) 552.
(^{2}) COM(2006) 193.
(^{3}) OJ L 198, 20.7.2006.
(^{4}) COM(2006) 234 and COM(2006) 235.

(2007–13). They take into account the new financial framework 2007–13 ([1]) and split the previous programme covering both health and consumer protection into two separate programmes. The latter was adopted by the European Parliament and the Council on 18 December ([2]).

On 21 June the Commission adopted a communication on the implementation of Directive 98/6/EC on consumer protection in the indication of prices of products offered to consumers ([3]). It found that, although the extent of its repercussions had not yet been clearly established, the directive had not given rise to any major transposition problems and had contributed to increasing the protection of consumer economic interests.

On 21 September the Commission adopted a communication on the implementation of Directive 97/7/EC on the protection of consumers in respect of distance contracts ([4]). It welcomed the adoption of transposition measures in all the Member States and saw no need at this stage to propose amendments to the directive.

Food safety, animal safety and animal welfare

Avian influenza

In 2006 avian influenza of the Asian type H5N1 was detected in wild birds in 14 Member States and in domestic poultry flocks in five Member States. In the European Union the virus was kept from spreading by immediate controls on all influenza outbreaks, and no human being was contaminated.

The measures for combating the H5N1 virus taken in 2005 were adapted to take account of developments in the epidemiological situation and complemented by enhanced surveillance and biosecurity measures in the Member States. The diagnostic methods for the disease have also been revised ([5]). Additional provisions to those of the directive on measures for the control of avian influenza were also laid down to prevent the spread of H5N1 in wild birds ([6]) and in poultry ([7]). The Commission also formally approved the vaccination plans for poultry at high risk of contamination submitted by the Netherlands, France and Germany. It also approved the vaccination plans submitted by 17 Member States to protect birds living in zoos.

---

[1] See Chapter I of this Report.
[2] Decision No 1926/2006/EC (OJ L 404, 30.12.2006).
[3] COM(2006) 325.
[4] COM(2006) 514.
[5] Decision 2006/437/EC (OJ L 237, 31.8.2006).
[6] Decision 2006/115/EC (OJ L 48, 18.2.2006).
[7] Decision 2006/135/EC (OJ L 52, 23.2.2006)

Animal welfare

On 23 January the Commission adopted a Community action plan on the protection and welfare of animals, identifying the broad guidelines for future initiatives over the period 2006–10 [1]. It also presented a strategic basis for the proposed action [2] to promote a coordinated approach throughout the Union.

In response to the concerns of European citizens over animal protection, on 20 November the Commission adopted a proposal for a regulation banning the placing on the market and the import to or export from the Community of cat and dog fur and products containing such fur [3]. The proposal also establishes a system for exchanging information on the methods of detecting the fur in question.

Aquaculture

On 4 April the Commission adopted a proposal for a regulation concerning the use of alien and locally absent species in aquaculture [4] with the aim of establishing a better balance between the economic development of this type of aquaculture and the preservation of ecosystems.

Community reference laboratories

On 23 May the Commission adopted a regulation amending Annex VII to Regulation (EC) No 882/2004, designating new Community reference laboratories (CRLs) [5]. The CRLs carry out various types of scientific analysis in accordance with Community law on food safety and animal health. An example of such work is the diagnosis of certain animal diseases, such as brucellosis or foot-and-mouth disease.

Spongiform encephalopathies

On 21 November following on from its 'roadmap' of 15 July 2005 [6], which set out possible future changes to European Union measures on transmissible bovine spongiform encephalopathies (TSEs) in the short, medium and long term, the Commission adopted a work programme (2006–07) on implementing the roadmap [7].

On 18 December the European Parliament and the Council laid down new rules for the prevention, control and eradication of certain TSEs [8].

---

[1] COM(2006) 13 (OJ C 49, 28.2.2006).
[2] COM(2006) 14 (OJ C 67, 18.3.2006).
[3] COM(2006) 684.
[4] COM(2006) 154 (OJ C 104, 3.5.2006).
[5] Regulation (EC) No 776/2006 (OJ L 136, 24.5.2006).
[6] COM(2005) 322.
[7] SEC(2006) 1527.
[8] Regulation (EC) No 1923/2006 (OJ L 404, 30.12.2006).

Plant protection products

On 12 July the Commission proposed new harmonised rules at Community level for plant protection products ([1]). The measures set out in the proposal for a regulation include clearer acceptance criteria and simplified procedures, simplified data protection rules, provisions on the replacement of certain active substances with safer products and a reduction in the number of tests and studies involving vertebrate animals.

Enzymes, aromas and additives

On 28 July the Commission adopted a set of legislative proposals ([2]) introducing for the first time harmonised Community legislation on food enzymes and improving the rules in force on aromas and additives. These documents are intended to clarify and update the relevant legislation on the matter and implement a simplified common authorisation procedure for food additives, aromas and enzymes based on the scientific assessments of the European Food Safety Authority.

Better training for safer food

On 20 September the Commission adopted a communication entitled 'Better training for safer food' ([3]), which deals with the question of training the staff of the competent authorities of the Member States and non-member countries who are in charge of carrying out checks to ensure food safety and consumer protection in the European Union. One option it considers is that of entrusting the management of a training programme to an executive agency.

Biotechnology

On 25 October the Commission adopted a report ([4]) on the implementation of Regulation (EC) No 1829/2003 on genetically modified food and feed ([5]). The report covers a range of issues, such as the authorisation procedure, labelling rules and the occurrence on the European Union market of unauthorised products. Particular emphasis is placed on the experience gained in the authorisation procedure and in the handling of unauthorised products.

---

[1] COM(2006) 388.
[2] COM(2006) 423, COM(2006) 425, COM(2006) 427 and COM(2006) 428.
[3] COM(2006) 519.
[4] COM(2006) 626.
[5] OJ L 268,18.10.2003.

Transport security and safety

Report on transport security and its financing

In August the Commission adopted a report on the financing of security measures in the aviation and maritime transport sectors (¹). According to the report, transport security costs can be significant and are currently largely borne by the users. The report provides clarification on the various financing mechanisms existing in the Member States and warns that the heterogeneity of approaches means that there is a possibility of some distortion of competition. According to the conclusions of the report, greater transparency relating to security taxes and charges would serve the interests of the users of transport services; in addition, the Commission feels that, in general, public funding of anti-terrorist measures in the transport sector does not constitute State aid.

Transport of dangerous goods

On 22 December the Commission drew up a proposal for a directive on the inland transport of dangerous goods (²). The proposal aims to streamline existing rules on the transport of dangerous goods by road and rail, and also to expand these rules to include inland waterway transport. At the same time, it recommends harmonising the rules where possible to make their application more uniform and safer, easier and less costly.

Maritime safety

Following the adoption of the third package of legislative measures for maritime safety (³) on 23 November 2005, the Committee of the Regions gave its opinion on all the measures on 15 June. It endorsed the proposals, believing that the package would increase maritime transport safety, but expressed concern about the administrative burden that the measures set out in the seven proposals might entail.

On 27 March the Commission adopted a proposal for a regulation on the accelerated phasing-in of double-hull or equivalent design requirements for single-hull oil tankers (⁴). The purpose of the proposal is to adapt the provisions of Regulation (EC) No 417/2002 (⁵), as amended (⁶), to the political declaration made to the International Maritime Organisation in 2003 by the presidency of the European Union, in which it announced that the Member States would not authorise single-hull tankers flying their flags to make use of any of the exemptions in Annex I to the Marpol 73/78 Convention.

(¹) COM(2006) 431.
(²) COM(2006) 852.
(³) COM(2005) 586, COM(2005) 587, COM(2005) 588, COM(2005) 589, COM(2005) 590, COM(2005) 592 and
       COM(2005) 593.
(⁴) COM(2006) 111.
(⁵) OJ L 64, 7.3.2002.
(⁶) OJ L 249, 1.10.2003.

Road safety

On 22 February the Commission adopted the mid-term review (¹) of the European road safety action programme (²). It found that faster progress had been made since road safety had become a political concern in the Member States. However, progress varied from one country to another, and the Commission considered that greater efforts were required to achieve the objective set in 2001 of halving the number of road deaths by 2010.

On 5 October the Commission adopted two proposals for directives of the European Parliament and of the Council on road infrastructure safety management (³) and on the retrofitting of mirrors to heavy goods vehicles registered in the Community (⁴).

On 20 December the European Parliament and the Council adopted the third directive on driving licences (⁵).

This proposed directive has three main objectives:

- fighting fraud by introducing a single licence model (plastic card), limiting the administrative validity of the licence to 10 years (with the possibility of extension up to 15 years) and providing for the introduction of an optional microchip;

- improving road safety by creating a licence for moped riders, reinforcing the principle of progressive access for the most powerful types of mopeds, redefining the categories for driving heavy vehicle–trailer combinations and setting up a system of initial qualification and obligatory periodic training for driving examiners; and

- facilitating free movement by reaffirming the principle of mutual recognition of licences within the European Union and harmonising the rules on the validity of licences and the periodicity of medical examinations for drivers of trucks and buses.

Air safety

On 19 May the Commission adopted Regulation (EC) No 768/2006 on the collection and exchange of information on the safety of aircraft using Community airports and the management of the information system (⁶), which implements Directive 2004/36/EC of the European Parliament and of the Council (⁷).

(¹) COM(2006) 74.
(²) COM(2001) 370.
(³) COM(2006) 569.
(⁴) COM(2006) 570.
(⁵) Directive 2006/126/EC (OJ L 403, 30.12.2006).
(⁶) OJ L 134, 20.5.2006.
(⁷) OJ L 143, 30.4.2004.

On 12 December the European Parliament and the Council signed Regulation (EC) No 1899/2006 on the harmonisation of technical requirements and administrative procedures in the field of civil aviation [1], amending Council Regulation (EEC) No 3922/91 [2]. A further amendment was adopted on 20 December [3].

On 22 March, pursuant to Regulation (EC) No 2111/2005 of 14 December 2005, the Commission adopted Regulation (EC) No 473/2006 [4] laying down implementing rules for the Community list of air carriers which are subject to an operating ban within the Community and Regulation (EC) No 474/2006 [5] establishing the Community list of air carriers which are subject to an operating ban within the Community. The Commission then adopted, on 20 June [6] and 12 October [7], two regulations amending Regulation (EC) No 474/2006 to update the Community list in question.

Aviation security

On 4 October the Commission adopted a regulation limiting the quantity of liquid that can be carried on board aircraft leaving Community airports and improving the procedures for screening passengers [8]. This decision constitutes the conclusion drawn by the Commission in the face of the new forms of terrorist threat revealed in the action taken on 10 August by the British authorities in charge of security at Heathrow airport. The other decisions on air security adopted by the Commission in 2006 concern in particular the introduction of a clause on new technologies [9], technical standards for radioscopic image equipment and explosive detection systems [10], and rules on the security of air cargo [11].

Supply chain security

On 27 February the Commission adopted a communication on enhancing supply chain security [12]. It considered that a first step towards improving the security of the entire supply chain was needed, and that the definition of a corresponding framework would stimulate interconnectivity between the various modes of transport and operators.

---

[1] OJ L 377, 27.12.2006.
[2] OJ L 373, 31.12.1991.
[3] Regulation (EC) No 1900/2006 (OJ L 377, 27.12.2006).
[4] OJ L 84, 23.3.2006.
[5] OJ L 84, 23.3.2006.
[6] Regulation (EC) No 910/2006 (OJ L 168, 21.6.2006).
[7] Regulation (EC) No 1543/2006 (OJ L 283, 14.10.2006).
[8] Regulation (EC) No 1546/2006 (OJ L 286, 17.10.2006).
[9] Regulation (EC) No 65/2006 (OJ L 11, 17.1.2006).
[10] Regulation (EC) No 1448/2006 (OJ L 271, 13.9.2006).
[11] Regulation (EC) No 831/2006 (OJ L 150, 3.6.2006).
[12] COM(2006) 79.

Energy security and installation safety

In the area of energy security and safety, the Commission proposed on 15 June that a further Community contribution be made to the European Bank for Reconstruction and Development for the Chernobyl Shelter Fund ([1]) in Ukraine.

On 24 July the Council adopted Directive 2006/67/EC ([2]) codifying Directive 68/414/EEC ([3]), which imposed an obligation on Member States to maintain minimum stocks of crude oil and/or petroleum products.

In December the Commission adopted a proposal for a directive on the European programme for critical infrastructure protection ([4]) and a communication on the protection of critical European infrastructure in the transport and energy sectors ([5]). The communication proposes to the Member States a set of criteria for identifying critical European energy and transport infrastructure.

Civil protection and disaster response

Flood management

On 18 January the Commission adopted a proposal for a directive on the assessment and management of floods ([6]), aimed at establishing a common framework for flood risk management at European Union level. Under the proposal, the Member States will assume responsibility for the following three tasks: preliminary flood risk assessment of their river basins and coastal areas, establishing flood risk maps identifying the areas at risk, and drawing up flood risk management plans for the areas identified.

Civil protection

On 26 January the Commission adopted a proposal for a decision establishing a Community civil protection mechanism ([7]). Its purpose is to strengthen the mechanism established by Council Decision 2001/792/EC, Euratom ([8]) on the basis of lessons learned in past emergencies, but also to provide a legal basis for additional support measures and action at Community level.

The main emergencies to which the Union responded via the Community civil protection mechanism in 2006 were the floods in central Europe and forest fires in

---

([1]) COM(2006) 305.
([2]) OJ L 217, 8.8.2006.
([3]) OJ L 308, 23.12.1968.
([4]) COM(2006) 787.
([5]) COM(2006) 786.
([6]) COM(2006) 15 (OJ C 67, 18.3.2006).
([7]) COM(2006) 29 (OJ C 67, 18.3.2006).
([8]) OJ L 297, 15.11.2001.

Spain, and, outside Europe, the earthquake and volcanic eruption in Indonesia and maritime pollution in Lebanon.

The Commission has also set up a daily monitoring and alert service for major disasters occurring worldwide ([1]), so that information can be shared easily between national crisis centres and the public.

Protection of the European Union's financial interests

In May the Commission proposed that the Pericles programme be extended until the end of 2013 ([2]). This exchange, assistance and training programme is aimed at protecting the euro against counterfeiting. Also in May, the Commission proposed amendments to the provisions on the investigations conducted by the European Anti-Fraud Office (OLAF) ([3]). In June it proposed amending the Hercule programme and extending it to the end of 2014 ([4]). The objective of this programme is to promote activities in the field of the protection of the Community's financial interests.

On 22 December the Commission proposed ([5]) amending Council Regulation (EC) No 515/97 ([6]) on mutual assistance between the administrative authorities of the Member States and cooperation between the latter and the Commission to ensure the correct application of the law on customs and agricultural matters. In order to enhance this cooperation, it advocated in particular the use of the customs information system database within the national systems and the creation of new instruments (customs files identification database; European central data directory containing data from the principal service providers in the international carriage of goods; permanent infrastructure for coordinating customs surveillance operations allowing representatives of the Member States to be hosted at OLAF).

General references and other useful links

- Directorate-General for Health and Consumer Protection:
  http://ec.europa.eu/dgs/health_consumer/index_en.htm

- Consumers:
  http://ec.europa.eu/consumers/index_en.htm

- Food safety:
  http://ec.europa.eu/food/food/index_en.htm

- Public health:
  http://ec.europa.eu/health/index_en.htm

- Transport:
  http://ec.europa.eu/transport/index_en.html

---

[1] http://ec.europa.eu/comm/environment/civil/micdaily/micdaily.doc.
[2] COM(2006) 243.
[3] COM(2006) 244.
[4] COM(2006) 339.
[5] COM(2006) 866.
[6] OJ L 82, 22.3.1997.

- European Maritime Safety Agency:
  http://emsa.europa.eu/
- Energy:
  http://ec.europa.eu/energy/index_en.html
- International Atomic Energy Agency:
  http://www.iaea.org/
- European Anti-Fraud Office:
  http://ec.europa.eu/anti_fraud/index_en.html

Chapter V

Europe as a global partner

Strengthening the Union's role as a global player

After the informal meeting of Heads of State or Government at Hampton Court in October 2005, it was agreed that the European Union needed to take steps to reinforce its external action and the link between internal and external policies, despite the setback to the Treaty establishing a Constitution for Europe. On 8 June the Commission therefore adopted a communication presenting a series of practical proposals which would not entail any amendments to the Treaty and are intended to bring greater coherence, effectiveness and visibility to Europe in the world (¹). The intention is to strengthen the Union's role as a global player through better strategic planning by holding informal meetings on each change of presidency of the European Council, improved cooperation between the Commission and the Council secretariat, and enhanced relations with the Member States through a staff exchange programme involving their diplomatic services and the Council secretariat.

Section 1

Proximity ties

The enlargement process

General approach

On 8 November the Commission adopted a communication entitled 'Enlargement strategy and main challenges 2006–07' together with a special report on the Union's capacity to integrate new members. The enlargement agenda covers the countries of the western Balkans and Turkey. Building on the European Union's existing strategy, it outlines an approach for drawing lessons from the fifth enlargement, supporting countries on their way to membership, fostering public support for further enlargement, addressing the enlargement challenges, and ensuring the Union's

---

(¹) COM(2006) 278.

integration capacity. More generally, in its communication of 10 May entitled 'A citizens' agenda — Delivering results for Europe' ([1]), the Commission recommended an intensification of the debate on the added value of enlargements and the European Union's absorption capacity.

At the European Council of 14 and 15 December the Heads of State or Government reached a renewed consensus on enlargement which provides for strict conditionality at all stages of the accession negotiations. Sensitive issues such as administrative and legal reforms and the fight against corruption needed to be addressed early in the negotiation process. The Union would avoid setting any time limits for accession until negotiations were approaching their conclusion. Finally, the European Council believed that the speed of enlargement needed to take account of the Union's capacity to absorb new members.

Bulgaria and Romania

On 16 May the Commission adopted a monitoring report on the state of preparedness for European Union membership of Bulgaria and Romania ([2]).

On 26 September, in its second monitoring report ([3]), it considered that both countries had made considerable efforts since the May report to complete their preparations for membership and that they were sufficiently prepared to meet the political, economic and *acquis* criteria by 1 January 2007. Many of the challenges set out in the May reports had been addressed since then. A number of sectoral issues had been resolved but, although there had been some progress in the areas of judicial reform and the fight against corruption, money-laundering and organised crime, further tangible results were needed. The new report identified the issues which require further work and drew attention to provisions in the *acquis* and the Accession Treaty which are designed to safeguard the proper functioning of European Union policies and institutions following accession. In line with the findings of this report, the Commission, after consulting the Member States, decided to set up a mechanism for cooperation and verification of progress in the areas of judicial reform and the fight against corruption, money-laundering and organised crime. Benchmarks referring to the particular circumstances of each country have been established for this purpose. The Commission report was welcomed by the Council on 17 October.

On 13 December the Commission established this mechanism to monitor progress made by Bulgaria and Romania in reforming the judiciary and fighting corruption and organised crime. These two new Member States will submit a progress report on the matter each year. The Commission will forward its comments and conclusions on these reports to the European Parliament and the Council.

---

[1] See Chapter I, Section 3, of this Report.
[2] COM(2006) 214.
[3] COM(2006) 549.

Turkey

On 23 January the Council adopted a decision on the principles, priorities and conditions contained in the accession partnership with Turkey (¹). The revised partnership includes a number of priorities relating to Turkey's capacity to meet the criteria defined by the Copenhagen European Council of 1993 and the requirements of the negotiating framework adopted by the Council in October 2005. The priorities, which concern legislation and its implementation, were chosen on the grounds that it was realistic to expect that Turkey could complete them.

On 10 April the Council approved the conclusion of an agreement with Turkey on its participation in European Union crisis management operations (²).

On 29 November the Commission adopted a communication (³) noting that Turkey had not fully implemented the additional protocol to the Ankara agreement, and that restrictions to the free movement of goods, including restrictions on transport, remained in force. The communication recommends in particular that, in the light of these circumstances, the Intergovernmental Conference on accession with Turkey should not open negotiations on eight chapters, and that no chapter should be provisionally closed until the Commission confirmed that Turkey had fulfilled the commitments contained in the additional protocol. The Council adopted the Commission's recommendations on 11 December.

Croatia

On 14 February the Council adopted a regulation (⁴) replacing the expression 'European partnership for Croatia' with 'accession partnership' to align it with the expression used to describe the partnership with Turkey. On 20 February it adopted a decision on the principles, priorities and conditions in the accession partnership with Croatia (⁵). This accession partnership updates the previous European partnership with Croatia on the basis of the findings of the Commission's 2005 progress report on this candidate country, and identifies new priorities for action. The new priorities are adapted to the country's specific needs and state of preparedness and will be updated as necessary. Croatia is now expected to develop a plan including a timetable and specific measures to address the accession partnership priorities. These priorities relate mainly to Croatia's capacity to meet the criteria defined by the Copenhagen European Council of 1993 and the conditions set for the stabilisation and association process.

(¹) Decision 2006/35/EC (OJ L 22, 26.1.2006).
(²) Decision 2006/482/CFSP (OJ L 189, 12.7.2006).
(³) COM(2006) 773.
(⁴) Regulation (EC) No 269/2006 (OJ L 47, 17.2.2006).
(⁵) Decision 2006/145/EC (OJ L 55, 25.2.2006).

Other western Balkan countries

The European Union's relations with the countries of the western Balkans maintained satisfactory progress in 2006, after the significant progress made in 2005.

On 27 January the Commission adopted a communication entitled 'The western Balkans on the road to the EU: consolidating stability and raising prosperity' ([1]). It considered that the perspective of accession to the European Union provides a powerful incentive for political and economic reform in the western Balkans and encourages reconciliation among the peoples of the region. It also considered that reinforcing the Union's policy for the region, especially in areas of mutual interest where there is a strong demand from the people of the region, such as justice, freedom and security, education and trade, is the best means to strengthen the credibility of the process and to lessen political risks. The Commission's objective is to promote stability, security and prosperity in the western Balkans through the progressive integration of the region into the European mainstream. The communication was endorsed by the foreign ministers of the European Union and the western Balkan countries in Salzburg on 11 March.

On 30 January the Council adopted decisions establishing European partnerships with the former Yugoslav Republic of Macedonia ([2]), Albania, Bosnia and Herzegovina, and Serbia and Montenegro including Kosovo ([3]). The partnerships are updated to define new priorities for action on the basis of the results of Commission reports on the preparations of the countries of the western Balkans to ease integration into the European Union ([4]), and on the Commission's opinion on the application from the former Yugoslav Republic of Macedonia for membership of the European Union ([5]).

President Barroso made his first visit to the western Balkans region between 15 and 18 February in the company of Commissioner Rehn. The President and Commissioner Rehn used the occasion to pass on a message of encouragement and confidence to the political leaders of the region. They reaffirmed the Commission's support for the prospect of European integration for the western Balkans. They urged the countries' Heads of State to step up their reform efforts in order to accelerate their progress on the road to the European Union.

On 9 January the Commission amended ([6]) for the eighth time a Council regulation imposing certain restrictive measures in support of effective implementation of the mandate of the International Criminal Tribunal for the former Yugoslavia (ICTY) ([7]).

([1]) COM(2006) 27.
([2]) Decision 2006/57/EC (OJ L 35, 7.2.2006).
([3]) Decisions 2006/54/EC, 2006/55/EC and 2006/56/EC (OJ L 35, 7.2.2006).
([4]) COM(2005) 553, COM(2005) 555 and COM(2005) 558 (OJ C 49, 28.2.2006).
([5]) COM(2005) 557 (OJ C 49, 28.2.2006).
([6]) Regulation (EC) No 23/2006 (OJ L 5, 10.1.2006).
([7]) Regulation (EC) No 1763/2004 (OJ L 315, 14.10.2004).

On 10 March the Council renewed further measures brought in for the same reason, targeting individuals who are engaged in activities which help persons at large continue to evade justice for crimes for which they have been indicted by the ICTY, or who are otherwise acting in a manner which could obstruct the ICTY's effective implementation of its mandate [1]. On 23 January [2] it repealed Common Position 96/184/CFSP [3] concerning arms exports to the former Yugoslavia.

On 6 April the Commission adopted a proposal for a regulation [4] on the European Agency for Reconstruction (EAR), set up to implement Community assistance to Serbia and Montenegro, including Kosovo, and the former Yugoslav Republic of Macedonia. As Regulation (EC) No 2667/2000, which established the Agency, expired on 31 December 2006, the Commission, on the basis of its December 2005 report on the future mandate of the Agency, proposed to discontinue the EAR, but to extend its existence for two years, until 31 December 2008, with its current mandate and status, so as to gradually phase out its activities under CARDS (Community assistance for reconstruction, development and stabilisation). The Council adopted the corresponding regulation [5] on 28 November.

On 13 November the Council adopted negotiating directives for the negotiation of visa facilitation and readmission agreements with Bosnia and Herzegovina, the former Yugoslav Republic of Macedonia, Montenegro and Serbia. At the same time the Council adopted a mandate for the negotiation of an agreement on visa facilitation with Albania, which already has a readmission agreement with the European Community. Negotiations were officially launched on 30 November with all countries concerned.

Former Yugoslav Republic of Macedonia

On 30 January the Council adopted a common position extending and amending restrictive measures against extremists in the former Yugoslav Republic of Macedonia [6]. These measures are aimed at preventing admission to the Union's territory of certain individuals who actively promote or take part in violent extremist activities challenging the Ohrid framework agreement's basic principles of stability, territorial integrity and the multi-ethnic character of the country and/or undermine and deliberately obstruct the implementation of the framework agreement by actions outside the democratic process.

On 20 February the Council extended and amended the mandate of the European Union Special Representative in the former Yugoslav Republic of Macedonia [7].

---

[1] Common Position 2006/204/CFSP and Decision 2006/205/CFSP (OJ L 72, 11.3.2006).
[2] Common Position 2006/29/CFSP (OJ L 19, 24.1.2006).
[3] OJ L 58, 7.3.1996.
[4] COM(2006) 162.
[5] Regulation (EC) No 1756/2006 (OJ L 332, 30.11.2006).
[6] Common Position 2006/50/CFSP (OJ L 26, 31.1.2006).
[7] Joint Action 2006/123/CFSP (OJ L 49, 21.2.2006).

Bosnia and Herzegovina

Negotiations for a stabilisation and association agreement (SAA) with Bosnia and Herzegovina were carried out in line with the negotiating directives adopted by the Council in November 2005. SAA technical negotiations were finalised in December 2006. The agreement will be submitted for signature once the country makes sufficient progress in the key areas indicated by the European Union, notably on police reform.

An economic dialogue with Bosnia and Herzegovina was also launched in January 2006, and a first meeting took place in April.

On 30 January the Council appointed Mr Christian Schwarz-Schilling to the post of European Union Special Representative in Bosnia and Herzegovina ([1]).

Albania

On 21 March the Commission proposed the signing and conclusion of a stabilisation and association agreement and an interim agreement with Albania ([2]). Both agreements were signed on 12 June ([3]). The interim agreement, which brings into force the trade-related provisions of the SAA pending its ratification, entered into force on 1 December.

Serbia and Montenegro, including Kosovo

In November 2005 the Commission presented a proposal for an updated European partnership with Serbia and Montenegro, including Kosovo. It was adopted by the Council in January 2006 (see above). After Montenegro proclaimed its independence in June, the Commission presented a new updated draft European partnership ([4]) for Montenegro alone. The proposal is based on the parts of the current European partnership for Serbia and Montenegro, including Kosovo, that cover Montenegro, which have been brought up to date by the addition of priorities arising from Montenegro's new competences, and the challenges resulting from its new status as an independent State.

On 3 May the Commission decided to freeze the negotiations on a stabilisation and association agreement (SAA) with Serbia and Montenegro as the authorities had failed to fulfil their commitment on the International Criminal Tribunal for the former Yugoslavia. The negotiations which were opened in October 2005 had progressed well until that point, but the Commission and the Council were always clear that both the pace and conclusion of the SAA negotiations would depend on full cooperation with the ICTY.

([1]) Joint Action 2006/49/CFSP (OJ L 26, 31.1.2006).
([2]) COM(2006) 138.
([3]) Decision 2006/580/EC (OJ L 239, 1.9.2006).
([4]) COM(2006) 654.

Following the proclamation of independence by Montenegro, on 24 July the Council adopted a mandate for the Commission to negotiate the stabilisation and association agreement with Montenegro, building on the results achieved previously in negotiations with the State Union. The negotiations were launched on 26 September.

On 10 April the Council adopted a joint action on the establishment of a European Union planning team regarding a possible European Union crisis management operation in the field of rule of law and possible other areas in Kosovo ([1]).

On 12 May the Commission proposed ([2]) providing exceptional Community financial assistance to Kosovo in the form of a grant with a view to supporting the development of a sound economic and fiscal framework, facilitating the continuation and strengthening of essential administrative functions, and addressing public investment needs. The assistance would be limited in time, complement support from the World Bank (through International Development Association funds) and other donors, and be conditional on progress in the implementation of a number of measures, in particular in the area of public finance, to be defined in close consultation with the International Monetary Fund and the World Bank. This assistance would provide crucial bridge support until Kosovo's status was resolved. It would be unrelated to new status arrangements and would not preempt the further Community and international support likely to be required upon status resolution beyond 2007. This exceptional assistance, which could total as much as EUR 50 million, was the subject of a Council decision on 30 November ([3]).

On 15 September the Council adopted a further joint action on the establishment of a European Union team to contribute to the preparations for the establishment of a possible international civilian mission in Kosovo, including a European Union Special Representative component ([4]).

European neighbourhood policy (ENP)

General approach

On 23 January the Council adopted a decision enabling countries covered by the European neighbourhood policy, and Russia, to benefit from the technical assistance and information exchange programme (TAIEX) ([5]).

On 24 May the Commission adopted an amended proposal for a regulation laying down general provisions establishing a European Neighbourhood and Partnership Instrument ([6]). The amended proposal was introduced in the wake of

---

[1] Joint Action 2006/304/CFSP (OJ L 112, 26.4.2006).
[2] COM(2006) 207.
[3] Decision 2006/880/EC (OJ L 339, 6.12.2006).
[4] Joint Action 2006/623/CFSP (OJ L 253, 16.9.2006).
[5] Decision 2006/62/EC (OJ L 32, 4.2.2006).
[6] COM(2004) 628.

the interinstitutional agreement of 17 May on the 2007–13 multiannual financial framework (¹). The corresponding regulation was adopted by the European Parliament and the Council on 24 October (²). The financial reference amount for implementation of the regulation over this period is set at EUR 11.181 billion.

On 28 November the Council decided to renew the mandate of the European Investment Bank to lend EUR 12.4 billion under the European neighbourhood policy. On 4 December the Commission adopted a communication on strengthening the European neighbourhood policy (³), which includes concrete proposals to this end in several areas. The communication is accompanied by a report on progress made by countries and sectors (⁴), covering the first seven countries to benefit from this policy, where ENP action plans have been implemented since 2005. The Commission also adopted a communication on 4 December on the participation of ENP partner countries in the work of Community agencies and in Community programmes.

Cooperation with the Mediterranean countries

A Euro-Mediterranean Summit, attended by Commissioner Ferrero-Waldner, was held in Tampere, Finland, on 27 and 28 November. Participants looked at the progress made in implementing the five-year work programme agreed at the Barcelona Summit in 2005. They also set out their priorities for 2007, which include: working together to defeat terrorism; the liberalisation of trade in services and agriculture; the right of establishment; regulatory convergence; enhanced investment; a ministerial conference on energy; a ministerial conference on migration; implementation of the Horizon 2020 initiative for the depollution of the Mediterranean; the launch by the Commission of a system of grants for students from the region and a ministerial conference on higher education; and the implementation of the action plan agreed at the first ministerial meeting in Istanbul in 2006 on strengthening the role of women in society.

Other Euro-Mediterranean conferences on more specific themes were held over the course of the year.

- On 24 March trade ministers from the European Union and Mediterranean countries met in Marrakech to promote trade and economic relations across the Mediterranean region. At this first ministerial conference since the Barcelona Summit of 2005 which marked the 10th anniversary of the process, the Euro-Mediterranean partners reiterated their commitment to the creation of a Euro-Mediterranean free trade zone by 2010.

(¹) See Chapter I of this Report.
(²) Regulation (EC) No 1638/2006 (OJ L 310, 9.11.2006).
(³) COM(2006) 726.
(⁴) SEC(2006) 1504.

- A Euro-Mediterranean conference of ministers for industry took place in Rhodes on 21 and 22 September. It reviewed progress made at political and technical levels, and action to be implemented to meet the challenges of globalisation. Participants also looked at the new perspectives offered by the Euro-Mediterranean partnership, the European Union's neighbourhood policy, and the extension of cooperation to areas such as innovation and the textile industry.

- A Euro-Mediterranean conference of ministers for agriculture took place in Strasbourg on 28 and 29 September. Participants stressed the interest of a common commitment, made by parliamentarians and professional associations on both sides of the Mediterranean, to promoting the coordination of agricultural policies and to strengthening cooperation between European and Mediterranean operators with a view to creating a common Euro-Mediterranean agricultural policy.

On 17 October the Commission presented a communication reviewing the Facility for Euro-Mediterranean Investment and Partnership, carried out in close cooperation with the European Investment Bank [1]. While stressing the positive contribution of this instrument to the channelling of funds, it recommended improving its ability to influence economic reforms.

On 14 February the Council concluded a Euro-Mediterranean association agreement with Lebanon [2]. The agreement, which entered into force on 1 April, is aimed at providing political dialogue to establish conditions for the gradual liberalisation of trade in goods, services and capital and at promoting economic, social, cultural, financial and monetary cooperation between the parties.

On 16 October the Council advocated the adoption, by the Association Council established by the agreement, of a recommendation on the implementation of an EU–Lebanon action plan. When Lebanon has completed its internal procedures, the action plan will be formally and jointly adopted by the Association Council. The action plan is a broad European neighbourhood policy tool for economic and political cooperation. In addition to the areas covered in the association agreement, it also provides for the implementation of cooperation in areas which fall within the competence of the Member States under the common foreign and security policy. The implementation of this action plan should help strengthen relations with Lebanon by stepping up economic integration, deepening political cooperation and increasing regulatory approximation between Lebanese law and the *acquis*.

On 7 June the Commission adopted a proposal [3] for a Council decision on the adoption by the Association Council established by the Euro-Mediterranean agreement of a recommendation on the implementation of the EU–Egypt action plan.

---

[1] COM(2006) 592.
[2] Decision 2006/356/EC (OJ L 143, 30.5.2006).
[3] COM(2006) 282.

The Commission, working closely with the Council, held exploratory talks with Egypt on a draft action plan covering a timeframe of three to five years. Its implementation should help fulfil the provisions in the association agreement and contribute to strengthening ties with Egypt, through a deepening of economic integration and political cooperation. As in the case of other Mediterranean countries, the action plan is a broad tool for economic and political cooperation, carrying to a further stage the commitments and objectives contained in the Euro-Mediterranean agreement.

The EU–Jordan Association Council met in Brussels on 14 November. It reviewed the development of bilateral relations between the two parties. The Union expressed its appreciation of Jordan's commitment, its long-standing contribution to the Euro-Mediterranean partnership and its participation in the five-year work programme, whose medium-term objectives include a political and security partnership, sustainable economic growth and reform, education and socio-cultural exchanges, migration, social integration, justice and security.

Further aspects of European Union policy towards other countries of the Mediterranean and Middle East are addressed below with regard to the Union's contribution to world security.

Cooperation with eastern European countries

Ukraine

Effective implementation of the 2005 ENP action plan progressed on the basis of annual implementation tools which set out comprehensive sets of priorities and timelines for 2006. The EU–Ukraine Cooperation Council and other relevant partnership and cooperation agreement structures reviewed the implementation of the action plan. Overall evaluations of progress were carried out in March and November.

In a resolution adopted on 6 April the European Parliament welcomed the democratic and transparent manner in which the parliamentary elections of 26 March had been held in Ukraine.

On 13 September the Commission adopted a recommendation on opening negotiations with Ukraine to draw up a new enhanced agreement to replace the current partnership and cooperation agreement which was signed in 1998 for a 10-year period.

After the meeting of the two Cooperation Council parties in Brussels on 14 September, the EU–Ukraine Summit was held in Helsinki on 27 October, attended by President Barroso and Commissioner Ferrero-Waldner. The summit notably reviewed progress on the joint initiatives launched in areas including energy, border issues and implementation of the 2005 EU–Ukraine action plan. Agreements on visa facilitation and the readmission of illegal immigrants were also initialled at the summit.

Progress was also noted on the transparent management of the national border between Ukraine and Moldova. After July, with the full support of both countries, the Union strengthened further the European Union Border Assistance Mission. Trilateral meetings on border issues were set up with both countries in January and November. At the November meeting, Ukraine and Moldova signed agreements on the exchange of customs and border-related information, in the presence of Commissioner Ferrero-Waldner.

Moldova

Effective implementation of the 2005 ENP action plan progressed on the basis of annual implementation tools which set out comprehensive sets of priorities and timelines for 2006. The EU–Moldova Cooperation Council and other relevant partnership and cooperation agreement structures reviewed the implementation of the action plan. Overall evaluations of progress were carried out in March and November.

From 1 January Moldova benefited from the generalised system of preferences plus (GSP+). Moldova and the Commission also made progress towards the possible granting of additional autonomous trade preferences to Moldova.

Progress was also noted on the transparent management of the national border between Ukraine and Moldova (see above).

The Commission continued to support efforts to resolve the conflict in Transnistria. It organised seminars for the Transnistrian business community in September and November to pass a clear message on the opportunities for trade with the European Union, and on the need in this regard to work within the official Moldovan framework.

The Commission also finalised preparations towards launching negotiations with Moldova on drawing up agreements on visa facilitation and readmission. The Council adopted negotiating directives to that effect on 19 December.

Belarus

Relations between the European Union and Belarus were frozen after the international condemnation of the presidential elections held on 19 March. Despite warnings from the international community, these elections were held in violation of international electoral standards, and the European Union reacted by imposing restrictive measures on certain officials of Belarus and on President Lukashenko [1]. The Council thereby froze all funds and economic resources belonging to persons responsible for the violations of international electoral standards and drew up a list of 36 persons concerned by the measures, including President Lukashenko.

[1] Common Position 2006/362/CFSP and Regulation (EC) No 765/2006 (OJ L 134, 20.5.2006).

On 21 November the Commission presented a paper setting out what the Union could bring to Belarus, were the country to engage in democratisation and respect for human rights and the rule of law. It contains concrete examples of how the people of Belarus could gain from a rapprochement between the European Union and Belarus within the framework of the European neighbourhood policy.

Cooperation with countries of the South Caucasus

Commissioner Ferrero-Waldner visited the South Caucasus on 16 and 17 February and 2 and 3 October to discuss ENP action plans, the 'frozen conflicts' in the region and issues related to energy security. During the ministerial troika visit on 2 and 3 October the ENP action plans with Armenia, Azerbaijan and Georgia were finalised. The texts were formally proposed by the Commission on 24, 25 and 26 October and adopted by the Cooperation Council meetings on 14 November in Brussels with each of the three countries. At these meetings, the Union representatives and the other parties reaffirmed their willingness to work together to fully exploit the new opportunities presented by the respective plans.

The EU–Armenia Cooperation Council took stock of developments in the South Caucasus and of political and economic reforms in Armenia. Energy issues, including progress in decommissioning the Medzamor nuclear power plant, were also discussed. The European Union addressed human rights and good governance issues as essential elements in the bilateral dialogue, stressing the importance of the next parliamentary elections in Armenia in spring 2007 being held in full compliance with commitments made to the Organisation for Security and Cooperation in Europe and the Council of Europe.

At the EU–Azerbaijan Cooperation Council, the Union expressed its concern at recent developments in Azerbaijan, especially in the field of freedom of the press and other media. A fruitful discussion on energy relations took place, in the aftermath of the signing by Presidents Barroso and Aliyev on 7 November of a memorandum of understanding on the establishment of an energy partnership between the Union and Azerbaijan.

The EU–Georgia Cooperation Council reviewed relations between the two parties, political and economic reforms in the country, and recent developments in relations between Georgia and Russia.

Strategic partnership with Russia

On 25 May an EU–Russia Summit was held in Sochi, Russia, in the presence of President Barroso. Participants reached agreement on an approach enabling the development of a new framework for relations between the European Union and Russia to replace the existing partnership and cooperation agreement. The summit also gave a fresh impetus to the implementation of the four common space roadmaps agreed between

Russia and the European Union. Agreements on easier issuing of visas and readmission were also signed.

After the summit, the European Parliament adopted a resolution on 15 June stressing the importance of a strengthened and enhanced partnership between the European Union and Russia, based on interdependence and shared interests in the development of all four common spaces. It underlined the strategic importance of cooperation on energy and the need to work together with Russia with a view to providing peace, stability and security, and fighting international terrorism and violent extremism, drugs, human trafficking and cross-border organised crime. Nonetheless, Parliament expressed disappointment at the lack of progress on conflict resolution in Transnistria and the South Caucasus, and the lack of willingness by the Russian authorities to engage with Belarus so as to start a genuine process of democratisation.

In a resolution adopted on 25 October Parliament paid tribute to the work and merits of Anna Politkovskaya, a Russian investigative reporter who had been murdered. It called on the Commission and the Member States to take a steadfast stand in the negotiations on a new partnership and cooperation agreement with Russia, insisting on the safeguarding of freedom of the press and respect for independent journalism in accordance with the relevant European standards.

On 25 November a second EU–Russia Summit was held in Helsinki attended by President Barroso. The participants reviewed the implementation of the common space roadmaps and in particular discussed the prospects for comprehensive and deep economic integration after Russia joined the World Trade Organisation. A memorandum of understanding was signed on the progressive abolition of Siberian overflight charges. Following this meeting the Prime Ministers of Norway and Iceland joined the Union and Russian leaders for a Northern Dimension Summit which approved a political declaration and a policy framework document for a new Northern Dimension policy beginning on 1 January 2007.

On 13 December the results of this second summit were the subject of a European Parliament resolution. On 16 November the European Parliament called for a Community Baltic Sea strategy to be drawn up for the Northern Dimension.

The EU–Russia Permanent Partnership Council met in Moscow in March and in Helsinki in October. The meetings covered justice and home affairs on both occasions, as well as transport, the environment, foreign affairs and energy.

On 22 December the Commission presented a report approving the functioning of facilitated transit for persons between the Kaliningrad region and the rest of Russia ([1]).

---

[1] COM(2006) 840.

General references and other useful links

- Directorate-General for Enlargement:
  http://ec.europa.eu/enlargement/index_en.htm
- Directorate-General for External Relations:
  http://ec.europa.eu/comm/external_relations/index.htm
- International Criminal Tribunal for the former Yugoslavia:
  http://www.un.org/icty/index.html
- European neighbourhood policy (ENP):
  http://ec.europa.eu/world/enp/index_en.htm
- Countries of the southern Mediterranean and of the Middle East:
  http://ec.europa.eu/comm/external_relations/med_mideast/intro/index.htm
- Barcelona process:
  http://ec.europa.eu/comm/external_relations/euromed/bd.htm
- EU–Russia relations:
  http://ec.europa.eu/comm/external_relations/russia/intro/index.htm
- EU–Ukraine relations:
  http://ec.europa.eu/comm/external_relations/ukraine/intro/index.htm

Section 2

The European Union in the global economy

International trade

Multilateral negotiations: Doha Round

In 2006 a recurring concern of the European Union was the continuation of the Doha Round following the modest results of the World Trade Organisation (WTO) Summit in Hong Kong in December 2005. On 4 April the European Parliament adopted a resolution on the need for an ambitious but balanced and realistic agreement to be concluded quickly. At the end of June the Council met in extraordinary session throughout an entire session of negotiations at ministerial level. In its conclusions of 12 June the Council had expressed the intention of also meeting for a negotiating session in July or August. This lasted only a few hours and no progress was made, with the result that the WTO Director-General, Pascal Lamy, proposed that the negotiations be suspended *sine die*. On 9 and 10 September a ministerial meeting was held in Rio de Janeiro, at the invitation of the G20 countries, to assess the reasons for this setback. It was attended by Commissioner Mandelson, who then visited the United States at the end of September for discussions with the American authorities on ways of relaunching the round. At the November General Council, Mr Lamy announced a 'flexible' resumption of work.

Dispute settlement

In 2006 the European Union was involved in 36 WTO disputes (18 as complainant, 18 as defendant), most of them with the United States (the European Union being the complainant in nine cases and the defendant in five). The most visible were the 'Airbus/Boeing' cases brought by the Union and the United States on alleged subsidies to these manufacturers of large civil aircraft. The Union and the United States filed updated panel requests on 20 and 31 January respectively. The year 2006 saw the first case brought by the Union against China over measures affecting imports of automobile parts (request for a panel made on 15 September). As regards cases in which the Union was the defendant, the WTO rejected the vast majority of the US claims concerning the Community customs regime (Appellate Body report of 13 November) and issued a ruling in a case brought by Argentina, Canada and the United States against the Union over an alleged *de facto* moratorium on the approval of GMOs (panel report of 29 September).

Trade policy instruments

On 30 November, 59 investigations had been opened concerning anti-dumping, anti-subsidy or safeguard measures. In all, 76 investigations were in hand. On the same date, 134 anti-dumping measures and 12 compensatory measures were in force, together with various commitments by 12 countries. In all, nine provisional anti-dumping measures and 13 definitive measures were imposed.

On 6 December the Commission adopted a Green Paper entitled 'Global Europe: Europe's trade defence instruments in a changing global economy' ([1]). This consultation seeks to determine the right balance in defending the interests of the various economic operators in the Community (consumers, distributors and retailers, industry and Member States). In the light of the response, the Commission intends to issue a communication with legislative proposals for adapting the use of trade defence mechanisms to the new requirements of the globalised economy.

Export credits

In August the Commission adopted a proposal for a new decision ([2]) to replace the Council decision of 22 December 2000, in order to incorporate into Community law the latest version of the Organisation for Economic Cooperation and Development (OECD) arrangement on officially supported export credits that came into effect at the beginning of December 2005.

([1]) COM(2006) 763.
([2]) COM(2006) 456.

Dual use

An amendment to Council Regulation (EC) No 1334/2000 (the principal regulation) setting up a Community regime for the control of exports of dual-use items and technology was adopted on 27 February ([1]). This amendment approved the most recent control list for exports of dual-use items and technology. On 18 December the Commission presented a communication on the review of the EC regime of controls on such exports ([2]). It also made proposals to amend/recast the regulation to incorporate the recommendations of the 2004 peer review of Member States' implementation of the regulation ([3]) and to align on the obligations set out by UN Resolution 1540 (2004) on export controls.

Access to external markets

The Commission continued to enhance the content of the free, interactive 'Market access' database ([4]) in order to provide even better information matching users' needs. A public consultation of interested parties was also launched in the autumn of 2006 in accordance with the communication of 4 October on the globalised economy, which indicated that European market access strategy would focus more clearly on the barriers of key importance for exporters ([5]).

Access to Union markets

In 2004 the Commission launched its new free online service, the 'export helpdesk for developing countries' ([6]), so demonstrating its resolve to help developing countries in their efforts to take their place in the world economy. Since then, and especially in 2006, the information provided by the service has been constantly expanded (in particular as regards health and phytosanitary requirements at both European and national levels). A strategy for promoting the export helpdesk was also put in place (presentations and workshops, new brochures in English, French, Portuguese and Spanish) so that all potential users could derive full benefit from this service.

Steel industry

On 13 November the Council adopted negotiating directives for agreements with Russia, Ukraine and Kazakhstan on quantitative limits for certain steel products. Negotiations on these agreements are in hand. On 11 December the Council adopted regulations containing unilateral measures setting quantitative limits on steel imports from these three countries to cover the interim period 1 January 2007 to the entry

---

([1]) Regulation (EC) No 394/2006 (OJ L 74, 13.3.2006).
([2]) COM(2006) 828.
([3]) COM(2006) 829.
([4]) http://ec.europa.eu/trade/index_en.htm.
([5]) COM(2006) 567.
([6]) http://exporthelp.europa.eu/.

into force of the agreements (¹). These measures include provisions to take account of European Union enlargement (transitional arrangements for shipments). On 18 December the Commission adopted a regulation continuing prior Community surveillance of certain iron and steel products until 31 December 2009 (²).

Textiles

On 14 September the Council authorised the Commission to negotiate an agreement with Belarus on trade in textile products. Once agreement had been reached, the Council adopted a decision on 19 December on the signing of the agreement and its provisional application from 1 January 2007.

A similar approach was adopted to the extension of a textiles agreement with Ukraine. On 27 November, once agreement had been reached with Ukraine, the Commission adopted a proposal for a Council decision on the signing of the agreement and its provisional application from 1 January 2007 to ensure legal certainty in this trade until Ukraine has completed the process of accession to the World Trade Organisation (³).

On 4 December the Council adapted the textile quotas for imports from third countries covered by agreements, protocols or other bilateral arrangements to take account of the requirements of Bulgaria and Romania in view of their accession to the Union as from 1 January 2007.

Customs union

On 17 May the Commission submitted to the European Parliament and the Council a proposal for a decision to establish an action programme for customs in the Community, to be known as 'Customs 2013' (⁴). The aim was to help the customs administrations of the participating countries to facilitate legitimate trade and to simplify and speed up customs procedures, whilst protecting the security and safety of citizens and the financial interests of the Community. Features of the programme were to be the development of a pan-European electronic customs environment, implementation of the modernised customs code or exchanges of information and best practice with the customs administrations of non-member countries.

Transatlantic relations

The 'transatlantic economic initiative' dates from the EU–US Summit in 2005. The follow-up in 2006 pursued the following objectives: to promote cooperation on standards and regulation, to facilitate opening and competitiveness of capital markets,

---

(¹) OJ L 360, 19.12.2006.
(²) Regulation (EC) No 1915/2006 (OJ L 365, 21.12.2006).
(³) COM(2006) 730.
(⁴) COM(2006) 201.

to encourage cooperation in efforts to combat money-laundering and the financing of terrorism, to stimulate innovation and technological development, to foster trade, travel and security and to promote energy efficiency, intellectual property rights, investment, competition policy, open public procurement and services.

On 1 June the European Parliament adopted a major resolution on improving relations between the European Union and the United States, replacing the existing transatlantic agenda by a Transatlantic Partnership Agreement (TPA), to enter into force in 2007. Parliament expects the TPA to broaden the current agenda in the political, economic and security fields.

In a resolution of 13 June, Parliament also expressed concern at the position of prisoners in the Guantánamo detention centre.

The EU–US Summit was held in Vienna on 21 June. The Union was represented by Wolfgang Schüssel, the Austrian Chancellor and President of the Council, Ursula Plassnik, the Austrian Foreign Minister, José Manuel Barroso, President of the Commission, Commissioners Ferrero-Waldner and Mandelson, and Xavier Solana, Secretary-General of the Council and High Representative for the CFSP. The United States was represented by the President, George Bush, and his Secretary of State, Condoleezza Rice. Four main topics were discussed: foreign policy, with a particular focus on Iran, the Middle East and promotion of democracy; energy, with a view to strengthening strategic cooperation between the European Union and the United States in this area and promoting good practice on the energy markets; the economy and trade, the main point discussed being progress towards conclusion of the Doha Round negotiations within the World Trade Organisation; and climate change and how best to deal with it. At this summit, a joint EU–US action plan was also launched on the overall strengthening of intellectual property rights by closer customs cooperation, especially through the exchange of information. A further result of the summit was renewal of the programme of cooperation in higher education and in education and vocational training.

Since the Court of Justice of the European Communities had struck down the agreement with the United States on the processing and transfer of PNR data by air carriers, the Commission recommended on 16 June ([1]) that the Council and the Commission jointly inform the United States that the agreement was being terminated. Termination took effect on 30 September. On 27 June the Council adopted negotiating directives with a view to substituting a new agreement on a suitable legal basis. This was concluded on 19 October and is provisionally applicable from that date until 31 July 2007, with provision for extension by mutual written consent of the two parties.

Canada and the European Union sought to deepen economic and trade relations. In 2006 a round of negotiations was held on the bilateral trade and investment

---

([1]) COM(2006) 335.

enhancement agreement. In May the two sides agreed to suspend the negotiations temporarily until the outcome of discussions on the WTO Doha Development Agenda was published (see above).

Relations with the countries of eastern Europe

Political and economic relations with the countries of eastern Europe and of the Balkans, the South Caucasus and central Asia are discussed in Section 1 of this chapter.

Relations with the other industrialised countries ([1])

General approach

On 25 January the Commission put forward a 'Thematic programme on cooperation with industrialised and other high-income countries' under the 2007–13 financial perspective ([2]). These partners, in relations with which the Union is pursuing strategic interests, are the main OECD countries that are not members of the European Union, certain Asian countries and territories and the countries of the Gulf Cooperation Council. Cooperation was to centre on five priorities: public diplomacy; promotion of economic partnerships, business collaboration and science and technology cooperation; people-to-people links, including the development of education cooperation; dialogues; and outreach. In June, in discussions between the European Parliament, the Council and the Commission on the package of instruments for cooperation with non-Union countries, it was agreed that cooperation with industrialised countries would be covered by a special instrument incorporating the content of the communication of 25 January.

G8 Summit

The Heads of State or Government met from 15 to 17 July in Saint Petersburg, together with Mr Barroso, President of the Commission, and Matti Vanhanen, Prime Minister of Finland and President of the Council. At the end of the summit, a declaration was adopted on combating pirating and counterfeiting, which threaten sustainable development, innovation and consumer health. The G8 leaders also adopted a declaration on world energy security, despite differences over nuclear energy and climate change and Russian unwillingness to ratify the Energy Charter.

Japan

The 15th EU–Japan Summit was held in Tokyo on 24 April. In addition to the President of the Commission, José Manuel Barroso, and Benita Ferrero-Waldner, the Union was represented by Wolfgang Schüssel, the Austrian Chancellor and President of the

---

[1] Relations with countries such as China and India are discussed in Section 3 of this chapter.
[2] COM(2006) 25.

Council, and Xavier Solana, Secretary-General of the Council and High Representative for the Common Foreign and Security Policy. The meeting centred on the political and economic aspects of EU–Japan relations, world problems, in particular as regards energy, and various international issues such as regional cooperation in east Asia and relations with China, the Korean peninsula, Russia, Iran and the Middle East.

South Korea

The third summit meeting between the European Union and South Korea was held in Helsinki on 9 September and attended by José Manuel Barroso, President of the Commission, Benita Ferrero-Waldner, Member of the Commission, Matti Vanhanen, Prime Minister of Finland and President of the Council, Xavier Solana, High Representative for the Common Foreign and Security Policy, and Roh Moo-hyun, the President of the Republic of Korea. In the economic field, the discussions covered ways of strengthening the already highly developed trade relations between the two sides. One possibility considered was that of opening negotiations on a bilateral free trade agreement. On the political level, the focus of the talks was on the developing situation on the Korean peninsula, inter-Korean relations and other international issues.

The summit also saw the signature of an agreement between the European Community and South Korea on development of the global navigation satellite system.

Switzerland

On 27 February the Council adopted various decisions with a view to concluding a number of agreements with Switzerland to allow it to take part in the Community programmes MEDIA Plus and MEDIA Training in the audiovisual field, in the European Environment Agency and the European Environment Information and Observation Network, and in statistical cooperation with the European Union. On 27 February the Presidents of the Council and the Commission also signed a memorandum of understanding on a Swiss contribution of CHF 1 billion over five years to the funding of projects to reduce socioeconomic disparities in the 10 new Member States of the Union. In view of this enlargement, changes were also made in sectoral bilateral agreements with Switzerland, for example on free movement of persons and public procurement.

On 15 May the Council approved an agreement on scientific and technological cooperation with Switzerland. On 10 August it approved an agreement on Swiss participation in the European Union's military operation (the EUFOR RD Congo operation) in support of the United Nations Mission in the Democratic Republic of Congo during the elections to be held in that country.

Countries of the European Economic Area

On 27 February the Council approved a draft administrative agreement on relations between the European Defence Agency and the Norwegian Ministry of Defence.

On 21 February (¹) the Council concluded a protocol making applicable to Iceland and Norway the criteria and mechanisms for establishing the State responsible for examining an application for asylum lodged in Iceland or Norway or in another Member State by a third-country national. On 27 June the Council approved the signature of an agreement on a procedure based on the European arrest warrant for transfer between the EU Member States and Iceland and Norway.

General references and other useful links

- Directorate-General for Trade:
  http://ec.europa.eu/trade/index_en.htm

- World Trade Organisation:
  http://www.wto.org/index.htm

- Doha Development Agenda:
  http://ec.europa.eu/trade/issues/newround/doha_da/index_en.htm
  http://www.wto.org/english/tratop_e/dda_e/dda_e.htm

- Directorate-General for External Relations:
  http://ec.europa.eu/comm/external_relations/index.htm

- EU–US relations:
  http://ec.europa.eu/comm/external_relations/us/intro/index.htm

Section 3

Contribution to international solidarity

Protection and promotion of common values beyond the borders of the European Union

On the international scene, the European Union's aims for 2006 in terms of common values were to strengthen the international framework for the protection of human rights, the rule of law and the promotion of democracy and to build confidence in the democratic process worldwide, notably through electoral observation missions.

On 25 January the Commission launched the idea of a 'thematic programme for the promotion of democracy and human rights worldwide under the 2007–13 financial perspective' (²). The programme follows on from the European initiative for democracy and human rights (EIDHR), the legal basis for which expires at the end of 2006. It has two strategic objectives: to enhance respect for human rights and fundamental freedoms where they are most at risk and provide support for victims of repression

---

(¹) Decision 2006/167/EC (OJ L 57, 28.2.2006).
(²) COM(2006) 23.

and abuse; and to strengthen the role of civil society in promoting human rights and democratic reform and support the development of political participation and representation.

More specifically, in 2006 almost EUR 35 million was provided under the EIDHR programme to finance 14 electoral observation missions organised by the Union. These missions were carried out in the following regions and countries:

- Asia/Pacific: Fiji (May); Aceh, Indonesia (December);

- Latin America and the Caribbean: Haiti (February–April); Bolivia (July); Mexico (July); Nicaragua (November); Venezuela (December);

- Middle East: Gaza Strip/West Bank (January); Yemen (September);

- Africa: Uganda (February), Democratic Republic of the Congo (July–October); Zambia (September); Mauritania (November–December): municipal/legislative elections.

A new financing instrument for the promotion of democracy and human rights worldwide, which will provide a legal basis for the above programme, was adopted by the European Parliament and the Council on 20 December (¹). The new instrument, like the EIDHR, has the specific mission of helping meet European Union policy objectives regarding the promotion of human rights and democracy in external relations, in accordance with the Treaty on European Union and as articulated in Commission communications, European Parliament resolutions and Council conclusions over the years. These objectives are of a global nature, reflected in European Union guidelines on human rights and echoed in different ways in the stabilisation and association process, the European neighbourhood policy and the European consensus on development, as well as in new regional initiatives, such as the strategy for Africa, the European Union strategic partnership with Latin America and European Union policy towards Asia. Like its predecessor, the new instrument is designed to complement the various other tools for implementation of Union policies on democracy and human rights, which range from political dialogue and diplomatic initiatives to financial and technical cooperation instruments. It also complements the more crisis-related interventions of the new stability instrument (see below).

On 10 April the Council signed a cooperation and assistance agreement between the European Union and the International Criminal Court (ICC) (²). The Union and the Court will cooperate closely where necessary and consult one another on matters of mutual interest. To this end they have agreed to establish appropriate regular contact in areas including attendance at meetings, exchange of information, testimony of European Union staff and cooperation between the European Union and the ICC prosecutor.

(¹) Regulation (EC) No 1889/2006 (OJ L 386, 29.12.2006).
(²) OJ L 115, 28.4.2006.

Support for the Court is a priority for the Union, which is determined to back the effective functioning of the Court and advance universal support for it by promoting the widest possible participation in the Rome Statute.

The European Parliament also continued its work in the human rights field, denouncing abuses case by case around the world, in Cambodia, Chad, Cuba, East Timor, Egypt, Guantánamo, Kazakhstan, Mauritania, North Korea, Peru, Somalia, Syria, Transnistria and Tunisia. A number of resolutions also identified human rights areas of particular concern, including homophobia, racism, trafficking in human beings, and violence against women and children. Parliament also set up a temporary committee to investigate the alleged use of Member States by the Central Intelligence Agency (CIA) for the transportation and illegal detention of prisoners and, together with the Council, expressed its approval of the creation of the United Nations Human Rights Council.

On 17 October the Council adopted the eighth European Union annual report on human rights.

Development policy

Financial perspective 2007–13

On 25 January, in the context of the broad objectives of the financial perspective for 2007–13, the Commission adopted four communications relating to development and aimed at strengthening the European Union's role in the world.

- The first communication proposes a plan for future thematic programming in the area of human and social development [1], identifying six wide-ranging areas of intervention: good health for all, knowledge and skills, employment and social cohesion, gender equality, children and youth, and culture.

- Focusing on a strategy to improve food security in order to achieve the millennium development goals, the second communication [2] sets out an approach for future intervention programmes complementing national programmes, and proposes three main objectives: supporting the delivery of international public goods contributing directly to food security and to the financing of global programmes; addressing food insecurity in countries or regions either where governments are not in place or not in control of parts of a country or where no country strategic framework is operational; and promoting innovative policies and strategies in the field of food security. The programmes (at continental, regional, national and local level) concentrate particularly on Africa.

[1] COM(2006) 18.
[2] COM(2006) 21.

- The third communication proposes a successor to current NGO cofinancing and decentralised cooperation ([1]). The new programme for 'non-State actors and local authorities in development' supports the right of initiative of all civil society organisations and local authorities of the Union and partner countries. It provides financing for their own initiatives, when geographical programmes are not the appropriate instrument, and complements the support available to them under other sectoral thematic programmes. Three main areas of action are highlighted: interventions in the field which promote an inclusive and empowered society; awareness-raising and education for development in the Union and acceding countries; and operations facilitating exchanges and coordination between stakeholder networks.

- The fourth communication, 'External action: thematic programme for environment and sustainable management of natural resources including energy' ([2]), seeks to address, through a single programme, the environmental dimension of development and other external policies and to help promote the Union's environmental and energy policies abroad.

Financial support for these thematic programmes will be provided through the general-purpose development cooperation and economic cooperation instrument, for which the Commission submitted an amended proposal for a regulation in the wake of the May interinstitutional agreement on the new financial framework for 2007–13 ([3]).

The regulation of the European Parliament and of the Council establishing the instrument was adopted on 18 December ([4]). It sets the instrument's financial allocation for the period 2007–13 at EUR 16.897 billion. Intervention is planned at two mutually reinforcing levels. The first is geographical and covers Asia, central Asia, Latin America, the Middle East and South Africa; the second is thematic and enables regional programmes to be strengthened in response to specific needs, such as migration, education and health. The African, Caribbean and Pacific (ACP) countries are also eligible for the thematic programmes, and a specific sum has been earmarked for ACP countries needing aid to adjust to the effects of the reform of the Union's sugar sector. The development cooperation instrument simplifies matters by replacing a range of instruments with a single financing instrument so that all intervention by the Union can be decided on the basis of the same principles and by a simpler decision-making procedure.

([1]) COM(2006) 19.
([2]) COM(2006) 20.
([3]) See Chapter I, Section 3, of this Report.
([4]) Regulation (EC) No 1905/2006 (OJ L 378, 27.12.2006).

On 15 November the European Parliament and the Council established a more specialised tool, the Instrument for Stability (^{1}), to deal with crisis situations in non-member countries.

Endowed with EUR 2.062 billion for the period 2007–13, this instrument is intended to contribute to stability by providing an effective response to help preserve, establish or re-establish conditions essential to the proper implementation of the Community's development and cooperation policies; it is also intended to help build capacity to address specific global and transregional threats having a destabilising effect and to ensure preparedness to address pre- and post-crisis situations.

Policy coherence for development

Bearing in mind its responsibility as the world's biggest donor, the European Union has focused on making aid more effective.

Hence the Commission proposed an aid effectiveness package on 2 March to improve the efficiency, coherence and impact of European Union development aid and comprising nine time-bound actions to be implemented jointly by the Commission and Member States. The package comprises three communications.

- 'European aid: delivering more, better and faster' (^{2}) sets out a specific action plan with a 2006–07 operational working agenda for each action.

- 'Increasing the impact of EU aid: a common framework for drafting country strategy papers and joint multiannual programming' represents one of the first tangible deliverables of the action plan. It proposes a joint European Union framework for the programming of development aid in order to improve its effectiveness.

- 'Financing for development and aid effectiveness — The challenges of scaling up European Union aid 2006–10' provides for the monitoring of the Union's performance against its commitments in terms of volume of aid and effectiveness of delivery.

In support of the aforementioned communications, the Commission revised and updated the European Union Donor Atlas 2006.

In April the European Parliament and the Council welcomed the progress made in development aid effectiveness.

Efforts for policy coherence continued with the Commission communication 'Governance in the European consensus on development — Towards a harmonised approach within the European Union' (^{3}), adopted on 30 August, which sets out

---

(^{1}) Regulation (EC) No 1717/2006 (OJ L 327, 24.11.2006).
(^{2}) COM(2006) 87.
(^{3}) COM(2006) 421.

the policy principles and plans for practical implementation in accordance with the European consensus on development policy. The communication comprises three parts. The first is centred on policies and takes into account all the dimensions of governance (political, economic, environmental and social) involved in assessing the governance situation and in supporting the democratic governance process in developing countries. The second part introduces two practical applications of this approach: the integration of an incentive approach to governance in the programming of the 10th European Development Fund by means of an 'incentive tranche' of EUR 2.7 billion; and support for the African peer-review mechanism under the New Partnership for Africa's Development (NEPAD) and the African Union. And the third part describes the Community approach as regards democratic governance in other developing countries.

The Commission also marked its support for the Paris Declaration of 2 March 2005 on aid effectiveness, an agreement between nearly 100 countries and 25 development agencies. Accordingly, 2006 saw the Commission delegations in the developing countries take part in the survey organised by the Organisation for Economic Cooperation and Development (OECD) to measure progress according to a dozen indicators introduced for the purpose.

Human and social development

The Commission has brought issues of health, education, gender equality, HIV/AIDS and children into development cooperation, in particular during the programming of the 10th EDF (see below). Since July the Commission has been co-chairing, for one year, the Education for All — Fast Track Initiative (FTI), which places it at the centre of international discussions on improving harmonisation between donors and aid effectiveness in the field of education. In close cooperation with the Member States, the Commission will be pursuing its efforts to strengthen the Union's collective role in the FTI. In 2006 the Commission also strengthened its role in the Global Fund to fight AIDS, Tuberculosis and Malaria (to which it has contributed a total of EUR 522.5 million over five years), with the appointment of a Commission representative as vice-chair of the board until April 2007.

On 21 December the Commission presented a communication entitled 'A European programme for action to tackle the critical shortage of health workers in developing countries (2007–13)' ([1]). It proposes designing a framework for the future monitoring of Community aid to this sector and using funding from the recently established development cooperation instrument (see above).

On 30 November the European Parliament adopted a resolution reiterating its concern at the spread of HIV/AIDS and other epidemics among the poorest peoples in the world.

([1]) COM(2006) 870.

International cooperation against drugs

The year saw the consolidation of the Paris Pact process, initiated in 2003, concerning heroin-trafficking routes, with two major initiatives in which the Commission played an active part: a ministerial conference in Moscow, which Ms Ferrero-Waldner attended for the Commission, and the launch of the second phase of the project supporting the process, for which the Commission will be the main financial backer. One of the major advances has been ensuring that the Paris Pact focuses not just on trafficking but on demand. In the framework of the pact, the Commission also took part in round-table meetings on Afghanistan and neighbouring countries and on the Gulf.

Other significant multilateral initiatives in which the Commission took part include the 49th session of the Commission on Narcotic Drugs (held in Vienna in March), the twice-yearly meetings of the Dublin Group (held in Brussels in February and July) and the conference on shared responsibility (held in London in November).

At bilateral level, the Union held its two high-level annual conferences on drugs with the Latin American and Caribbean countries (held in Vienna in March) and with the Andean region (held in Brussels in September). There were also meetings of the troika with the United States, Russia, the western Balkans and Ukraine.

Though most cooperation projects continue to focus on Afghanistan and the Andean region, and to a lesser extent on eastern Europe, central Asia, the Caucasus and the Balkans, a number of global initiatives (support for NGOs' efforts in the developing countries, help with the analysis of current international efforts, etc.) and interregional initiatives (in Latin America, the Caribbean, the Muslim world, trafficking between Latin America and Africa, etc.) were also launched to plug gaps in national and regional programmes.

Humanitarian aid

Under its humanitarian aid policy, the Commission provides assistance to the victims of natural or man-made disasters in third countries on the sole basis of humanitarian needs. In 2006 the Commission's response to humanitarian crises in over 60 countries was channelled through 90 funding decisions, totalling EUR 671 million.

The Commission's policy is to pay particular attention to 'forgotten' crises, i.e. situations where major humanitarian needs receive little attention from donors (reflected in the level of official aid received) and low media coverage. In 2006 the total support allocated to forgotten crises (the Sahrawi refugees in Algeria, Chechnya and its neighbouring republics, the separatist conflict in Jammu and Kashmir, Nepal and Burma/Myanmar) amounted to EUR 66.4 million, representing 11% of the amounts committed in 2006 for geographical decisions.

While 2005 saw major natural disasters, 2006 saw the severe worsening of several longstanding complex crises, as in Darfur, the Democratic Republic of the Congo, Sri Lanka and the occupied Palestinian territories. The Commission also had to respond rapidly to the sudden, short but highly complex Lebanon crisis in July/August.

In these situations the Commission needed to call on the European Union's emergency reserve as it has more or less systematically in recent years. This proved necessary three times during 2006, for Sudan (Darfur), Lebanon and the occupied Palestinian territories, for a total of EUR 140 million, leading to an increase of 35 % of its initial budget (EUR 495 million).

Main humanitarian aid operations

In 2006 the Commission allocated, through the Humanitarian Aid DG (ECHO), EUR 670.5 million to humanitarian aid operations.

The main operations financed are set out by region in Table 1.

Table 1

Humanitarian aid financing decisions (2006 budget) by geographical area (at 30 November 2006)		*(EUR)*
Africa, Caribbean, Pacific		**322 060 000**
Horn of Africa (^{1})	161 050 000	
African Great Lakes (^{2})	84 050 000	
West Africa (^{3})	56 150 000	
Caribbean, Pacific, Indian Ocean	1 610 000	
Southern Africa (^{4})	19 200 000	
New Independent States (Caucasus, Tajikistan)		**33 000 000**
Middle East		**134 000 000**
North Africa		**10 900 000**
Asia		**86 327 000**
Latin America		**18 600 000**
Thematic funding and grants		**20 500 000**
Technical assistance (experts and imprests)		**19 000 000**
Dipecho — Operational support and disaster prevention		**19 050 000**
Other expenses (audits, evaluations, information and communication, etc.)		**7 116 852**
Total 2006		**670 553 852**

(^{1}) Djibouti, Eritrea, Ethiopia, Kenya, Somalia, Sudan and Uganda.
(^{2}) Burundi, Democratic Republic of the Congo, Rwanda and Tanzania.
(^{3}) Chad, Côte d'Ivoire, Guinea, Guinea-Bissau, Liberia, Mali, Mauritania, Niger and regional epidemic decision.
(^{4}) Angola and Zimbabwe.

Disaster preparedness

The Commission supports disaster preparedness interventions in several regions of the world. In 2006 it supported interventions in the context of the Dipecho programmes in the Caribbean, Latin America, central Asia, south-east Asia and south Asia. Specific interventions, such as the drought preparedness decision for the Horn of Africa, were launched in 2006. The Commission aims at integrating and mainstreaming disaster preparedness in its relief interventions when and where appropriate, and continues to work with other Commission departments and relevant stakeholders for integration of disaster risk reduction in sustainable development interventions.

Evaluation of the Humanitarian Aid DG (ECHO)

Although it has already been thoroughly evaluated twice during its existence, the Humanitarian Aid DG (ECHO) was evaluated for a third time in 2006 (covering 2000–05). The entire life of ECHO has now been evaluated as far back as its foundation in 1992–93.

The evaluation, which acknowledges the prominent role of the Humanitarian Aid DG (ECHO) in the international humanitarian and donor community, focuses on the structure of the DG, its method of operation and its international presence. While there are many points for reflection contained in the report, it is already clear that among the priorities will be the qualitative strengthening of operational and coordination capacity of the humanitarian services of the Commission ([1]).

Regional approaches

Financial framework and management of cooperation with the African, Caribbean and Pacific (ACP) countries and overseas countries and territories (OCT)

At its meeting in Port Moresby (Papua New Guinea) on 1 and 2 June, the ACP–EC Council of Ministers agreed to set the aggregate amount of Community aid to the ACP countries for the period 2008–13 at EUR 21.966 billion from the 10th European Development Fund (EDF). The European Investment Bank is to allocate up to EUR 2 billion from its own resources.

Detailed rules for implementing this new financial framework at Community level were established on 17 July by an internal agreement between the Representatives of the Governments of the Member States meeting within the Council ([2]). The internal agreement allocated EUR 286 million from the 10th EDF to the overseas countries and territories (OCT) associated with the Community. It also allocated EUR 430 million to the Commission for support expenditure incurred in the programming and

---

[1] The report can be consulted at http://ec.europa.eu/echo/evaluation/partners_en.htm#echo.
[2] OJ L 247, 9.9.2006.

implementation of the EDF. The total resources allocated to the 10th EDF thus come to EUR 22.682 billion, an increase of more than 30 % over the ninth EDF ([1]).

EDF operations undertaken for the benefit of the ACP States and OCT in 2006 came to a total of EUR 3.4 billion. The breakdown of this amount is given in Table 2.

Table 2

EDF operations for the benefit of the ACP States and OCT in 2006	(EUR)
Operation regions	**Amount decided for 2006**
Africa	2 019 297 729
Caribbean	224 019 564
Pacific	10 251 728
OCT	77 800 813
Non-geographical programmes	1 076 490 081
Total 2006	**3 407 859 915**

Partnership with the ACP countries

In the framework of economic and trade cooperation, the Commission presented a number of regional partnership strategies concerning ACP countries. These strategies will bring the Union's relationship with the regions into line with the development policy statement adopted in December 2005 and the revised Cotonou Agreement of 2005. They will also help fulfil its commitments on aid effectiveness.

Trade negotiations between the Union and the six regions of the ACP countries for the economic partnership agreements provided for in the Cotonou Agreement continued in 2006. Discussions focused on the links between trade, development and regional integration.

Africa

On 13 July, in the framework of the European Union's strategy for Africa adopted in 2005, the Commission presented a communication entitled 'Interconnecting Africa: the EU–Africa partnership on infrastructure'. The aim of the partnership is to substantially increase European Union investment in African infrastructure and in the delivery of transport, energy, water, and information and communication technology services.

On 20 October the Commission adopted a communication specifically concerning the Horn of Africa, which, as part of the Union's strategy for Africa, proposes a regional political partnership for peace, security and development in the Horn ([2]). The main

---

([1]) Decision No 1/2006 of the ACP–EC Council of Ministers (OJ L 247, 9.9.2006).
([2]) COM(2006) 601.

objectives of this strategy are to address the root causes of regional instability, introduce confidence-building measures and promote conflict prevention. It provides a political framework for concrete regional initiatives and programmes.

The Secretary-General of the Council and High Representative for the Common Foreign and Security Policy and the Commission jointly prepared a European Union concept for strengthening African capabilities for the prevention, management and resolution of conflicts. This initiative was endorsed by the Council in its conclusions of 13 November.

On 22 and 23 November Mr Frattini and Mr Michel, respectively Vice-President and Member of the Commission, attended the first EU–Africa ministerial conference on migration and development, which was held in Tripoli (Libya).

The first edition of the European Development Days (EDD), organised by the Commission in Brussels from 13 to 17 November, addressed the theme of 'Africa on the move'. Events included a political forum, a business forum and art exhibitions.

At its December summit, the European Council stressed its commitment to working towards a joint EU–Africa strategy to be adopted at the second Europe–Africa Summit in 2007. The European Council also welcomed the successful conduct of the first democratic elections in the Democratic Republic of the Congo in more than 40 years. It likewise expressed support for the comprehensive peace agreement in Sudan and for the negotiating process initiated by the League of Arab States in Somalia in June. It also expressed its concern at the continuing obstacles to the peace process in Côte d'Ivoire.

At bilateral level, two communications adopted by the Commission on 28 June focused on the European Union's relations with South Africa.

- The first, 'Towards an EU–South Africa strategic partnership' ([1]), proposes a comprehensive, coherent and coordinated long-term framework for the Union's relations with South Africa, taking account of its traumatic past, its role as an anchor country in the region and its unique position on the continent and on the global scene, while building on the millennium development goals package, the European consensus on development and the European Union strategy for Africa. The partnership will be based on: bringing Member States, the Community and South Africa together in a single and coherent framework with clearly and jointly defined objectives, covering all areas of cooperation and associating all stakeholders; moving from political dialogue to strategic political cooperation and shared objectives on regional, African and international issues; enhancing existing economic and trade cooperation; and extending cooperation to the social, cultural and environmental fields.

([1]) COM(2006) 347.

- The second ([1]) identifies a number of issues to be examined with a view to amending the agreement on trade, development and cooperation with South Africa. The Council adopted the relevant negotiating directives on 28 November.

Relations with the Democratic Republic of the Congo were particularly important in 2006 as the country made its way towards greater stability and democracy. These developments were borne out by the presidential and legislative elections in July and October. The Union also paid very close attention to developments in the political and humanitarian situation in Sudan's Darfur region.

Caribbean

On 2 March the Commission adopted a communication on an EU–Caribbean partnership for growth, stability and development ([2]) proposing a long-term strategy for the Caribbean and examining how existing European Union development cooperation policy and instruments can be used more effectively in order to ensure that the Caribbean does not become a pole of insecurity but achieves its long-term development goals in a self-sustaining manner. The proposal builds on and integrates previous Commission papers, in particular the millennium development goals package and the European consensus. The objectives will be pursued under a new EU–Caribbean partnership with three interrelated facets: shaping political partnership, addressing economic opportunities and vulnerabilities, and promoting social cohesion and the fight against poverty.

On 10 April the Council adopted conclusions listing the principles that should form the basis of the partnership.

Pacific

On 29 May the Commission adopted a communication entitled 'EU relations with the Pacific Islands — A strategy for a strengthened partnership' ([3]), which the Council endorsed in its conclusions of 17 July. This is the first formal strategy in the 30 years of EU–Pacific relations. It aims to strengthen political dialogue, provide greater focus for development cooperation and improve the effectiveness of aid delivery. The proposed strategy, which reflects the growing environmental, political and economic importance of the Pacific region, is constructed around three main proposals: building stronger political relations on interests of common concern, such as global political security, trade, economic and social development and the environment; focusing development cooperation on areas where the Pacific has important needs and where the European Union has a comparative advantage and a good track record, such as the sustainable management of natural resources, regional cooperation and good

---

[1] COM(2006) 348.
[2] COM(2006) 86.
[3] COM(2006) 248.

governance; increasing the efficiency of aid delivery, notably by making more use of direct budgetary aid and working more closely with other partners, in particular Australia and New Zealand. The strategy will bring the Union's relationship with the Pacific into line with the development policy statement adopted by the institutions in December 2005 and with the revised Cotonou Agreement of 2005. It will also help fulfil the Union's commitments on aid effectiveness in this region.

Cooperation with Asia

The importance of economic cooperation with Asia was highlighted by the Council in the conclusions adopted on 20 March.

The Council particularly stressed the importance it attaches to proper monitoring and evaluation arrangements and local coordination, all of which allow the effectiveness of European Union assistance to be measured and enhanced. It expressed support for the Commission in its efforts further to improve and simplify procedures for its external action programmes.

The 10th anniversary of the ASEM process of Asia–Europe meetings was celebrated in 2006 at the sixth Asia–Europe Summit, held in September in Helsinki and attended by the Heads of State or Government of the 25 European Union Member States and of 13 Asian countries, and by Mr Barroso and Ms Ferrero-Waldner for the Commission. The main issues addressed were promoting multilateralism, strengthening economic cooperation and controlling climate change. North Korea and democracy in Myanmar (Burma) were also discussed. The participants adopted the Helsinki declaration on the future of their informal dialogue.

At bilateral level, Helsinki was also the setting for a summit with China on 9 September. Items on the agenda included the strengthening of cooperation, environmental and climate change issues, readmission and human rights, and economic and trade-related aspects of energy security. The day before the summit the European Parliament adopted a resolution expressing its concerns regarding the human rights situation in China. The political summit was followed by a business summit focusing on cooperation in innovation-related matters.

On 24 October the Commission adopted a communication entitled 'EU–China: closer partners, growing responsibilities' ([1]). The new strategy seeks to respond to China's emergence as a global economic and political power. The communication sets out a comprehensive approach, identifying as priorities: support for China's transition towards a more open and plural society; sustainable development, in particular in relation to energy, climate change and international develpment; trade and economic relations; strengthening bilateral cooperation, including on science and technology,

---

([1]) COM(2006) 631.

and migration; and the promotion of international security, both in east Asia and beyond, and more broadly on non-proliferation issues.

The communication was accompanied by a working paper advocating a new strategy for building the Union's trade and investment relationship with China ([1]).

To enhance Sino-European cooperation in science and technology, Mr Potočnik, Member of the Commission, and Mr Wu Zhongze, Chinese Deputy Science and Technology Minister, launched 'China–EU Science and Technology Year, 2007' in Brussels on 11 October.

European Union economic and trade relations with India were the subject of an important Parliament resolution adopted on 28 September with a view to pursuing implementation of the joint action plan adopted in 2005 for the strategic partnership between the European Union and India, itself adopted in 2004.

The seventh EU–India Summit was held in Helsinki on 13 October. In the framework of their strategic partnership and following the report of the high-level group on trade advocating closer trade relations, the partners discussed a bilateral agreement on free trade and investment. Politically, they reaffirmed their support for multilateralism and fighting terrorism. In addition to action against global warming, they discussed the importance of the international thermonuclear experimental reactor, in which India became a partner on 21 November, and the international satellite navigation system.

The Union showed its support for the millennium goals by continued support for India's health and education sectors.

The sensitive situations in Aceh (Indonesia) and Myanmar (Burma) were the subject of specific measures by the Union in the framework of implementation of the common foreign and security policy ([2]).

Cooperation with Latin America

New impetus was given in 2006 to relations between the European Union and Latin America, not only by the conclusion of trade and association agreements but also by the development of forums for specialised dialogue.

On 27 February the Council welcomed the Commission communication 'A stronger partnership between the European Union and Latin America' ([3]) and underlined that the Union's aim was to continue cooperating closely with Latin America in order to promote joint values and interests and work together for peace and security,

---

([1]) COM(2006) 632.
([2]) See Section 4 of this chapter.
([3]) COM(2005) 636.

the protection and promotion of human rights, and the strengthening of citizen participation and democracy. The main aims of the strategic partnership with the region are to ensure social cohesion and sustainable development, including environmental protection and the strengthening of international environmental governance, and to encourage regional integration and stability.

This year was also marked by three summits in Vienna.

- On 12 May the 25 Heads of State or Government of the European Union and their 33 counterparts from Latin America and the Caribbean held their fourth summit. The overall theme was 'strengthening the bi-regional strategic association' and the agenda included discussions on such key policy issues as the promotion of social cohesion, regional integration and multilateralism. Bilateral and regional meetings completed the in-depth dialogue.

- On 13 May the EU–Mexico Summit afforded an opportunity to take stock of the progress made since the Guadalajara Summit in 2004 and to decide on ways of continuing to strengthen the association between the Union, Latin America and the Caribbean. The summit's main achievements were the opening of negotiations with a view to an association agreement with Central America and the decision to launch in 2006 a process leading to negotiations for an association agreement with the Andean Community.

- Also on 13 May, at the summit between the European Union and Chile, the two parties expressed the wish to strengthen relations and agreed to do this via the association agreement and to ask their respective authorities to look at ways of strengthening the association process in all the sectors covered by the bilateral relationship.

On 5 July the European Economic and Social Committee delivered an opinion on relations between the European Union and the Andean Community ([1]) in which it expressed the wish that the European Commission and the Secretariat-General of the Andean Community, with the cooperation of the Committee and the Andean advisory councils, promote a regular civil society forum where social organisations and associations from both regions could expound their views on EU–Andean Community relations.

On an operational level, most of the projects and programmes approved in 2006 for cooperation with Latin America focused on strengthening social cohesion, regional integration, institution building and economic cooperation. Financial commitments for these projects and programmes totalled EUR 330 million.

General references and other useful links

- Directorate-General for External Relations:
  http://ec.europa.eu/comm/external_relations/index.htm

([1]) OJ C 309, 16.12.2006.

- EuropeAid Co-operation Office:
  http://ec.europa.eu/europeaid/index_en.htm

- Human rights:
  http://ec.europa.eu/comm/external_relations/human_rights/intro/index.htm

- Development cooperation and Directorate-General for Development:
  http://ec.europa.eu/development/index_en.htm

- Millennium development goals (MDGs):
  http://www.un.org/millenniumgoals/

- Directorate-General for Humanitarian Aid (ECHO):
  http://ec.europa.eu/echo/index_en.htm

- Relations with ACP countries:
  http://www.acpsec.org/

- Cotonou Partnership Agreement:
  http://ec.europa.eu/development/body/cotonou/index_en.htm

- Relations with Mediterranean countries:
  http://ec.europa.eu/comm/external_relations/med_mideast/intro/index.htm

- Relations with Asia:
  http://ec.europa.eu/comm/external_relations/asia/index.htm
  http://ec.europa.eu/europeaid/projects/asia/index_en.htm

- Relations with Latin America:
  http://ec.europa.eu/comm/external_relations/la/index.htm
  http://ec.europa.eu/europeaid/projects/amlat/index_fr.htm

Section 4

Contribution to security in the world

Common foreign and security policy (CFSP)

Arms trade

On 27 February the Council updated ([1]) the common military list of the European Union covered by the Union's code of conduct on arms exports.

In a resolution adopted on 15 June with a view to the 2006 Review Conference on the United Nations Programme of Action to Prevent, Combat and Eradicate the Illicit Trade in Small Arms and Light Weapons, and towards the establishment of an international arms trade treaty, the European Parliament called on the States party to the Conference to agree a set of global principles on arms transfers.

([1]) OJ C 66, 17.3.2006.

The Council conclusions of 11 December welcomed the formal start of the process for drawing up an international arms trade treaty following action taken by the UN General Assembly.

Implementation of the CFSP

On 10 April the Council adopted guidelines on the appointment, mandate and financing of European Union special representatives (EUSRs). It agreed to extend the standard duration of their mandates to one year and to keep the necessary flexibility to respond to specific needs relating to a specific mandate. Each representative would be asked to submit a regular progress report and a full report on the implementation of their mandate.

On 16 November the Council underlined the importance of promoting gender equality in the context of the CFSP and the European Security and Defence Policy (ESDP) at all levels. It invited the Member States to nominate more female candidates for upcoming appointments to special representative and head of mission posts.

The joint actions and common positions adopted by the Council in implementing the CSFP during the year concerned:

- in the Balkans:
  - repeal of Common Position 96/184/CFSP concerning arms exports to the former Yugoslavia [1],
  - renewal of measures in support of effective implementation of the mandate of the International Criminal Tribunal for the former Yugoslavia [2],
  - implementation of Common Position 2004/694/CFSP on further measures in support of the effective implementation of the mandate of the International Criminal Tribunal for the former Yugoslavia [3],
  - extension of the validity of Common Position 2004/694/CFSP on further measures in support of the effective implementation of the mandate of the International Criminal Tribunal for the former Yugoslavia [4],
  - appointment of the European Union special representative in Bosnia and Herzegovina [5],
  - amendment of the mandate of the European Union special representative in Bosnia and Herzegovina [6],

---

[1] Common Position 2006/29/CFSP (OJ L 19, 24.1.2006).
[2] Common Position 2006/204/CFSP (OJ L 72, 11.3.2006).
[3] Decisions 2006/205/CFSP (OJ L 72, 11.3.2006) and 2006/484/CFSP (OJ L 189, 12.7.2006).
[4] Common Position 2006/671/CFSP (OJ L 275, 6.10.2006).
[5] Joint Action 2006/49/CFSP (OJ L 26, 31.1.2006).
[6] Joint Action 2006/523/CFSP (OJ L 205, 27.7.2006).

— appointment of a European Union force commander for the European Union military operation in Bosnia and Herzegovina ([1]),

— conclusion of the Agreement between the European Union and the former Yugoslav Republic of Macedonia on the participation of the former Yugoslav Republic of Macedonia in the European Union military crisis management operation in Bosnia and Herzegovina (Operation Althea) ([2]),

— implementation of Joint Action 2005/824/CFSP on the European Union Police Mission in Bosnia and Herzegovina ([3]),

— extension of the mandate of the head of mission/police commissioner of the European Union Police Mission in Bosnia and Herzegovina ([4]),

— extension and amendment of Common Position 2004/133/CFSP on restrictive measures against extremists in the former Yugoslav Republic of Macedonia ([5]),

— extension and amendment of the mandate of the European Union special representative in the former Yugoslav Republic of Macedonia ([6]),

— establishment of a European Union planning team regarding a possible European Union crisis management operation in the field of rule of law and possible other areas in Kosovo ([7]),

— establishment of a European Union team to contribute to the preparations of the establishment of a possible international civilian mission in Kosovo, including a European Union special representative component ([8]),

— extension of the mandate of the head of mission of the European Union Monitoring Mission ([9]),

— extension and amendment of the mandate of the European Union Monitoring Mission ([10]),

— amendment and extension of Joint Action 2006/304/CFSP on the establishment of a European Union Planning Team (Kosovo), referred to above ([11]),

— extension of the mandate of the head of the European Union planning team (Kosovo) ([12]);

• in the South Caucasus:

— appointment of the European Union special representative for the South Caucasus ([13]),

---

([1]) Decision 2006/497/CFSP (OJ L 196, 18.7.2006).
([2]) Decision 2006/477/CFSP (OJ L 188, 11.7.2006).
([3]) Decision 2006/865/CFSP (OJ L 335, 1.12.2006).
([4]) Decision 2006/979/CFSP (OJ L 365, 21.12.2006).
([5]) Common Position 2006/50/CFSP (OJ L 26, 31.1.2006).
([6]) Joint Action 2006/123/CFSP (OJ L 49, 21.2.2006).
([7]) Joint Action 2006/304/CFSP (OJ L 112, 26.4.2006).
([8]) Joint Action 2006/623/CFSP (OJ L 253, 16.9.2006).
([9]) Decision 2006/866/CFSP (OJ L 335, 1.12.2006).
([10]) Joint Action 2006/867/CFSP (OJ L 335, 1.12.2006).
([11]) Joint Action 2006/918/CFSP (OJ L 349, 12.12.2006).
([12]) Decision 2006/980/CFSP (OJ L 365, 21.12.2006).
([13]) Joint Action 2006/121/CFSP (OJ L 49, 21.2.2006).

- conclusion of the Agreement between the European Union and the Government of Georgia on the status in Georgia of the European Union special representative for the South Caucasus and his/her support team (¹),
- further contribution of the European Union to the conflict settlement process in Georgia/South Ossetia (²),

- in central Asia:

  - extension of the mandate of the European Union special representative for central Asia and amendment of Joint Action 2005/588/CFSP (³),
  - appointment of a new European Union special representative for central Asia (⁴),
  - renewal of certain restrictive measures against Uzbekistan (⁵);

- in Asia:

  - extension of the mandate of the special representative of the European Union for Afghanistan (⁶),
  - extension of the Agreement between the European Union and the Government of Indonesia on the tasks, status, privileges and immunities of the European Union Monitoring Mission in Aceh (Indonesia) and its personnel (⁷),
  - amendment and extension on several occasions of Joint Action 2005/643/CFSP on the European Union Monitoring Mission in Aceh (Indonesia) (⁸),
  - renewal of restrictive measures against Myanmar (Burma) (⁹),
  - participation by the European Union in the Korean Peninsula Energy Development Organisation (¹⁰),
  - adoption of restrictive measures against the Democratic People's Republic of Korea (¹¹);

- in Africa:

  - extension of the mandate of the European Union special representative for the African Great Lakes Region (¹²),

---

(¹) Decision 2006/366/CFSP (OJ L 135, 23.5.2006).
(²) Joint Action 2006/439/CFSP (OJ L 174, 28.6.2006).
(³) Joint Action 2006/118/CFSP (OJ L 49, 21.2.2006).
(⁴) Decision 2006/670/CFSP (OJ L 275, 6.10.2006).
(⁵) Common Position 2006/787/CFSP (OJ L 318, 17.11.2006).
(⁶) Joint Action 2006/124/CFSP (OJ L 49, 21.2.2006).
(⁷) Decisions 2006/201/CFSP (OJ L 71, 10.3.2006), 2006/448/CFSP (OJ L 176, 30.6.2006) and 2006/666/CFSP (OJ L 273, 4.10.2006)
(⁸) Joint Actions 2006/202/CFSP (OJ L 71, 10.3.2006), 2006/407/CFSP (OJ L 158, 10.6.2006) and 2006/607/CFSP (OJ L 246, 8.9.2006).
(⁹) Common Position 2006/318/CFSP (OJ L 116, 29.4.2006).
(¹⁰) Common Position 2006/244/CFSP (OJ L 88, 25.3.2006).
(¹¹) Common Position 2006/795/CFSP (OJ L 322, 22.11.2006).
(¹²) Joint Action 2006/122/CFSP (OJ L 49, 21.2.2006).

— amendment and extension of Joint Action 2004/847/CFSP on a European Union Police Mission in Kinshasa (Democratic Republic of the Congo) regarding the Integrated Police Unit ([1]),

— amendment and extension of Joint Action 2005/355/CFSP on the European Union mission to provide advice and assistance for security sector reform in the Democratic Republic of the Congo ([2]),

— the European Union military operation in support of the United Nations Organisation Mission in the Democratic Republic of the Congo during the election process ([3]),

— launching of the European Union military operation in support of the United Nations Organisation Mission in the Democratic Republic of the Congo during the election process (Operation EUFOR RD Congo) ([4]),

— setting up of the Committee of Contributors for the European Union military operation in support of the United Nations Organisation Mission in the Democratic Republic of the Congo during the election process ([5]),

— acceptance of third States' contributions to the European Union military operation in support of the United Nations Organisation Mission in the Democratic Republic of the Congo during the election process ([6]),

— amendment of restrictive measures against the Democratic Republic of the Congo ([7]),

— contribution by the Swiss Confederation to the European Union military operation in support of the United Nations Organisation Mission in the Democratic Republic of the Congo during the election process ([8]),

— participation of the Swiss Confederation in the European Union military operation in support of the United Nations Organisation Mission in the Democratic Republic of the Congo during the election process ([9]),

— amendment of Joint Action 2004/847/CFSP on the European Union Police Mission in the Democratic Republic of the Congo ([10]),

— implementation of Common Position 2005/411/CFSP concerning restrictive measures against Sudan ([11]),

([1]) Joint Action 2006/300/CFSP (OJ L 111, 25.4.2006).
([2]) Joint Action 2006/303/CFSP (OJ L 112, 26.4.2006).
([3]) Joint Action 2006/319/CFSP (OJ L 116, 29.4.2006).
([4]) Decision 2006/412/CFSP (OJ L 163, 15.6.2006).
([5]) 2006/492/CFSP — Political and Security Committee Decision MONUC SPT/2/2006 (OJ L 194, 14.7.2006).
([6]) 2006/499/CFSP — Political and Security Committee Decision MONUC SPT/1/2006 (OJ L 197, 19.7.2006).
([7]) Common Position 2006/624/CFSP (OJ L 253, 16.9.2006).
([8]) Decision 2006/675/CFSP (OJ L 276, 7.10.2006).
([9]) Decision 2006/676/CFSP (OJ L 276, 7.10.2006).
([10]) Joint Actions 2006/868/CFSP (OJ L 335, 1.12.2006) and 2006/913/CFSP (OJ L 346, 9.12.2006).
([11]) Decision 2006/386/CFSP (OJ L 148, 2.6.2006).

— renewal and revision of the mandate of the European Union special representative for Sudan ([1]),

— implementation of Joint Action 2005/557/CFSP on the European Union civilian–military supporting action to the African Union mission in the Darfur region of Sudan ([2]),

— appointment of a military adviser to the European Union special representative for Sudan ([3]),

— appointment of a head of the European Union police team/police adviser to the European Union special representative for Sudan ([4]),

— renewal of restrictive measures against Côte d'Ivoire ([5]),

— implementation of Common Position 2004/852/CFSP concerning restrictive measures against Côte d'Ivoire ([6]),

— renewal of the restrictive measures imposed against Liberia ([7]),

— amendment and extension of certain restrictions against Liberia ([8]),

— renewal of restrictive measures against Zimbabwe ([9]),

— conclusion of the Agreement between the European Union and the Gabonese Republic on the status of the European Union-led forces in the Gabonese Republic ([10]);

• in Latin America and the Caribbean:

— implementation of Joint Action 2002/589/CFSP with a view to a European Union contribution to combating the destabilising accumulation and spread of small arms and light weapons in Latin America and the Caribbean ([11]);

• in the Middle East:

— extension of the mandate of the European Union special representative for the Middle East peace process ([12]),

— amendment and extension of Joint Action 2005/190/CFSP on the European Union Integrated Rule of Law Mission for Iraq, EUJUST Lex ([13]),

---

([1]) Joint Action 2006/468/CFSP (OJ L 184, 6.7.2006).
([2]) Decisions 2006/486/CFSP (OJ L 192, 13.7.2006) and 2006/725/CFSP (OJ L 296, 26.10.2006).
([3]) 2006/634/CFSP — Political and Security Committee Decision Darfur/3/2006 (OJ L 258, 21.9.2006).
([4]) 2006/756/CFSP — Political and Security Committee Decision Darfur/4/2006 (OJ L 309, 9.11.2006).
([5]) Common Position 2006/30/CFSP (OJ L 19, 24.1.2006).
([6]) Decisions 2006/172/CFSP (OJ L 61, 2.3.2006) and 2006/483/CFSP (OJ L 189, 12.7.2006).
([7]) Common Position 2006/31/CFSP (OJ L 19, 24.1.2006).
([8]) Common Position 2006/518/CFSP (OJ L 201, 25.7.2006).
([9]) Common Position 2006/51/CFSP (OJ L 26, 31.1.2006).
([10]) Decision 2006/475/CFSP (OJ L 187, 8.7.2006).
([11]) Decision 2006/1000/CFSP (OJ L 367, 22.12.2006).
([12]) Joint Action 2006/119/CFSP (OJ L 49, 21.2.2006).
([13]) Joint Actions 2006/413/CFSP (OJ L 163, 15.6.2006) and 2006/708/CFSP (OJ L 291, 21.10.2006).

— prohibition on the sale or supply of arms and related material and on the provision of related services to entities or individuals in Lebanon in accordance with UNSC Resolution 1701 (2006) (¹),

— temporary reception by Member States of the European Union of certain Palestinians (²),

— amendment and extension of Joint Action 2005/889/CFSP on establishing a European Union border assistance mission for the Rafah crossing point (³),

— implementation of Joint Action 2005/797/CFSP on the European Union Police Mission for the Palestinian territories (⁴);

- in eastern Europe:

— restrictive measures against certain officials of Belarus and repealing Common Position 2004/661/CFSP (⁵),

— implementation of Common Position 2006/276/CFSP concerning restrictive measures against certain officials of Belarus (⁶),

— renewal of restrictive measures against the leadership of the Transnistrian region of the Republic of Moldova (⁷),

— implementation of Common Position 2004/179/CFSP concerning restrictive measures against the leadership of the Transnistrian region of the Republic of Moldova (⁸),

— extension of the mandate of the European Union special representative for Moldova (⁹);

- other subjects and regions:

— updating of Common Position 2001/931/CFSP on the application of specific measures to combat terrorism (¹⁰),

— conclusion of the Agreement between the European Union and the Republic of Turkey establishing a framework for the participation of the Republic of Turkey in European Union crisis management operations (¹¹),

— conclusion of the Agreement between the European Union and the Republic of Croatia on security procedures for the exchange of classified information (¹²),

---

(¹) Common Position 2006/625/CFSP (OJ L 253, 16.9.2006).
(²) Common Position 2006/755/CFSP (OJ L 308, 8.11.2006).
(³) Joint Action 2006/773/CFSP (OJ L 313, 14.11.2006).
(⁴) Decision 2006/807/CFSP (OJ L 329, 25.11.2006).
(⁵) Common Position 2006/276/CFSP (OJ L 101, 11.4.2006).
(⁶) Common Position 2006/362/CFSP (OJ L 134, 20.5.2006) and Decision 2006/718/CFSP (OJ L 294, 25.10.2006).
(⁷) Common Position 2006/95/CFSP (OJ L 44, 15.2.2006).
(⁸) Decision 2006/96/CFSP (OJ L 44, 15.2.2006).
(⁹) Joint Action 2006/120/CFSP (OJ L 49, 21.2.2006).
(¹⁰) Common Positions 2006/231/CFSP (OJ L 82, 21.3.2006), 2006/380/CFSP (OJ L 144, 31.5.2006) and 2006/1011/CFSP (OJ L 379, 28.12.2006).
(¹¹) Decision 2006/482/CFSP (OJ L 189, 12.7.2006).
(¹²) Decision 2006/317/CFSP (OJ L 116, 29.4.2006).

— signing of an Agreement between the European Union and the United States of America on the processing and transfer of passenger name record data by air carriers to the United States Department of Homeland Security ([1]),

— adaptation of Decision 96/409/CFSP on the establishment of an emergency travel document, in order to take account of the accession of Bulgaria and Romania to the European Union ([2]).

European security strategy and European security and defence policy

General approach

On 11 December, following a conference held in Brussels on 21 November, the Council adopted an action plan on civilian aspects of the ESDP with a view to the improvement of civilian capabilities.

On 16 November the European Parliament commented on the implementation of the European security strategy in the context of the ESDP, noting that the strategy adopted in 2003 was an excellent analysis of the threats to the modern world. It supported the idea that the best means of attaining the objectives of the strategy was 'effective multilateralism', based on international institutions and international law. Given the developments in the geopolitical situation, Parliament considered that the strategy should be revised to include other challenges, such as growing energy competition, natural disasters and the security of the Union's external borders. It also put forward a series of proposals on other aspects of the strategy (the concentration of efforts on the geographical neighbourhood, strategic transport, the creation of a European equipment market, a joint intelligence system, etc.).

Security sector reform

On 24 May the Commission adopted a communication entitled 'A concept for European Community support for security sector reform' ([3]). The communication notes that the Community is engaged in support for reform in this sector in over 70 countries through both geographical and thematic programmes. The need for a more coherent and common European Union concept on reform across the three pillars was raised by Member States and the Commission in order to contribute to more effective European Union external action in this area. Based on current support in different countries and regional settings, and on the relevant policy frameworks under which the European Community supports security sector reform, the Commission notes the principles for the Community's engagement in this reform and puts forward Community

---

[1] Decision 2006/729/CFSP/JHA (OJ L 298, 27.10.2006).
[2] Decision 2006/881/CFSP (OJ L 363, 20.12.2006).
[3] COM(2006) 253.

perspectives on how to strengthen overall Union support for it based on the added value it provides. In order to strengthen the Community's contribution to overall Union support, the Commission recommends: strengthening policy and programming dialogue; integrating security sector reform in country and regional strategy papers, action plans and programming tools; ensuring coordinated planning; strengthening overall implementation of European Union support; developing tools for planning and implementation; expanding the expertise and pool of experts for field missions and programmes; developing sector-specific training for the mainstreaming of security sector reform; and strengthening cooperation with international partners.

The Commission communication was approved by the Council on 12 June. The Council considers that it complements the European Union's concept for ESDP support to security sector reform adopted in November 2005 and that the two concepts constitute a policy framework. It also believes that this reform should be based on principles that draw on the OECD Development Assistance Committee's definition of reform. The Council and the Commission later approved a joint concept paper.

Weapons of mass destruction

On 27 February the Council adopted a joint action in support of the Biological and Toxin Weapons Convention under the European Union's strategy against the proliferation of weapons of mass destruction ([1]). This will give immediate and practical application to some elements of the European strategy adopted in December 2003. On the same day the Council also adopted a European Union action plan on biological and toxin weapons to underpin the joint action by introducing measures to be taken by Member States in the event of violation of the Biological and Toxin Weapons Convention within the European Union. The European Parliament adopted a resolution on 16 November calling for a stronger commitment on the part of the Union in favour of strengthening the convention.

On 20 March the Council set out the European Union's position on the updating and improvement of the system of non-proliferation of weapons of mass destruction ([2]), in the light of the forthcoming conference in Geneva from 20 November to 8 December and the meeting of the preparatory committee from 26 to 28 April.

It also set out a clear position on nuclear testing ([3]). The Council confirmed its support for the work of the Preparatory Commission of the Comprehensive Nuclear-Test-Ban Treaty Organisation (CTBTO). The aims are to improve operational performance of the verification system set up by the Preparatory Commission, to improve the capacity of CTBT signatory States to fulfil their verification responsibilities and to enable them to

---

([1]) Joint Action 2006/184/CFSP (OJ L 65, 7.3.2006).
([2]) Common Position 2006/242/CFSP (OJ L 88, 25.3.2006).
([3]) Joint Action 2006/243/CFSP (OJ L 88, 25.3.2006).

benefit fully from their participation in the treaty regime and from potential civil and scientific applications.

In support of implementation of the United Nations Security Council Resolution 1540 (2004) ([1]), the Council decided to implement International Atomic Energy Agency projects under the European Union strategy against the proliferation of weapons of mass destruction ([2]).

On 11 December the Council adopted a concept paper on the monitoring and enhancement of implementation of the European Union's strategy against the proliferation of weapons of mass destruction with the aim of establishing a cooperative working method within the Union.

European Defence Agency (EDA)

In the second year since its establishment in 2004, the Agency started to deliver concrete results. In relation to the European defence equipment market, a voluntary, intergovernmental regime on defence procurement entered into force on 1 July to which 22 Member States subscribed; an electronic bulletin board for the publication of contracting opportunities was launched; a code of best practice in the supply chain was agreed as were mutual agreements on security of information and security of supply. An initial long-term vision for European defence capability and capacity needs was drawn up and endorsed by the EDA Steering Board on 3 October as a reasonable foundation for the Agency's medium-to-long term agendas; as a follow-up, an ESDP capability development plan would be prepared. In line with the Hampton Court agenda of October 2005 to 'spend more, spend better, and spend more together' on defence research and technology, on 13 November the EDA Steering Board launched the first 'joint investment programme' with 19 contributors, including 18 participating Member States plus Norway, and a budget of over EUR 54 million in the area of force protection. The Commission is represented in the EDA structures and close cooperation between Commission departments and the Agency has been developed aiming at complementarity and synergies (e.g. software defined radio) while keeping with the respective institutional responsibilities.

In its six-monthly review of developments in the ESDP, the Council noted with satisfaction that Member States had fulfilled the required commitments concerning battlegroups, for which the European Union will reach full operational capability by 1 January 2007. In conclusions adopted on 13 November, it noted the report submitted by the Head of the European Defence Agency on its activities and welcomed the results achieved.

([1]) Joint Action 2006/419/CFSP (OJ L 165, 17.6.2006).
([2]) Joint Action 2006/418/CFSP (OJ L 165, 17.6.2006).

Middle East peace process

Palestinian territories

The prospect of a solution to the Israeli–Palestinian crisis and a sustainable peace in the region appeared positive following the Israeli disengagement from Gaza in 2005. But the situation in the region deteriorated during 2006 and the prospect of a lasting peace seems once again to be distant.

Elections to the Palestinian Legislative Council held on 25 January were conducted in a free and fair manner. The Council urged Hamas, the winners of the election, and all other factions to commit themselves to three principles: to renounce violence, to recognise Israel's right to exist, and to accept existing agreements. It stressed the need for the continuous commitment of all parties to the pursuit of a peaceful solution with Israel, and underlined that violence and terror are incompatible with democratic processes. The new Hamas-led Palestinian government refused to commit itself to these three principles and a humanitarian, economic and financial crisis ensued in the territories. On 15 May the Council supported the creation of a temporary international mechanism (TIM) designed to deliver assistance directly to the Palestinian people. The mechanism, which was endorsed by the European Council in June, has three 'windows' covering the health sector, utilities and social allowances.

At its meeting on 15 May the Council called for an early engagement between the Israeli Prime Minister and the President of the Palestinian Authority, to relaunch the process towards a negotiated settlement of the Israeli–Palestinian conflict. On 1 June the European Parliament adopted a resolution expressing its serious concern over the deteriorating situation in the West Bank and Gaza Strip and called on the Israeli government to resume the transfer of withheld Palestinian tax and customs revenues which had been blocked since January 2006. On 17 July, following the capture of an Israeli soldier in the Gaza Strip, the Council called for his immediate and unconditional release. It urged Israel not to resort to disproportionate action, to avoid the destruction of civilian infrastructure and to release elected members of the Palestinian government and legislature which it had detained. On 15 September, in the face of a worsening humanitarian crisis in the Palestinian territories, the Council welcomed the extension of the temporary international mechanism for a further three months. The Commission allocated approximately EUR 100 million to the TIM bringing the total made available from the Community budget to the Palestinian territories in 2006 to EUR 329 million. In a resolution adopted on 16 November the European Parliament reiterated its concern over the situation in Gaza.

Lebanon

In mid-July, following the abduction of two Israeli soldiers by Hezbollah forces on the Israeli–Lebanese border, the Council called for their immediate and unconditional release and for the cessation of all attacks on Israeli towns and cities.

On 1 August the Council expressed its utmost concern at the Lebanese and Israeli civilian casualties and human suffering, the destruction of civilian infrastructure and the increased number of internally displaced persons following the escalation of violence. It condemned both the rocket attacks by Hezbollah on Israel and the death of innocent civilians, mostly women and children, caused by Israeli air strikes. The Council underlined the European Union's commitment to support Lebanon's sovereignty and its long-term political and economic partnership with Europe. The Commission used the rapid reaction mechanism to respond to an appeal made by developing countries to help repatriate their citizens from Lebanon. The EUR 11 million it allocated assisted in evacuating the most vulnerable people.

Following the adoption of United Nations Security Council Resolution 1701 (2006), on 25 August the Council welcomed Member States' willingness to contribute to the reinforcement of the United Nations interim force in Lebanon designed to maintain a ceasefire between Israel and Hezbollah. It reiterated its determination to bring humanitarian relief to the people of Lebanon and, to this end, urged Israel to remove its air and sea blockade of Lebanon.

On 15 September the Council welcomed the early deployment of the Lebanese army in southern Lebanon. It adopted a common position banning the sale or supply of arms and related material and the provision of related services to entities or individuals in Lebanon in accordance with United Nations Security Council Resolution 1701 (2006) (¹). On 25 September it also adopted a regulation concerning restrictive measures against Lebanon (²).

Following the summer fighting, the Commission conducted joint missions with the Member States to evaluate the damage and requirements with a view to assessing Lebanon's current priorities. It pledged to contribute to the country's economic recovery and reconstruction effort. A total of EUR 42 million was committed for that purpose in 2006.

Iran

The European Union's relations with Iran over the course of 2006 were marked by the nuclear dispute between Iran and the international community. On 30 January the Council urged Iran to refrain from all uranium enrichment-related and reprocessing activities until international confidence in the peaceful nature of its nuclear programme was restored. It stressed that the European Union did not question Iran's right to nuclear energy for peaceful purposes.

(¹) Common Position 2006/625/CFSP (OJ L 253, 16.9.2006).
(²) Regulation (EC) No 1412/2006 (OJ L 267, 27.9.2006).

After the repeated unsuccessful calls for negotiation by the European Union and the international community, the International Atomic Energy Agency (IAEA) Board of Governors decided to refer Iran to the United Nations Security Council.

On 20 March the Council regretted that Iran had failed to implement in full the measures deemed necessary by the IAEA Board and once more urged iran to fully suspend all enrichment-related and reprocessing activities. It also expressed its dismay at the deteriorating human rights situation in Iran and condemned the use of violence against peaceful protesters on International Women's Day.

Mr Solana, Secretary-General of the Council and High Representative for the CFSP, presented a package of proposals on Iran, including European Union support for the development of a civilian nuclear programme following an agreement with China, France, Germany, Russia, the United Kingdom and the United States. However, on 17 July, following the Iranian government's refusal, the Council indicated that it would be forced to return to the UN Security Council to make the decisions of the IAEA Board of Governors mandatory.

Reconstruction process

Iraq

Although there was continuing insecurity in Iraq throughout the year, progress was made on the formation of a government of national unity. The situation was closely monitored by the Council, which issued a number of statements including, on 15 September, its appreciation of the progress made since the launching of the so-called 'Compact process' on 27 July. It confirmed the European Union's support for this process to mobilise the international community to support Iraq in its efforts to forge its own national vision of reconstruction. A trade and cooperation agreement is being negotiated between the European Community and Iraq.

On 17 October the Council extended ([1]) until 31 December 2007 the mandate of the European Union Integrated Rule of Law Mission for Iraq, EUJUST Lex, which had been set up to meet the urgent training needs of the Iraqi criminal justice system.

On 7 June the Commission presented a communication entitled 'Recommendations for renewed European Union engagement with Iraq' ([2]). Although the objectives set out in a previous communication adopted in June 2004 ([3]) were still valid, the Commission recommended new objectives to strengthen the European Union's engagement with Iraq. These included: helping to improve security conditions by promoting the rule of law and a culture of respect for human rights, assistance to the

---

([1]) Joint Action 2006/708/CFSP (OJ L 291, 21.10.2006).
([2]) COM(2006) 283.
([3]) COM(2004) 417.

national authorities to improve basic services, efforts to promote the establishment of a functioning administration, and support for mechanisms preparing the ground for Iraq's economic recovery and prosperity. The Commission also considered it vital for the European Union to work with other regional and international stakeholders.

On 12 July and 21 November the Commission approved two packages of measures to support reconstruction in Iraq. These brought the total of Community aid to Iraq to EUR 200 million in 2006.

Post-tsunami reconstruction

The European Union played a leading role in the international response to reconstruction following the tsunami which devastated several Asian countries in December 2004. The Commission alone committed EUR 123 million in humanitarian aid and EUR 350 million in medium- and long-term rehabilitation and reconstruction. The Community support focused on the three worst affected countries: Indonesia, Sri Lanka and the Maldives.

In Indonesia the post-tsunami reconstruction process was well under way. The consolidation of the Aceh peace process, with significant support from the European Union, provided a strong political basis for sustainable reconstruction. The Multi-Donor Fund — an initiative led by the European Union — gathered around EUR 520 million in grants (85 % from the Community and Member States). For Sri Lanka, despite the recent deterioration of the security situation, the Union in cooperation with other donors has committed more than EUR 100 million for the recovery of communities, rebuilding the major infrastructure and management of the environment. The Maldives was the most affected country in per capita terms, and the Union provided assistance (EUR 17 million) for the immediate restart of livelihoods on affected atolls, and support to the longer-term regional development strategy ('Safe island' programme) with a focus on environmental infrastructure and strengthening community services. Finally, the Commission undertook a number of projects at a regional level (EUR 27 million) in all Indian Ocean countries (including India and Thailand), to share experience and implement best practices for the recovery of the environment and local communities in a sustainable way.

General references and other useful links

- External relations:
  http://ec.europa.eu/comm/external_relations/index.htm

- Common foreign and security policy (CFSP):
  http://ec.europa.eu/comm/external_relations/cfsp/intro/index.htm

- United Nations:
  http://www.un.org/

- International Atomic Energy Agency:
  http://www.iaea.org/

- Council website devoted to European security and defence policy (ESDP):
  http://www.consilium.europa.eu/cms3_fo/showPage.asp?lang=en&id=261&mode=g&name=

- European Defence Agency:
  http://eda.europa.eu/

- Civilian operations:
  http://ec.europa.eu/comm/external_relations/cfsp/fin/pja.htm

- Rebuilding Iraq:
  http://ec.europa.eu/comm/external_relations/iraq/intro/index.htm

- Multi-Donor Trust Fund for Iraq:
  http://www.irffi.org/

- Middle East peace process:
  http://ec.europa.eu/comm/external_relations/mepp/index.htm

Chapter VI

Life of the institutions and other bodies

European Parliament

Composition of Parliament

The distribution of the 732 seats among the political groups at 31 December was as follows:

- European People's Party (Christian Democrats) and European Democrats (EPP–ED),
  chaired by Mr Poettering 264
- Socialist Group in the European Parliament (SPE),
  chaired by Mr Schulz 200
- Alliance of Liberals and Democrats for Europe (ALDE),
  chaired by Mr Watson 90
- Union for Europe of the Nations (UEN),
  co-chaired by Ms Muscardini and Mr Crowley 44
- Greens/European Free Alliance (Greens/EFA),
  co-chaired by Ms Frassoni and Mr Cohn-Bendit 42
- Confederal Group of the European United Left/Nordic Green Left (GUE/NGL),
  chaired by Mr Wurtz 41
- Independence and Democracy (ID),
  co-chaired by Mr Bonde and Mr Farage 23
- non-attached (NI) 28

Statute of Members

On 6 July Parliament adopted a resolution on modification of the Protocol on Privileges and Immunities. It recalled the Council's undertaking to consider an earlier parliamentary request that the protocol be reviewed when an instrument was adopted laying down the regulations and general conditions governing the performance of the duties of Members. It said that the review of the protocol should form an integral part of the overall compromise on a Statute for the Members, in line with Parliament's resolution of 23 June 2005, and called on the Council to ensure that Parliament was involved in the Intergovernmental Conference called for the purpose.

Parliament amended its Rules of Procedure with regard to standards for the conduct of Members in order to prevent extreme forms of public demonstration on its premises. It also amended Articles 3 and 4 of the Rules of Procedure so as to clarify its power to deal with any cases of manifest incompatibility between membership of Parliament and the holding of other offices.

Parliament's work

A breakdown of Parliament's work in 2006 is given in Table 3.

In 2006 Parliament addressed 6 075 questions to the Commission: 5 327 written questions, 87 oral questions with debate and 661 during question time. Parliament addressed 1 024 questions to the Council: 549 written questions, 45 oral questions with debate and 430 during question time.

Parliament adopted a report on the handling of petitions since the 2004 enlargement, in which it emphasises the fact that the petitions lodged by European citizens provide it with a vital opportunity to monitor the application of Community law in practical ways and take appropriate action where necessary. Parliament received some 1 000 new petitions in 2006; a steadily growing proportion concerned the protection of the environment, which has now become the biggest single issue in petitions. In only one third of these new cases did Parliament ask the Commission to study the circumstances complained of in more detail: many petitions are inadmissible, or can be dealt with direct by Parliament itself. But it was evidence of far-reaching interinstitutional cooperation in hundreds of cases where the Committee on Petitions had the help of the Commission — repeatedly so in areas where Community law is developing fast.

With regard to the strategic objective of prosperity, Parliament debated a wide variety of issues, including: the broad economic policy guidelines for 2006 and the guidelines for the employment policies of the Member States; a new partnership for entrepreneurship and growth, manufacturing industry in the Union, and in particular the situation in the European footwear industry; an information society for growth and employment; a European social model for the future; the reform of State aid 2005–09; public–private partnerships, and Community law on public procurement and concessions; services of general interest; future patent policy in Europe; the implications of signing the Hague Securities Convention; European contract law and the revision of the *acquis*; public finances in economic and monetary union; the enlargement of the euro area, and the 2006 annual report on the euro area; the financial and stock exchange sectors; mortgage credit; mergers in the single market; sustainable development strategy; the application of Directive 96/71/EC concerning the posting of workers, and of the postal directive; the Galileo programme; nanosciences and nanotechnologies (2005–09);

an integrated European action programme for inland waterway transport NAIADES; measures to promote tourism; and a European qualifications framework.

Energy was a major focus of debate this year: security of energy supply in the European Union; energy efficiency; the failure of the European electricity network; the use of renewable energy sources for heating and refrigeration; the Energy Community Treaty; the Green Paper entitled 'A European strategy for sustainable, competitive and secure energy'; and the strategy for biomass and biofuels.

On the legislative front, two of the major items that have marked the sixth parliamentary term, namely the REACH system for chemicals and the services directive, were brought to a conclusion when they were approved at second reading (co-decision); and the seventh framework programme for research was approved, with its rules for participation and specific programmes. But the House rejected the Commission proposal on market access to port services — which the Commission subsequently withdrew — and the Commission proposal on voluntary modulation of direct payments under the commmon agricultural policy — which was referred back for further consideration by the parliamentary committee responsible.

As regards the solidarity objective, the subjects considered by Parliament included: demographic challenges and solidarity between the generations; cohesion policy in support of growth and jobs (strategic guidelines 2007–13); the economic and social consequences of company restructuring in Europe, especially in the motor industry; social protection and inclusion; the effects of globalisation on the internal market; homophobia and the increase in racist and homophobic violence in Europe; fighting trafficking in human beings, and forced prostitution during the 2006 football World Cup; the right to freedom of speech and respect for religious beliefs; a framework strategy for non-discrimination and equal opportunities for all; equality between women and men in the European Union, and the future of the Lisbon strategy from the point of view of the gender perspective; women in international politics; the situation of disabled people in the enlarged European Union (the European action plan 2006–07); the transitional arrangements restricting the free movement of workers on European Union labour markets; a new framework strategy for multilingualism, and measures to promote multilingualism and language learning in the European Union; the crisis of the Equitable Life Assurance Society — on 18 January Parliament decided to set up a committee of inquiry to investigate alleged contraventions or maladministration in the application of Community law in the case; climate change; establishing a scheme for greenhouse gas emission allowance trading (national allocation plans 2008–12); the protection of the environment through criminal law, and the consequences of the judgment of the Court of Justice of 13 September 2005 in Case C-176/03 *Commission v Council*; the financing of environmental protection (LIFE+ and Natura 2000); the thematic strategies for the urban environment and protection and conservation of the marine environment; improving the economic situation in the fishing industry; the sugar and milk sectors; and risk and crisis management in the agricultural sector.

Also as regards solidarity there were important legislative developments, including the setting-up of a European Institute for Gender Equality (compromise agreement at second reading in December); the establishment of a European Globalisation Adjustment Fund (agreement at first reading in December); and the establishment of a European Union Agency for Fundamental Rights.

As regards the strategic objective of security, Parliament expressed its views on such current issues as progress towards an area of freedom, security and justice in 2005; the interception of bank transfer data from the SWIFT system by the US secret services; the use and protection of passenger data, the EU–US agreement on the use of passenger name records (PNR) and the Council framework decision on the protection of personal data processed in the framework of police and judicial cooperation in criminal matters; evaluation of the European arrest warrant (recommendation to the Council); protection of the Communities' financial interests and the fight against fraud (2004); pandemic influenza preparedness and response planning in the European Community; counterfeiting of medicinal products; lessons for the future on the 20th anniversary of the Chernobyl disaster; the UN 2006 review conference on small arms; the Convention on the Prohibition of Biological and Toxin Weapons, cluster bombs and conventional arms; violent video games; road safety: bringing eCall to citizens; the alleged use of European countries by the CIA for the transportation and illegal detention of prisoners — on 18 January Parliament decided to set up a temporary committee to consider the matter; measures to improve road safety and safety measures in transport, and the financing of such measures; the deployment of the European rail signalling system ERTMS/ETCS; external aviation policy; World Health Day; HIV/AIDS ('time to deliver'); breast cancer; a strategy for improving the mental health of the population; immigration issues (common policy on immigration, the integration of immigrants in the European Union, the mutual information procedure for asylum and immigration, and the role and place of immigrant women in the European Union); natural disasters (fires, droughts and floods) and a rapid response and preparedness instrument for major emergencies/European initiative in the field of civil protection.

As regards the Union as a global partner, Parliament reviewed the outlook for the common foreign policy in 2006. There were major debates on particular countries and regions of the world, discussing: the situation in the Middle East; the situation in Darfur, in south-east Turkey, in Moldova (Transnistria) and in Georgia (South Ossetia); the elections in Belarus and Ukraine; relations with the United States, including a transatlantic partnership agreement; relations with Russia, China and India; a stronger partnership between the European Union and Latin America; economic and trade relations between the European Union and Mercosur with a view to the conclusion of an interregional association agreement; the European neighbourhood policy; Euro-Mediterranean policy; a Baltic Sea strategy for the Northern Dimension; visa policy for the countries of the western Balkans; the outlook for Bosnia and Herzegovina; the European Union's preparedness for its future role in Kosovo; the conclusion of the stabilisation and association agreement with Albania; the confrontation between

Iran and the international community regarding nuclear facilities; the European Union's policy towards the Cuban government; the North Korean nuclear test; and the implementation of the European security strategy in the context of the European security and defence policy.

Various aspects of development policy and external trade were considered, and in particular the European Union's generalised system of preferences; the WTO ministerial conference in Hong Kong, and the suspension of negotiations on the Doha Development Agenda; the strategic review of the International Monetary Fund; the revision of the Cotonou Agreement and setting of the amount for the 10th EDF; new financial instruments for development in connection with the millennium goals; the development impact of economic partnership agreements; aid effectiveness and corruption in developing countries; fair trade and development; and the links between development and migration, and development and the media.

Human rights were also repeatedly on the agenda: more specifically, Parliament discussed the human rights and democracy clause in European Union agreements; the annual European Union reports on human rights in the world 2005 and 2006; the 62nd session of the UN Commission on Human Rights; the situation of prisoners at Guantánamo; Chechnya after the elections and civil society in Russia; and EU–Russia relations following the murder of the Russian journalist Anna Politkovskaya.

The House returned again and again to the subject of enlargement, debating both the principles and the practical steps being taken. On the general aspects it adopted a resolution on the Commission's 2005 enlargement strategy paper, and also considered the Commission communication on the enlargement strategy and main challenges 2006–07, and the institutional aspects of the European Union's capacity to integrate new Member States. In June and November it adopted resolutions on the accession of Bulgaria and Romania, and discussed the progress being made by the two countries in April, May and September.

In September the European Parliament adopted a resolution on Turkey's progress towards accession. In January it approved an amendment to the relevant Council regulation to change the name of the partnership with Croatia from 'European partnership' to 'accession partnership', so as to align it on the name of the partnership with Turkey, as both are candidate countries which have started accession negotiations.

Parliament's relations with the other institutions

On the interinstitutional front, Parliament debated the work programmes and achievements of the Austrian and Finnish Presidencies, the preparations for the European Councils in Brussels on 15 and 16 June and 14 and 15 December, and their outcome. It also discussed the preparations for the spring European Council on 23 and 24 March, and its outcome, in the context of the Lisbon strategy; the Commission's contributions to the June European Council ('A citizens' agenda — Delivering results for Europe' and 'The period of reflection and Plan D'); the outcome of the informal European Council in Lahti on 20 October; the 2005 activity report of the European Investment Bank; the 2004 annual report on the activities of the European Ombudsman (in the presence of the Ombudsman, Mr Diamandouros); and the Court of Auditors 2005 annual report, presented by its President, Mr Weber.

On the budgetary front, Parliament adopted the 2007 budget and approved the discharge for 2004. It played a central role in the conclusion of an interinstitutional agreement on budgetary discipline and sound financial management (financial perspective 2007–13). It approved a Council regulation amending the financial regulation applicable to the general budget of the European Communities, and adopted a resolution on the recovery of Community funds.

On the political and institutional front Parliament expressed its position on a great many issues of current political importance, such as: the period of reflection (a resolution on the period of reflection: the structure, subjects and context for an assessment of the debate on the European Union, and a resolution addressed to the June European Council on the next steps for the period of reflection); the European communication strategy; European political parties; the operating framework for the European regulatory agencies; better lawmaking (resolutions on the annual report 'Better lawmaking 2004', on monitoring the application of Community law, on a strategy for the simplification of the regulatory environment, on the outcome of the screening of legislative proposals pending before the legislator, and on the implementation, consequences and impact of the internal market legislation in force); openness and transparency measures, with specific reference to the openness of the meetings of the Council when acting in its legislative capacity, and to access to the institutions' papers; and 'comitology' procedures (Parliament decision on the conclusion of an interinstitutional agreement taking the form of a joint statement, and consequent amendment of Article 81 of Parliament's Rules of Procedure).

At the December part-session the Sakharov Prize was awarded to Aliaksandr Milinkevich, leader of the Belarusian opposition. The President of Austria, Heinz Fischer, addressed a special sitting of the European Parliament in February, as did Horst Köhler, President of Germany, in March; Edward Fenech-Adami, President of Malta, in April; Evo Morales Ayma, President of Bolivia, Mahmoud Abbas, President of the Palestinian Authority, and Karolos Papoulias, President of Greece, in May; Tarja Halonen, President of Finland, and Ellen Johnson Sirleaf, President of Liberia, in September; László Sólyom, President of Hungary, in October; Mikheil Saakashvili, President of Georgia, and Sheik Hamad Bin Khalifa Al-Thani, Emir of the State of Qatar, in November. At a meeting of the Conference of Presidents open to all Members and held in the chamber in September, Parliament had an exchange of views with Fouad Siniora, Prime Minister of Lebanon.

Table 3

Parliamentary proceedings from January to December — Resolutions and decisions adopted

| | Legislation | | | | | | | Budget and discharge | Other procedures | | | | Total |
| | Consultation (1) | Cooperation | | Co-decision | | | Approved | | Own-initiative procedures | Resolutions (Articles 103, 108) | Human rights | Miscellaneous | |
		First reading	Second reading	First reading (2)	Second reading (3)	Third reading							
January	7			1	1	2			8	10	3	1	33
February I				1		2			4	4			11
February II	5			2	1	1	2		8	5	2		26
March I	8			3				1	9	7	3		31
March II	2			1			3		5	4			15
April I	3			4	1	2	1		9	5	3	1	28
April II	6			1			1	25	6	1		1	41
May I	16			5	2		1	2	11	1	3	2	43
May II	2			3	2			1	8	1			17
June	9			5	5				7	9	3		35
July	11			4	5	2	2		12	5	3	1	45
September I	9			2			2		8	9	3		33
September II	7			3	1		1	4	13	4		1	34
October I	17			5					3	2		1	28
October II	6			3	7		1	5	9	11	3	2	47
November I	12			3	1				11	3	3	3	36
November II	12			5	1				4	2		1	25
December	26			22	10	1		2	5	7	3	4	80
Total 2006	**158**	**0**	**0**	**74**	**34**	**10**	**13**	**40**	**140**	**90**	**32**	**18**	**608**

(1) Including 72 cases in which Parliament proposed amendments to the Commission proposal.
(2) Including 52 cases in which Parliament proposed amendments to the Commission proposal.
(3) Including 18 cases in which Parliament amended the Council's common position.

Parliament invited various members of the European Council to debate the future of Europe, notably Guy Verhofstadt, Prime Minister of Belgium, in May, and Bertie Ahern, the Irish Prime Minister, in November. In the form of statements made by the President of Parliament and the presidents of the political groups, the House sent powerful political messages, in July, marking 70 years since General Franco's *coup d'état* in Spain and, in October, commemorating the Hungarian uprising in 1956; a third such issue was the peace process in Spain, which was the subject of statements by Parliament (the President and the presidents of the political groups), the Commission and the Council.

Staffing

At 31 December the establishment plan of Parliament's Secretariat comprised 4 883 permanent posts and 116 temporary posts.

Cooperation between the European Parliament and the Commission

In December the European Parliament adopted two resolutions, by very large majorities, approving the appointment of the new Members of the Commission designated by Romania and Bulgaria, namely Leonard Orban and Meglena Kuneva.

At the December part-session the European Parliament approved, likewise by a large majority, a resolution on the Commission's legislative and work programme for 2007. The resolution welcomed improvements made by the Commission, and put forward a great many suggestions.

European Ombudsman

The European Ombudsman, Mr P. Nikiforos Diamandouros, acting on the basis of Article 195 of the EC Treaty, opened some 170 inquiries into cases of suspected maladministration on the part of the Commission. These cases focused mainly on the question of transparency (access to documents), disputes regarding invitations to tender and grants, recruitment and personnel matters, the role of the Commission as guardian of the Treaties, and traditional types of administrative problem such as letters answered late or not at all. About 15 % of inquiries in recent years have led to criticism by the Ombudsman: more and more often the Ombudsman has proposed that the complainant and the Commission reach a settlement of their dispute. In order to enhance political responsibility, it is now no longer the Secretary-General of the Commission that replies to the Ombudsman in an inquiry, but instead the Commissioner responsible.

Council and European Council

Council

The Council was chaired by Austria in the first half of 2006 and by Finland in the second half. It held a total of 62 meetings in its various configurations.

The Council amended its Rules of Procedure twice:

- on 23 January, in order to update for 2006 the table of population of the Member States used to calculate weightings for qualified majority voting in the Council;

- on 15 September, in order to improve public access to information on its activities, especially by means of broadcasts of its public deliberations and debates over the Internet, in line with the policy formulated by the European Council at its meeting of 15 and 16 June ([1]).

At 31 December the establishment plan of the General Secretariat of the Council comprised 3 461permanent posts and 340 temporary posts.

European Council

The European Council held four meetings in 2006.

23 and 24 March

The European Council met in Brussels with Mr Schüssel, the Austrian Chancellor, in the chair. The meeting focused on the launch of an energy policy for Europe, explicit targets to be inserted in the conclusions regarding the Lisbon strategy, and support for the approach being taken in Parliament to the services directive. The meeting approved a pact for gender equality. A debate on the future of Europe was concerned mainly with the enlargement of the Union.

15 and 16 June

The European Council met in Brussels with Mr Schüssel, the Austrian Chancellor, in the chair. A major item in the discussions was the Treaty establishing a Constitution for Europe, and a timetable was approved providing for a report exploring possible future developments to be submitted in June 2007, based on extensive consultations with the Member States. The European Council asked the Commission and the Council to prepare a set of actions with respect to energy policy that would enable it to adopt a prioritised action plan in spring 2007.

Informal meeting in Lahti, 20 October

The Heads of State or Government of the Union met in Lahti, Finland, at the invitation of the Finnish Presidency. Essentially they discussed three subjects: energy, innovation and immigration. On energy, they asked Russia immediately to apply the principles of the Energy Charter, which they said should be included in the new bilateral agreement that the Union and Russia were to negotiate in 2007. On innovation, they stressed the need for the Union to follow a global strategy that would reinforce European

---

([1]) See 'Transparency' in Chapter I of this Report.

competitiveness on the world market. Immigration was a problem that concerned the whole European Union, they said, calling for solidarity on the part of everyone.

14 and 15 December

The European Council met in Brussels under Finnish chairmanship. It concentrated on two main issues: enlargement strategy, where it had before it a Commission report on the European Union's capacity to integrate new members; and migration, with special reference to legal migration, illegal immigration, border controls and solidarity mechanisms, subjects on which the Commission was asked to make proposals. The Commission was also asked to draw up proposals with regard to innovation, and specifically intellectual property rights, joint technology initiatives and standardisation. The meeting outlined priority measures to ensure the security of the Union's energy supplies. It also discussed external relations, in particular the Middle East, Africa and the European neighbourhood policy.

Commission

Synthesis of policy achievements in 2005

The Commission issued two summaries of its policy achievements the previous year.

- On 14 March, in parallel with the presentation of the annual policy strategy for 2007 (see below), the Commission approved a synthesis of policy achievements entitled 'Policy achievements in 2005' [1]. This report gives a brief description of the Commission's contribution in 2005 to the realisation of its five-year strategic objectives, namely to promote prosperity, solidarity, security and a stronger Europe in the world.

- On 7 June it adopted a report entitled 'Synthesis of the Commission's management achievements in 2005' [2]. This report summarises the progress made in 2005 towards fully developing the performance potential of the Commission's management and control systems in areas such as: promoting the Commission's accountability, by taking a more coherent approach based on 'families' of related departments; applying the principles of accrual-based accounting to the budget of the Union; enhancing effective performance management, notably via the introduction of a Commission-wide methodology on risk management; and reinforcing the Commission's monitoring capacity, by means of simplification measures and the improvement of internal control strategies.

---

[1] COM(2006) 124.
[2] COM(2006) 277.

Mid-term review of the 2006 legislative and work programme

On 30 August the Commission submitted a short review ([1]) of the initiatives taken in the first eight months of the year under its 2006 legislative and work programme ([2]), presented in October 2005. The Commission noted that the implementation rate was 39 %, owing in particular to the large number of items carried over to the last quarter, and stressed its determination to undertake a major effort to ensure that all the initiatives that were scheduled for adoption by the end of 2006 would be submitted in time.

Strategic planning and programming for 2007

On 14 March, as the first stage in its annual policy cycle, the Commission adopted its annual policy strategy for 2007 ([3]). Subtitled 'Boosting trust through action', the paper establishes the policy priorities for each of the Commission's four strategic objectives (see above).

On 24 October the Commission presented its legislative and work programme for 2007 ([4]). To develop this programme, it has had the benefit of the reactions from the European Parliament, the Council and the other institutions to its annual policy strategy for 2007. For the first time, the Commission sets out 21 strategic initiatives which will be at the core of its political delivery in 2007. It also lists a series of priority initiatives to be adopted over the next 12 to 18 months. The approach is underpinned by two further innovations: in line with the undertaking given to Parliament, the programme takes full account of the initiatives linked to the better regulation objective, and also sets out a list of priorities for connecting with the citizens.

Continuity of business at the Commission

On 12 July the Commission approved a framework for business continuity management in the Commission ([5]). This is intended to allow it to prepare for major potential disruptions such as terrorist attacks, the threat of a global flu pandemic, or threats to staff, buildings or IT systems.

The objectives are: to develop the Commission's resilience to such threats, in particular by establishing the necessary plans and procedures and by strengthening its infrastructure where necessary; to ensure that the Commission and its departments are able to continue operating, by identifying critical and essential functions, services and infrastructure that need to be restored within certain time limits and the key staff necessary for this purpose; to raise staff awareness of business continuity requirements;

([1]) SEC(2006) 1052.
([2]) COM(2005) 531.
([3]) COM(2006) 122.
([4]) COM(2006) 629.
([5]) SEC(2006) 898.

and to maintain and improve the Commission's business continuity management on an ongoing basis.

Legislative activity

The Commission met 43 times during the year. It sent 482 proposals for directives, regulations and decisions and made seven recommendations. It also presented 324 communications and reports, 10 Green Papers and two White Papers. In addition to the new initiatives, programmes and action plans adopted by the Commission, the debates launched and the ongoing activities pursued under its work programme for 2006, these figures include proposals for routine management instruments (especially in the fields of agriculture, fisheries, customs and commercial policy) and proposals for consolidating existing legislation.

Relations with national parliaments

In February 2005 Ms Wallström presented the Commission with 10 concrete targets for relations with national parliaments, one of which was an annual report on the subject; on 22 March 2006 the Commission adopted its first such report, the 'Annual report 2005 on the relations with the national parliaments' ([1]). The report reviews progress on the achievement of these objectives in 2005, including such things as visits to national parliaments by Members of the Commission, and greater accessibility to national parliaments in the performance of their institutional responsibilities.

In 2006 the Commission continued to pursue these objectives, with attendance at meetings of the permanent representatives of the national parliaments, high-level participation in the Conference of European Affairs Committees of the parliaments of the European Union (COSAC) and in meetings between national parliaments and the European Parliament organised by COSAC, and the drafting of a newsletter.

In its communication to the European Council 'A citizens' agenda — Delivering results for Europe', adopted on 10 May ([2]), the Commission expressed its wish to 'transmit directly all its new proposals and consultation papers to the national parliaments, inviting them to react so as to improve the process of policy formulation'.

The European Council of 15 and 16 June welcomed this commitment by the Commission and called on it to examine with all due attention the observations made by the national parliaments. The Commission departments worked out a procedure for the transmission of documents to all the national parliaments, and the Commission approved principles for handling opinions they might express ([3]). Since October national parliaments have sent the Commission 50 sets of observations on

---

([1]) SEC(2006) 350.
([2]) COM(2006) 211. See Chapter I, Section 3, of this Report.
([3]) SEC(2006) 1252.

27 proposals; the observations are concerned mainly with questions of subsidiarity and proportionality.

Staff policy and human resources management

In 2006 the Commission had 18 205 permanent administrative posts and 366 temporary administrative posts, and 3 792 permanent research posts. There were also 1 913 permanent posts and 120 temporary posts for offices attached to the Commission, and 679 and 2 559 posts in decentralised bodies and executive agencies respectively.

There are 11 Commission officials currently seconded to national administrations and international organisations under the staff exchange scheme, and 1 134 national experts are working at the Commission. In 2006, 214 national civil servants had the opportunity to see the working of the Commission from the inside under its 'structural' in-service training scheme.

In the run-up to the new enlargement of the Union on 1 January 2007, the Commission proposed special measures for the recruitment of officials from Bulgaria and Romania. The necessary regulation was adopted by the Council on 28 November ([1]).

On 26 April the Commission adopted a package of measures for the well-being at work of its staff. The central element is a multiannual action plan 2006–09, aiming at improving health and safety at work in all Commission premises, increased support for spouses and families, better reconciliation of professional and private life, and a human resources policy geared to individualised assistance to staff members and improvement of their work environment.

The other measures in the package are:

- a policy on absence for medical reasons and invalidity;

- a harmonised policy for health and safety at work for all Commission staff;

- a policy on protecting the dignity of the person and preventing psychological harassment and sexual harassment.

Court of Justice and other courts

Appointments to the Court of Justice

The following were appointed to the Court of Justice in 2006:

- as judges: Mr Tizzano, Mr Bay Larsen, Ms Lindh, Mr Bonichot, and Mr von Danwitz;

- as advocates-general: Ms Sharpston, Ms Trstenjak, Mr Mengozzi, Mr Bot and Mr Mazák.

([1]) Regulation (EC, Euratom) No 1760/2006 (OJ L 335, 1.12.2006).

Case-law of the Court of Justice

The *Cresson* case was the first in which the Court had to clarify the obligations of a Member of the Commission under Article 213 of the Treaty (¹). The Court found that it was a circumvention of the relevant rules to recruit someone as a visiting scientist so that they could in reality act as a personal adviser, when they would not have been eligible for recruitment as a personal adviser. Having regard to her personal involvement in the appointment, Ms Cresson had to be held responsible for the circumvention and misapplication of the rules.

The Court delivered two important judgments on social policy.

• The Court clarified the application of the principle of equal treatment for men and women, a fundamental principle of Community law, in the case of *Sarah Margaret Richards* (²), which concerned eligibility for retirement at 60 where the person concerned had had gender reassignment surgery. The Court said that the Member States retained the power to organise their social security systems, but that when exercising that power they had to comply with Community law. The Court compared the situation of the male-to-female transsexual with that of women 'who had always been women', and found that there was indeed discrimination.

• In the *Yvonne Watts* case (³) the Court stressed the need to find a balance between the management and policy constraints on the provision of hospital care by the Member States and the requirements of the freedoms established by the EC Treaty. It reviewed the strict criteria for determining whether it was legitimate to refuse to authorise reimbursement of the cost of hospital treatment in another Member State.

In the case of the *Sellafield* nuclear fuel reprocessing plant (⁴), the Court based its judgment partly on Article 292 of the EC Treaty; this was the first time that article had been invoked and applied. The Court said that it had exclusive jurisdiction to decide any dispute regarding the interpretation and application of Community law, and held that Ireland had failed to fulfil its obligations when it brought a dispute between itself and the United Kingdom on questions that were essentially questions of Community law before an arbitral tribunal provided for in the Law of the Sea Convention.

The Court delivered two important judgments concerning the right to vote in elections to the European Parliament (⁵). It had to consider whether the United Kingdom was entitled to grant the right to vote to nationals of non-Member States, and whether the Netherlands was entitled to exclude its own nationals resident in an overseas territory.

(¹) Case C-432/04.
(²) Case C-423/04.
(³) Case C-372/04.
(⁴) Case C-459/03.
(⁵) Cases C-145/04 and C-300/04.

It held that the United Kingdom could extend the vote to nationals of non-Member States under certain conditions. But it found that sufficient justification had not been put forward for the exclusion in the second case.

In *Traghetti del Mediterraneo* the Court had to consider the non-contractual liability of the Member States ([1]). A Member State might incur non-contractual liability where there was a breach of Community law attributable to a national court. National legislation could not restrict this liability in a general manner, as it purported to do in the case before the Court.

In the field of police cooperation, the Court delivered two judgments clarifying the principle of *ne bis in idem* in Article 54 of the Convention implementing the Schengen Agreement ([2]). The Court clarified the effect of the principle and applied it to a case of acquittal on the ground that the prosecution was time-barred, and to a case of acquittal for lack of evidence.

Appointments to the Court of First Instance

In 2006 Mr Moavero Milanesi, Mr Wahl and Mr Prek were appointed judges of the Court of First Instance.

Staffing of the courts

At 31 December the Court of Justice, the Court of First Instance and the Civil Service Tribunal had 1 346 permanent posts and 411 temporary posts.

Court of Auditors

Annual report

On 24 October the President of the Court of Auditors presented its annual report for 2005 to the European Parliament ([3]). The report speaks of considerable progress made by the Commission in introducing its new accruals-based accounting system, but finds weak internal controls for most European Union expenditure, both within Member States and at the Commission, and a high incidence of errors in the underlying transactions.

Special reports

The special reports produced by the Court of Auditors in 2006 concerned:

- the contribution of the European Social Fund in combating early school leaving;

([1]) Case C-173/03.
([2]) Cases C-467/04 and C-150/05.
([3]) OJ C 263, 31.10.2006.

- the performance of projects financed under Tacis in the Russian Federation;

- the European Commission humanitarian aid response to the tsunami;

- Phare investment projects in Bulgaria and Romania;

- the MEDA programme;

- the environmental aspects of the Commission's development cooperation;

- rural development investments;

- the effectiveness of the European Union support for fruit and vegetable producers' operational programmes;

- translation expenditure incurred by the Commission, the Parliament and the Council;

- *ex post* evaluations of Objectives 1 and 3 programmes 1994–99 (Structural Funds).

Specific annual reports

The specific annual reports produced by the Court of Auditors in 2006 concerned the annual accounts of the various European Union bodies and agencies for 2005.

Opinions

In 2006 the Court of Auditors issued opinions on various legislative proposals with financial implications, including the proposal for a decision on the system of the European Communities' own resources and the draft amendments to the financial regulation applicable to the general budget of the European Communities.

European Economic and Social Committee

The year 2006 was a productive one for the Committee, whose membership was renewed in October, when it also elected its new President, Mr Dimitris Dimitriadis of Greece, from the employers' group.

As always, the Committee put forward positions on all Community policies, delivering more than 170 opinions. But it sought to express its views especially on the subjects central to the European agenda.

Just before the spring European Council it delivered opinions on the Lisbon strategy, dealing with the hot political issue of 'flexicurity', or the attempt to strike the right balance between business flexibility and the security that has to be guaranteed to employees. It also commented on the sustainable development strategy, the challenges of climate change and television without frontiers.

The Committee made intensive efforts to cooperate more closely with similar bodies in Member States, and made a major contribution to the strategy aimed at communicating Europe ([1]).

The President and Members of the Commission played an active part in the Committee's work. Mr Barroso addressed the plenary session in March, when he concentrated on the Lisbon strategy, a subject at the heart of the European agenda. Ms Wallström presented the Commission's communication strategy to the plenary in July, and at the February plenary Mr Almunia spoke on the revision of the Stability and Growth Pact. At the April session Mr Špidla outlined the main initiatives the Commission intended to put forward in the social sphere, namely the roadmap for equality between women and men, the new European Globalisation Adjustment Fund, the response to the challenge of demographic trends, and the Green Paper on modernising labour law.

Cooperation between the Commission and the Committee proceeded on two fronts, the ordinary institutional consultation provided for in the Treaty, which requires the Commission to consult the Committee on a range of subjects, and the application of the cooperation protocol signed on 7 November 2005 by Mr Barroso and the then President of the Committee, Ms Sigmund.

In the course of 2006 the Commission and the Committee sought especially to build on two central elements in the 2005 protocol.

- Major efforts were undertaken with regard to programming. On the basis of the Commission's work programme for 2007 the Commission sent the Committee a list of dossiers for optional consultation, in order to facilitate the programming of the Committee's work. The Committee's programming was also to be made more selective.

- The Commission continued to pay close attention to the follow-up to opinions, and in its three-monthly reports gave even greater prominence to the Committee's main opinions, especially the exploratory opinions.

The Commission and the Committee also worked towards the signature at the beginning of 2007 of the addendum to the cooperation protocol of 2005 which was to deal with the European Union's communication policy.

Committee of the Regions

The Committee of the Regions had a busy year. In February it renewed its membership and elected its new President, Mr Delebarre, the socialist mayor of Dunkirk. It also adopted a resolution on its political guidelines for the period 2006–08.

([1]) See Chapter I, Section 2, of this Report.

The Committee expressed views on a variety of common policies; these included opinions on territorial pacts, the Hague programme, the implementation of the European Youth Pact, and services of general interest.

Several Members of the Commission attended meetings of the Committee, confirming the importance the Commission attaches to its work. Mr Barroso took part in the 'structured dialogue' in December, where the debate with the Committee and associations of local and regional authorities was intense and positive. At the plenary session in April Mr Barrot spoke on the subject of urban mobility and Ms Hübner on the need for cooperation between the Commission and the Committee with regard to the implementation of cohesion policy. Ms Hübner was the first Member of the Commission to take part in a question and answer session following a formula suggested by the Committee, and gave detailed answers to the 12 questions put to her. Ms Wallström addressed the plenary session in June, concentrating on the period of reflection on the future of the Union.

The Committee held the fourth 'Open Days' event this year, in cooperation with the Commission. The event has become an essential focus for the regional and local dimension. The Commission worked hard to ensure its success. The proceedings were opened by Mr Barroso himself, and three vice-presidents and seven other commissioners took part.

The year 2006 saw the beginning of the implementation of the cooperation protocol signed by the Commission and the Committee on 17 November 2005.

Two aspects were given special prominence.

- On programming, the Commission and the Committee identified subjects of common interest, based on the work programme for 2007.

- On the follow-up of opinions, special emphasis was given to outlook opinions. At the 'structured dialogue' in December, Mr Barroso gave a political response to two Committee opinions, one concerning public–private partnerships, the other on the situation of unaccompanied minors.

The Commission and the Committee also worked towards the signature at the beginning of 2007 of the addendum to the cooperation protocol of 2005 which was to deal with the European Union's communication policy.

European Central Bank

The European Central Bank (ECB) continued to pursue a monetary policy aimed at maintaining price stability in the euro area. Over the period January to December, the ECB's Governing Council raised key interest rates by 125 basis points, with the ECB's minimum bid rate in main refinancing operations reaching the level of 3.5 % in December. By ensuring price stability, monetary policy is contributing to the promotion of growth and employment in the euro area. Real GDP growth considerably strengthened in 2006, compared with 2005. Overall, amid significant volatility, in particular in the second part of the year, prices on average remained elevated over the year. In conducting its monetary policy, the ECB continued to ensure transparency by explaining the economic and monetary assessment underlying policy decisions in regular press conferences given by the ECB President, in its monthly bulletin and in other publications and speeches of Governing Council members. In addition, in line with the ECB's statutory reporting obligations, the ECB President appeared before the Committee on Economic and Monetary Affairs of the European Parliament and at a plenary session of the European Parliament.

The ECB examined whether the non-euro area Member States fulfilled the necessary conditions for adoption of the euro in two convergence reports ([1]). The first, published in May 2006, examined Lithuania and Slovenia, following requests from the authorities of these Member States. The second, published in December 2006, examined the other non-euro area Member States (excluding Denmark and the United Kingdom). Taking into account the ECB's and the European Commission's May 2006 convergence reports, and upon a proposal from the Commission, the Council decided to abrogate Slovenia's derogation on 11 July, allowing it to adopt the euro on 1 January 2007. The ECB, together with Banka Slovenije, undertook the necessary preparations for the entry of Slovenia into the Eurosystem, including a joint communication campaign on the euro banknotes and coins.

Target, one of the world's largest payment systems, continued to contribute to the integration of the euro money market and to play an important part in the smooth implementation of the single monetary policy. Work is currently under way on Target2, the next generation of the system, which is scheduled to go live in November 2007. Furthermore, the ECB is exploring the setting-up of a new service that would allow for the harmonised settlement of securities transactions in euro in central bank money (Target2–Securities). The ECB continued to cooperate closely with the European Commission in the process leading to the realisation of the single euro payments area (SEPA) and to encourage the European banking industry and the other relevant stakeholders to create the conditions for the introduction of SEPA as of 2008 and its realisation by the end of 2010.

The ECB continued its work in the field of prudential supervision and financial stability, inter alia by monitoring and analysing the main developments in banking and finance, developing new areas of cooperation between central banks and other supervisory authorities, and contributing to the further development of the framework for financial regulation. In the context of the Eurosystem arrangements for financial stability, the Eurosystem central banks carried out a stress-testing exercise relating to the ability of the Eurosystem to address effectively a financial crisis with the potential for systemic

---

([1]) See also 'Economic and monetary union' in Chapter II, Section 1, of this Report.

implications across several euro area countries. The conduct of the exercise confirmed the preparedness of the system for dealing with potentially systemic events that affect the euro area's financial system and contributed to the improvement of the existing arrangements for managing financial crises in the European Union.

The ECB continued to monitor the progress of financial integration in the euro area and published the second annual assessment of the degree of integration of financial markets in the euro area. This assessment is based on a set of financial integration indicators that are published semi-annually on the ECB's website ([1]).

The ECB, assisted by the national central banks, continued to develop, collect, compile and disseminate a broad range of statistics. In May the ECB, together with Eurostat, published for the first time annual European accounts for institutional sectors. In September the ECB launched on the Internet its statistical data warehouse, a new online data delivery service for a wide range of users of euro area statistics ([2]).

Following the successful introduction of euro banknotes in 2002, the ECB continued its work on planning the second series, to be issued gradually towards the end of the current decade.

The ECB continued to take part in the activities of a number of European and international institutions and forums. The President of the Eurogroup and a member of the European Commission participated in meetings of the Governing Council. The President and the Vice-President of the ECB also participated in meetings of the Eurogroup, which continued to serve as an important forum for an open and informal policy dialogue between the ECB, the finance ministers of the euro area countries and the Commission.

The ECB continued to deliver opinions on legislative proposals by the Community and the Member States in its fields of competence. The ECB's activities are explained in detail in the reports it has drawn up in accordance with its statutory obligations.

European Investment Bank

In 2006 the European Investment Bank (EIB) granted loans totalling EUR 45.8 billion: EUR 39.9 billion in the Member States of the European Union and EUR 5.9 billion in partner countries.

([1]) http://www.ecb.eu/.
([2]) http://sdw.ecb.eu/.

Agencies

Regulatory agencies

In 2006 the completion of the legislative process allowed two new regulatory agencies to be set up; they will be operational from the beginning of 2007.

- A European Chemicals Agency was established by a Parliament and Council regulation adopted on 18 December ([1]) in connection with the REACH project (registration, evaluation, authorisation and restriction of chemicals) ([2]). It is to be based in Helsinki, Finland.

- A European Institute for Gender Equality was set up by a Parliament and Council regulation adopted on 20 December ([3]). It will be based in Vilnius, Lithuania.

The proposal to set up a European Union Agency for Fundamental Rights was the subject of an opinion delivered by the European Parliament (single reading) on 30 November. The Council is expected finally to adopt the regulation towards the end of January 2007.

The draft interinstitutional agreement on the operating framework for the European regulatory agencies, which the Commission put forward in 2005 ([4]), was the subject of statements by the Council and the Commission at the sitting of the European Parliament on 15 November 2006. The Council considered that this was an important question and that there was a need for legislation that would bring real added value. The Commission said it was open to suggestions and would study any solution the Council proposed. But it felt that an interinstitutional agreement was the most appropriate legal instrument for laying down across-the-board rules of good governance that would provide a framework for the establishment, operation and supervision of regulatory agencies.

Executive agencies

On 26 October the Commission set up the Trans-European Transport Network Executive Agency.

The Education, Audiovisual and Culture Executive Agency, which was set up in 2005 ([5]), had its responsibilities broadened in 2006.

([1]) Regulation (EC) No 1907/2006 (OJ L 396, 30.12.2006).
([2]) See 'Product policy' in Chapter II, Section 2, of this Report.
([3]) Regulation (EC) No 1922/2006 (OJ L 403, 30.12.2006). See also 'Gender equality' in Chapter III, Section 1, of this Report.
([4]) COM(2005) 59.
([5]) Decision 2005/56/EC (OJ L 24, 27.1.2005).

Legislative activity

Co-decision

In 2006 the Commission presented 109 proposals for adoption by the co-decision procedure. The European Parliament and the Council for their part signed — or reached a consensus on them prior to signing — 91 legislative acts, for most of which the procedure was in progress before 1 January.

The number of proposals on which agreement was reached at first reading grew to 54, i.e. more than half. Although the list of proposals concluded without the need for a second reading mainly includes technical proposals, consolidations and proposals on relations with third countries, it also includes a number of subjects of wide public interest such as the Community action for the European Capital of Culture event for the years 2007–19, the European Globalisation Adjustment Fund, the European Monitoring Centre for Drugs and Drug Addiction, the European Neighbourhood and Partnership Instrument to strengthen cooperation and economic integration between the Union and the partner countries, and the European Maritime Safety Agency in the field of response to pollution caused by ships.

A third of the legislative proposals (31 acts) were adopted with two readings. This testifies once again to the political will of the two branches of the legislature to reach agreement on important and sensitive dossiers without going through the conciliation procedure. A number of dossiers were concluded (essentially under the Finnish Presidency, though the negotiations had often been begun under the Austrian Presidency), among them the services directive, the European Chemicals Agency, and the system of registration, evaluation, authorisation and restriction of chemicals (REACH). For the European scientific community a major step was the adoption of the seventh framework programme of the European Community for research, technological development and demonstration activities (2007–13).

The conciliation procedure was used in six cases, mainly in the environmental sphere. They concerned public access to information and access to justice under the Aarhus Convention, the treatment and disposal of batteries and accumulators, the protection of groundwater, and the legal framework for an infrastructure for spatial information in the European Community (Inspire), which would focus on environmental surveillance. Mention should also be made of two dossiers which were linked in negotiation: one concerned climate change due to fluorinated greenhouse gases, and the other air pollution by emissions from air conditioning systems in motor vehicles.

Interinstitutional cooperation was boosted this year with the conclusion of negotiations on the revision of the joint declaration of 1999 on practical arrangements for the co-decision procedure. The negotiation resulted in the codification of a number of practices, more effective and transparent handling of agreements at first and second reading, and the strengthening of proper cooperation between the three institutions throughout the procedure.

'Comitology'

On 17 July the Council amended (^{1}) the decision laying down the procedures for the exercise of implementing powers conferred on the Commission (^{2}) to add a new procedure: regulatory procedure with scrutiny. This procedure will allow the legislator to oppose the adoption of quasi-legislative measures, namely measures of general scope 'amending' non-essential elements of basic instruments adopted by co-decision, if it considers that the draft exceeds the implementing powers provided for in the basic instrument, is incompatible with the aim or the content of that instrument or fails to respect the principles of subsidiarity or proportionality. The European Parliament, the Council and the Commission also adopted a joint statement (^{3}) containing a list of legal instruments already in force to be given priority for adjustment under the new procedure. The Commission adopted the 25 proposals in question on 22 December (^{4}).

On 9 August the Commission presented its annual report on the working of committees, covering the year 2005 (^{5}). For the first time the report includes a section on the case-law of the Court of Justice relating to issues of comitology.

Statistical data

Figures for legislative acts adopted, repealed or expiring in 2006 can be found in the EUR-Lex database (^{6}).

General references and other useful links

- European Parliament:
  http://www.europarl.europa.eu/

- Council of the European Union:
  http://www.consilium.europa.eu/

- European Council:
  http://www.consilium.europa.eu/cms3_fo/showPage.asp?id=432

- European Commission:
  http://ec.europa.eu/index_en.htm

(^{1}) Decision 2006/512/EC (OJ L 200, 22.7.2006).
(^{2}) Decision 1999/468/EC (OJ L 184, 17.7.1999).
(^{3}) OJ C 255, 21.10.2006
(^{4}) COM(2006) 902, COM(2006) 903, COM(2006) 904, COM(2006) 905, COM(2006) 906, COM(2006) 907, COM(2006) 908, COM(2006) 909, COM(2006) 910, COM(2006) 911, COM(2006) 912, COM(2006) 913, COM(2006) 914, COM(2006) 915, COM(2006) 916, COM(2006) 917, COM(2006) 918, COM(2006) 919, COM(2006) 920, COM(2006) 921, COM(2006) 922, COM(2006) 923, COM(2006) 924, COM(2006) 925 and COM(2006) 926.
(^{5}) COM(2006) 446.
(^{6}) http://eur-lex.europa.eu/en/index.htm.

- Sites of the Members of the Commission:
  http://ec.europa.eu/commission_barroso/index_en.htm
- Annual policy strategy:
  http://ec.europa.eu/atwork/programmes/index_en.htm
- European Ombudsman:
  http://ombudsman.europa.eu/home/en/default.htm
- Court of Justice, Court of First Instance and European Civil Service Tribunal:
  http://curia.europa.eu/
- Court of Auditors:
  http://eca.europa.eu/
- European Economic and Social Committee:
  http://eesc.europa.eu/
- Committee of the Regions:
  http://cor.europa.eu/
- European Central Bank:
  http://www.ecb.int/home/html/index.en.html
- European Investment Bank:
  http://www.bei.org/
- Agencies:
  http://europa.eu/agencies/community_agencies/index_en.htm
- Co-decision site:
  http://ec.europa.eu/codecision/index_en.htm
- Register of comitology:
  http://ec.europa.eu/transparency/regcomitology/registre.cfm?CL=en

Chapter VII

Budget and financial activities

Implementation of the 2006 budget

The 2006 budget, the last one covered by the 2000–06 financial framework, was adopted by the European Parliament on 15 December 2005 ([1]).

The commitment appropriations amounted to EUR 120.6 billion, corresponding to 1.08 % of the gross national income (GNI) of the 25 Member States. The payment appropriations totalled EUR 107.4 billion, corresponding to 0.96 % of GNI.

Six amending budgets were adopted in the course of the year. A breakdown of the appropriations, taking account of the amending budgets, is included in the annex (colour pages) to this Report.

Preparation of the 2007 budget

The preparation of the budget for the financial year 2007 took the form of:

- a preliminary draft approved by the Commission on 3 May;
- a draft established by the Council on 17 July;
- a first reading by the European Parliament on 26 October;
- a second reading by the Council on 30 November.

Parliament finally adopted the budget at second reading on 14 December.

The 2007 budget is the first budget covered by the 2007–13 financial framework ([2]).

([1]) OJ L 78, 15.3.2006.
([2]) See 'Financial perspective' in Chapter I of this Report.

Financial regulation

In May the Commission presented an amended proposal ([1]) for revising the 2002 financial regulation applicable to the general budget of the European Communities ([2]). After a successful conciliation procedure between the Council and Parliament in November, the revised regulation was finally adopted by the Council on 13 December ([3]).

The revision was a major step to further simplify the rules, thereby enabling easier access to European Union funding, to improve transparency and to tighten scrutiny of the budget. Under the new provisions, the names of beneficiaries of agricultural and structural funds will have to be disclosed to the public. The Commission will also have a new tool to prevent fraud and corruption with the setting-up of a central database of organisations excluded from European Union funding. National authorities have also committed themselves to put in place efficient internal control systems and make the necessary checks on European Union funds under their management. Annual audit summaries by the Member States will provide the Commission with better assurance as to the proper implementation of the European Union budget.

The revision was complemented by a series of proposed changes to the related implementing rules ([4]), some of which came into force in August ([5]). On 4 July the Commission adopted a proposal on the changes stemming from the revision itself ([6]).

Own resources decision

Following the conclusions of the European Council in December 2005 the Commission presented a new proposal for an own resources decision in March ([7]). The proposal includes changes to the VAT calculation and collection mechanisms, the GNI resource and the United Kingdom rebate. The Council decision will take effect retroactively from 1 January 2007, once it has been adopted unanimously by the Council and ratified by all the Member States.

---

[1] COM(2006) 213.
[2] Regulation (EC, Euratom) No 1605/2002 (OJ L 248, 16.9.2002).
[3] Regulation (EC, Euratom) No 1995/2006 (OJ L 390, 30.12.2002).
[4] Regulation (EC, Euratom) No 2342/2002 (OJ L 357, 31.12.2002).
[5] Regulation (EC, Euratom) No 1248/2006 (OJ L 227, 19.8.2006).
[6] SEC(2006) 865.
[7] COM(2006) 99.

Annual accounts

The Commission presented its first accrual-based financial statements for the year 2005.

General references and other useful links

- Budget website:
  http://ec.europa.eu/budget/index_en.htm

Institutions and other bodies

European Parliament
Secretariat
Centre européen, plateau du Kirchberg
L-2929 Luxembourg
Tel. (352) 43 00-1

Council of the European Union
General Secretariat
Rue de la Loi 175
B-1048 Brussels
Tel. (32-2) 285 61 11

European Commission
Rue de la Loi 200
B-1049 Brussels
Tel. (32-2) 29-91111

Court of Justice, Court of First Instance and Civil Service Tribunal
Boulevard Konrad Adenauer
L-2925 Luxembourg
Tel. (352) 43 03-1

European Court of Auditors
12, rue Alcide De Gasperi
L-1615 Luxembourg
Tel. (352) 43 98-1

European Economic and Social Committee
Rue Belliard 99
B-1040 Brussels
Tel. (32-2) 546 90 11

Committee of the Regions
Rue Belliard 101
B-1040 Brussels
Tel. (32-2) 282 22 11

European Investment Bank
100, boulevard Konrad Adenauer
L-2950 Luxembourg
Tel. (352) 43 79-1

European Central Bank
Kaiserstraße 29
D-60311 Frankfurt am Main
Tel. (49-69) 13 44-0

European Ombudsman
1, avenue du Président-Robert-Schuman
BP 403 FR
F-67001 Strasbourg Cedex
Tel. (33) 388 17 23 13

European Data Protection Supervisor
Rue Wiertz 60
B-1047 Brussels
Tel. (32-2) 283 19 00

Decentralised bodies
of the European Union

http://publications.europa.eu/code/en/en-390500.htm

- **Community regulatory agencies (first pillar)**
  — Community Fisheries Control Agency (CFCA)
  — Community Plant Variety Office (CPVO)
  — European Agency for Reconstruction (EAR)
  — European Agency for Safety and Health at Work (OSHA)
  — European Agency for the Management of Operational Cooperation at the External Borders (Frontex)
  — European Aviation Safety Agency (EASA)
  — European Centre for Disease Prevention and Control (ECDC)
  — European Centre for the Development of Vocational Training (Cedefop)
  — European Chemicals Agency (ECA)
  — European Environment Agency (EEA)
  — European Food Safety Authority (EFSA)
  — European Foundation for the Improvement of Living and Working Conditions (Eurofound)
  — European GNSS Supervisory Authority
  — European Institute for Gender Equality
  — European Maritime Safety Agency (EMSA)
  — European Medicines Agency (EMEA)
  — European Monitoring Centre for Drugs and Drug Addiction (EMCDDA)
  — European Monitoring Centre on Racism and Xenophobia (EUMC)
  — European Network and Information Security Agency (ENISA)
  — European Railway Agency (ERA)

— European Training Foundation (ETF)

— Office for Harmonization in the Internal Market (Trade Marks and Designs) (OHIM)

— Translation Centre for the Bodies of the European Union (CdT)

- **Proposed Community agency in 2006 (first pillar)**
  - European Fundamental Rights Agency (EFRA)

- **European Union agencies (second and third pillars)**
  - European Agency for the Enhancement of Judicial Cooperation (Eurojust)
  - European Defence Agency (EDA)
  - European Police College (CEPOL)
  - European Police Office (Europol)
  - European Union Institute for Security Studies (EUISS)
  - European Union Satellite Centre (EUSC)

- **Executive agencies**
  - Education, Audiovisual and Culture Executive Agency
  - Executive Agency for the Public Health Programme
  - Intelligent Energy Executive Agency

The European Union in 2006

Member States of the European Union

Candidate countries

Source: Communication DG

Summary of appropriations for commitments (by policy area)

Title	Budget 2005 (¹)		Budget 2006 (¹)	
	Commitments EUR	Human resources (²)	Commitments EUR	Human resources (²) (³)
01 Economic and financial affairs	400 201 998	538	468 476 353	572
02 Enterprise	381 316 768	1 045	399 828 648	1 052
03 Competition	89 127 373	867	98 657 766	900
04 Employment and social affairs	11 427 816 628	909	11 938 359 782	926
05 Agriculture and rural development	53 184 651 245	1 243	54 595 078 891	1 320
06 Energy and transport	1 415 885 043	1 161	1 467 018 844	1 165
07 Environment	325 818 542	694	346 198 192	701
08 Research	3 307 806 914	1 779	3 525 524 298	1 736
09 Information society	1 375 250 095	1 146	1 425 305 907	1 189
10 Direct research	366 418 287	2 347	330 209 495	2 356
11 Fisheries	1 019 875 616	366	1 073 914 748	386
12 Internal market	73 581 959	584	75 206 248	614
13 Regional policy	27 295 029 985	692	28 735 564 828	707
14 Taxation and customs union	120 565 947	564	130 398 219	607
15 Education and culture	943 498 200	661	1 007 494 882	638
16 Press and communication	187 460 083	959	205 327 888	1 014
17 Health and consumer protection	480 756 056	946	558 930 694	967
18 Area of freedom, security and justice	596 866 914	443	608 476 896	505
19 External relations	3 332 510 399	2 734	3 476 284 050	2 705
20 Trade	76 103 566	857	82 796 875	634
21 Development and relations with African, Caribbean and Pacific (ACP) States	1 230 912 686	1 943	1 300 607 197	2 094
22 Enlargement	2 002 707 239	570	2 325 171 524	611
23 Humanitarian aid	643 832 369	176	515 103 476	190
24 Fight against fraud	57 967 048	418	65 745 124	417
25 Commission's policy coordination and legal advice	213 065 957	1 709	214 995 745	1 722
26 Administration	646 475 623	4 037	660 329 166	4 105
27 Budget	1 369 627 564	657	1 159 929 327	692
28 Audit	10 746 818	104	11 547 110	105
29 Statistics	131 264 213	797	132 987 886	811
30 Pensions	899 771 000		945 245 000	
40 Reserves	13 000 000		229 000 000	
Total Commission	**113 619 912 135**	**30 946**	**118 109 715 059**	**31 441**
Other institutions (excluding pensions)	**2 336 205 081**		**2 460 056 437**	
Grand total	**115 956 117 216**		**120 569 771 496**	

Source: Budget DG

(¹) Amending budgets.
(²) Covers both regular and support staff.
(³) 2006 preliminary draft budget.

Figures by financial perspective headings, in commitment appropriations (aggregate)

Appropriations of commitments		Budget 2005 EUR	Financial perspective 2006 EUR	Budget 2006 EUR
1. AGRICULTURE		**49 026 450 000**	**52 618 000 000**	**50 190 720 000**
	Margin	*2 412 550 000*		*2 427 280 000*
Agricultural expenditure (excluding rural development)		42 185 450 000	44 847 000 000	42 419 720 000
Rural development and accompanying measures		6 841 000 000	7 771 000 000	7 771 000 000
2. STRUCTURAL OPERATIONS		**42 420 297 444**	**44 617 000 000**	**44 555 004 990**
	Margin	*20 702 556*		*61 995 010*
Structural Funds		37 288 364 455	38 523 000 000	38 522 922 880
Cohesion Funds		5 131 932 989	6 094 000 000	6 032 082 110
3. INTERNAL POLICIES		**9 150 458 408**	**9 385 000 000**	**9 399 462 774**
	Margin	*−138 458 408*		*−14 462 774*
4. EXTERNAL ACTION		**5 444 000 000**	**5 269 000 000**	**5 544 000 000**
	Margin	*−325 000 000*		*−275 000 000*
5. ADMINISTRATION		**6 292 922 368**	**6 708 000 000**	**6 656 924 362**
	Margin	*67 077 632*		*51 075 638*
6. RESERVES		**236 000 000**	**458 000 000**	**458 000 000**
	Margin	*210 000 000*		*0*
Guarantee reserve		223 000 000	229 000 000	229 000 000
Emergency aid reserve		13 000 000	229 000 000	229 000 000
7. PRE-ACCESSION STRATEGY		**2 081 000 000**	**3 566 000 000**	**2 692 159 038**
	Margin	*1 391 000 000*		*873 840 962*
Sapard pre-accession instrument		250 300 000		300 000 000
ISPA pre-accession instrument		525 700 000		585 000 000
Phare pre-accession instrument		898 800 000		977 300 000
Turkey		286 200 000		479 500 000
European Union Solidarity Fund		0		91 559 038
Economic development of Turkish Cypriot Community		120 000 000		258 800 000
8. COMPENSATION		**1 304 988 996**	**1 074 000 000**	**1 073 500 332**
	Margin	*11 004*		*499 668*
Appropriations for commitments — Total		**115 956 117 216**	**123 695 000 000**	**120 569 771 496**
	Margin	*3 637 882 784*		*3 125 228 504*
Compulsory expenditure		45 078 212 878		45 006 877 332
Non-compulsory expenditure		70 877 904 338		73 102 837 727
Appropriations for payments — Total		**105 684 514 081**	**119 292 000 000**	**107 378 469 621**
	Margin	*8 550 485 919*		*11 913 530 379*
Compulsory expenditure		45 119 231 878		45 023 454 332
Non-compulsory expenditure		60 565 282 203		59 894 958 852
Appropriations for payments as % of GNI		**1.00 %**	**1.07 %**	**0.96 %**

Source: Budget DG

Breakdown by type of revenue

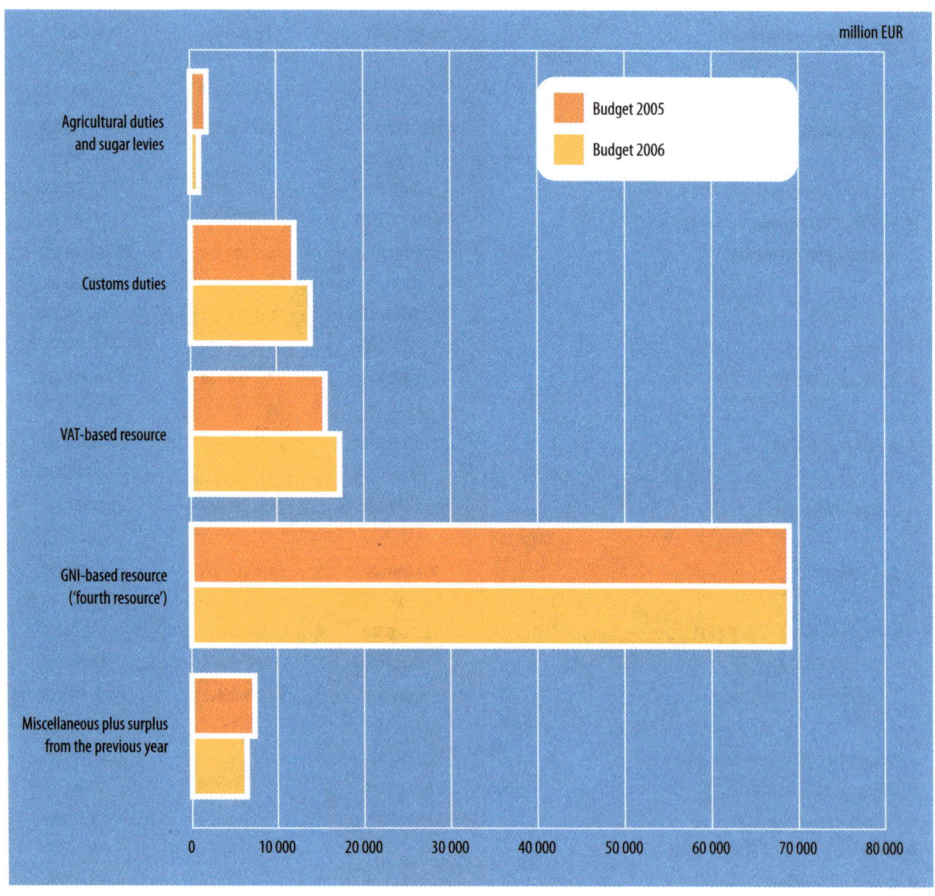

Type of revenue	Budget 2005		Budget 2006	
	Million EUR	%	Million EUR	%
Agricultural and sugar levies	1 913.20	1.8	1 014.00	0.9
Customs duties	12 030.80	11.4	13 874.90	12.9
VAT-based resource	15 556.05	14.7	17 200.28	16.0
GNI-based resource ('fourth resource')	68 884.10	65.2	68 921.21	64.3
Miscellaneous plus surplus from the previous year	7 299.90	6.9	6 368.08	5.9
Total	**105 684.05**	**100.0**	**107 378.47**	**100.0**

Source: Budget DG

European Commission

General Report on the Activities of the European Union — 2006

Luxembourg: Office for Official Publications of the European Communities

2007 — 230 pp. — 16.2 × 22.9 cm

ISBN 92-79-02100-1

Price (excluding VAT) in Luxembourg: EUR 25

The *General Report on the Activities of the European Union* is published annually by the Commission as required by Article 212 of the EC Treaty and Article 125 of the EAEC Treaty.

The Report is presented to the European Parliament and provides a general picture of Community activities over the past year.